Hardware technology has been evolving too quickly lately for someone like me, who buys lots of software and games. You can just throw out videos and laserdiscs when you get DVDs, but if you have just one good game for a system, you have to keep the whole console. I have so many adapters and cables, I can't keep them straight!

— Riku Sanjo

Author Riku Sanjo and artist Koji Inada were both born in Tokyo in 1964. Sanjo began his career writing a radio-controlled car manga for the comic **Bonbon**. Inada debuted with **Kussotare Daze!!** in **Weekly Shonen Jump**. Sanjo and Inada first worked together on the highly successful **Dragon Quest–Dai's Big Adventure. Beet the Vandel Buster**, their latest collaboration, debuted in **Monthly Shonen Jump** in 2002 and was an immediate hit, inspiring an action-packed video game and an animated series on Japanese TV.

BEET THE VANDEL BUSTER
VOL. 12
The SHONEN JUMP Manga Edition

STORY BY RIKU SANJO
ART BY KOJI INADA

Translation/Naomi Kokubo
Touch-Up & Lettering/Mark McMurray
Design/Andrea Rice
Editor/Shaenon K. Garrity

Editor in Chief, Books/Alvin Lu
Editor in Chief, Magazines/Marc Weidenbaum
VP of Publishing Licensing/Rika Inouye
VP of Sales/Gonzalo Ferreyra
Sr. VP of Marketing/Liza Coppola
Publisher/Hyoe Narita

Published by VIZ Media, LLC
P.O. Box 77064
San Francisco, CA 94107

SHONEN JUMP Manga Edition
10 9 8 7 6 5 4 3 2 1
First printing, October 2007

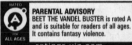

THE WORLD'S
MOST POPULAR MANGA

www.shonenjump.com

www.viz.com

SHONEN JUMP Manga Edition

Volume 12

Story by **Riku Sanjo**
Art by **Koji Inada**

CHARACTERS

BEET

The hero of the story. He sets out on a journey to save the world from Vandels. He has received five Saiga, or spirit weapons, from his heroes, the Zenon Warriors.

POALA

Beet's childhood friend has an unyielding spirit. She is skilled at Kenjutsu, the art of the samurai sword, as well as the Divine Attack.

KISSU

An old friend of Beet's, he is a genius and a master of the Divine Attack. He's trying to redeem himself after working for Vandels.

MILFA

Milfa is one of the Broad Busters, an elite class of high-level Busters. She has an extremely upbeat personality and is a huge fan of the Zenon Warriors.

SLADE

Although he acts cold and rude, he cares about Beet and has a friendly rivalry with him as a Buster.

NOA

A seven-star Vandel who has studied both Vandels and humans carefully. He dislikes fighting.

HYSTARIO

A seven-star Vandel widely feared as "The Evil Blade." He can regenerate and seems immortal.

BARON

A seven-star Vandel known as the "King of the Sky." Humans call him "Sir Baron" out of respect for his noble fighting style.

GALA

A high-spirited girl who lives in Sankmeel.

THE WINGED KNIGHT

A mysterious Buster who appears when Beet is in a crisis.

SHAGIE

The "world's busiest Vandel," he is in charge of evaluating and supervising all Vandels. He is the Chief of the Dark House of Sorcery.

STORY ++

"Vandels"...In this story, that's what we call evil creatures with magical powers. One day they appeared on the surface of the Earth, releasing monsters and destroying whole nations. People called this seemingly endless era "The Dark Age." Beet, a young boy who believes in justice, binds himself to a contract and becomes a Vandel Buster. Early in his career, Beet stumbles into a battle between the Zenon Warriors and a Vandel named Beltorze, where he suffers a fatal injury. He miraculously survives by receiving the Saiga of the Zenon Warriors. Carrying on the Zenon Warriors' dream of peace, Beet sets out with his friends on a quest to destroy all Vandels.

The Beet Warriors have arrived at Sankmeel, a country in the wilderness. As soon as they find a moment to relax, a powerful Vandel, Sir Baron, arrives to battle Beet. To demonstrate his power, Sir Baron strikes Poala down with a single blow. Kissu flees in terror. Now Beet must face the enemy alone...

Beet™ The Vandel Buster

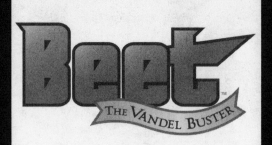

12

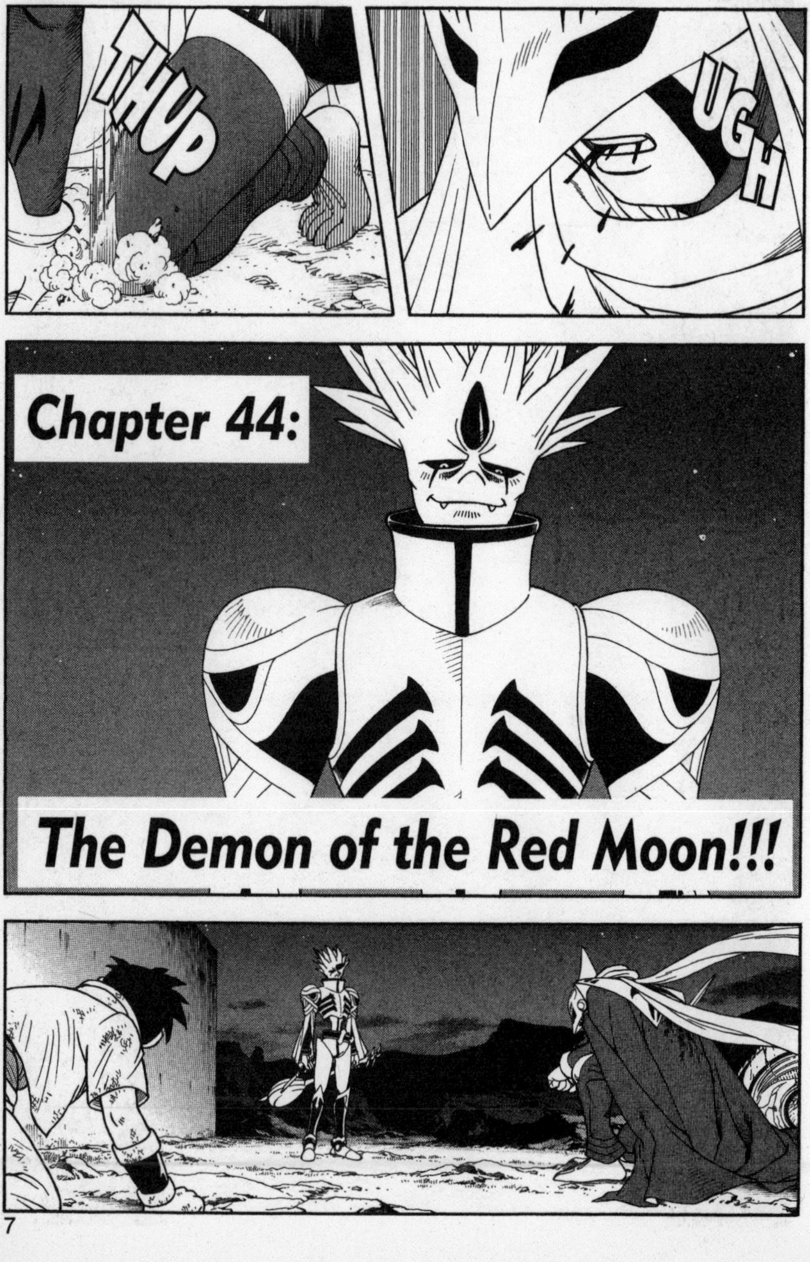
UGH
THUP
Chapter 44:
The Demon of the Red Moon!!!

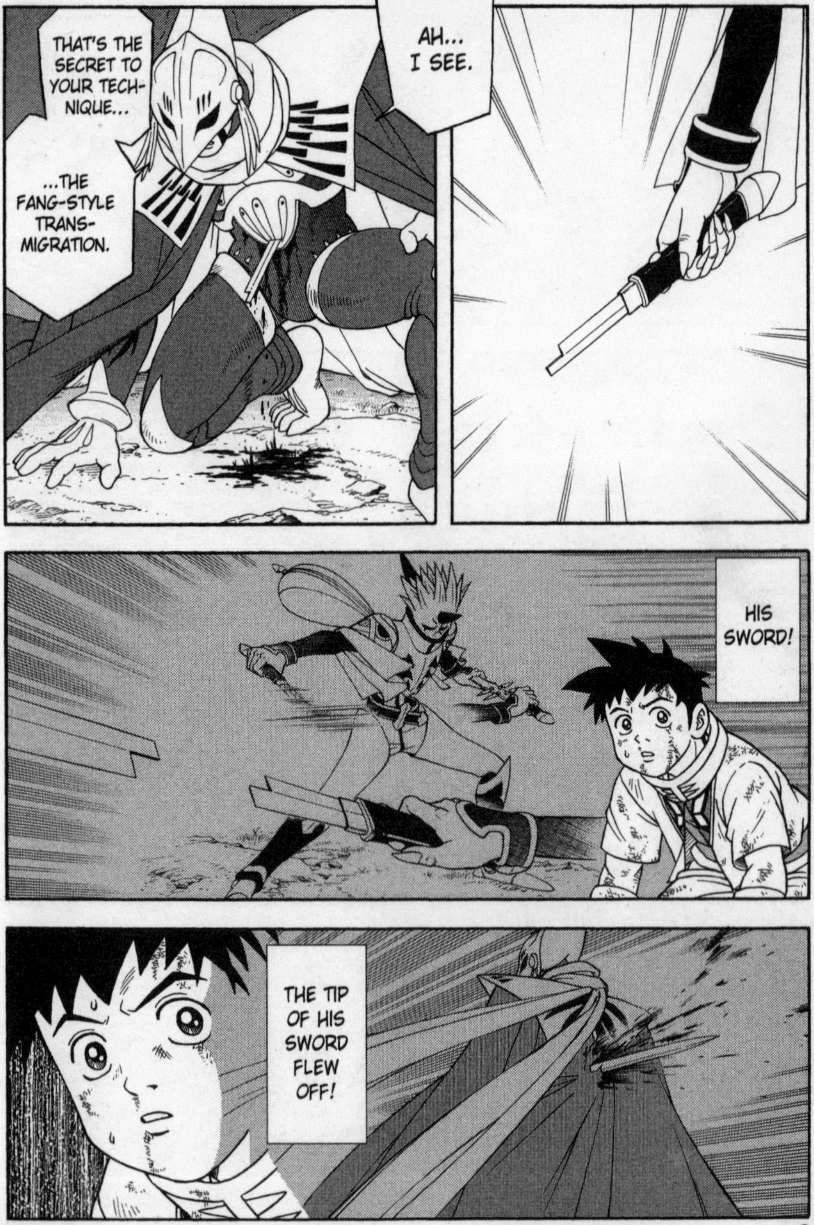
AH... I SEE.
THAT'S THE SECRET TO YOUR TECH-NIQUE...
...THE FANG-STYLE TRANS-MIGRATION.
HIS SWORD!
THE TIP OF HIS SWORD FLEW OFF!

READ THIS WAY

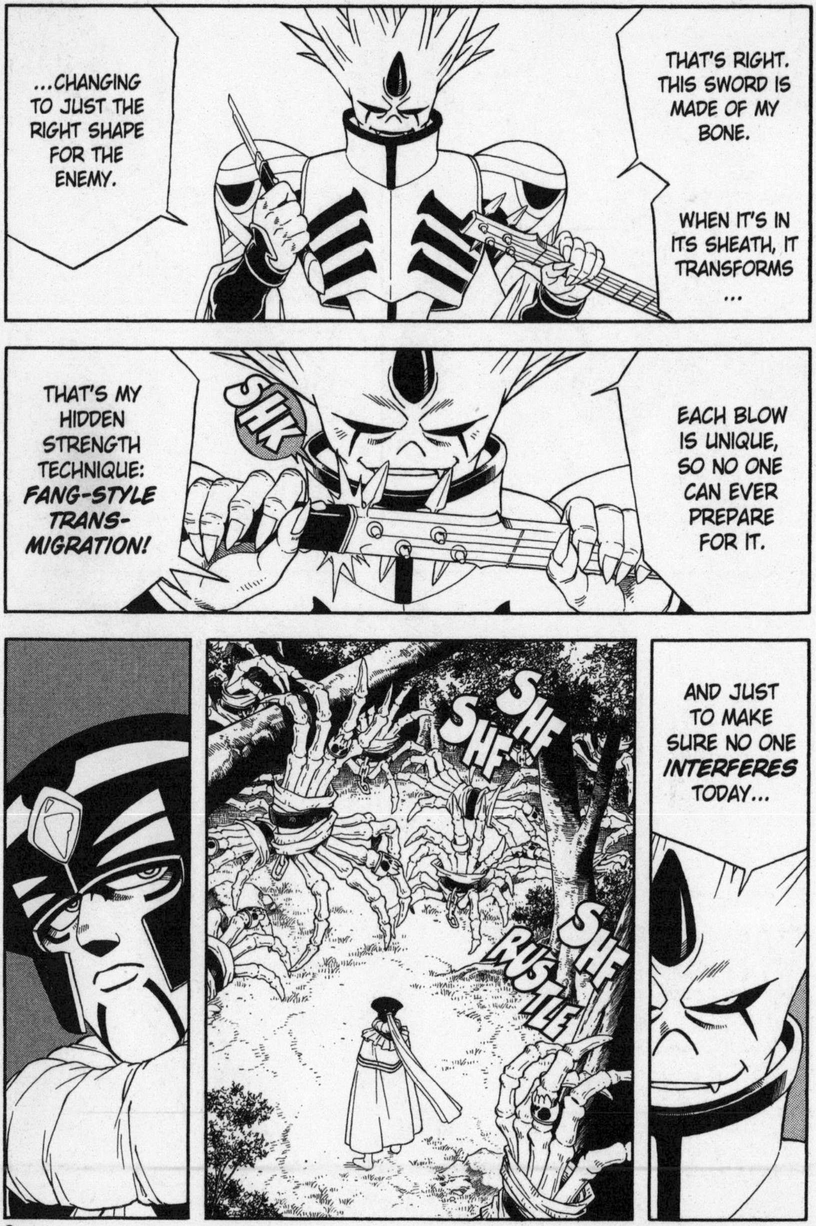
THAT'S RIGHT. THIS SWORD IS MADE OF MY BONE.
WHEN IT'S IN ITS SHEATH, IT TRANSFORMS ...
...CHANGING TO JUST THE RIGHT SHAPE FOR THE ENEMY.
EACH BLOW IS UNIQUE, SO NO ONE CAN EVER PREPARE FOR IT.
SHK
THAT'S MY HIDDEN STRENGTH TECHNIQUE: *FANG-STYLE TRANS-MIGRATION!*
AND JUST TO MAKE SURE NO ONE *INTERFERES* TODAY...
SHF SHF
SHF
RUSTLE

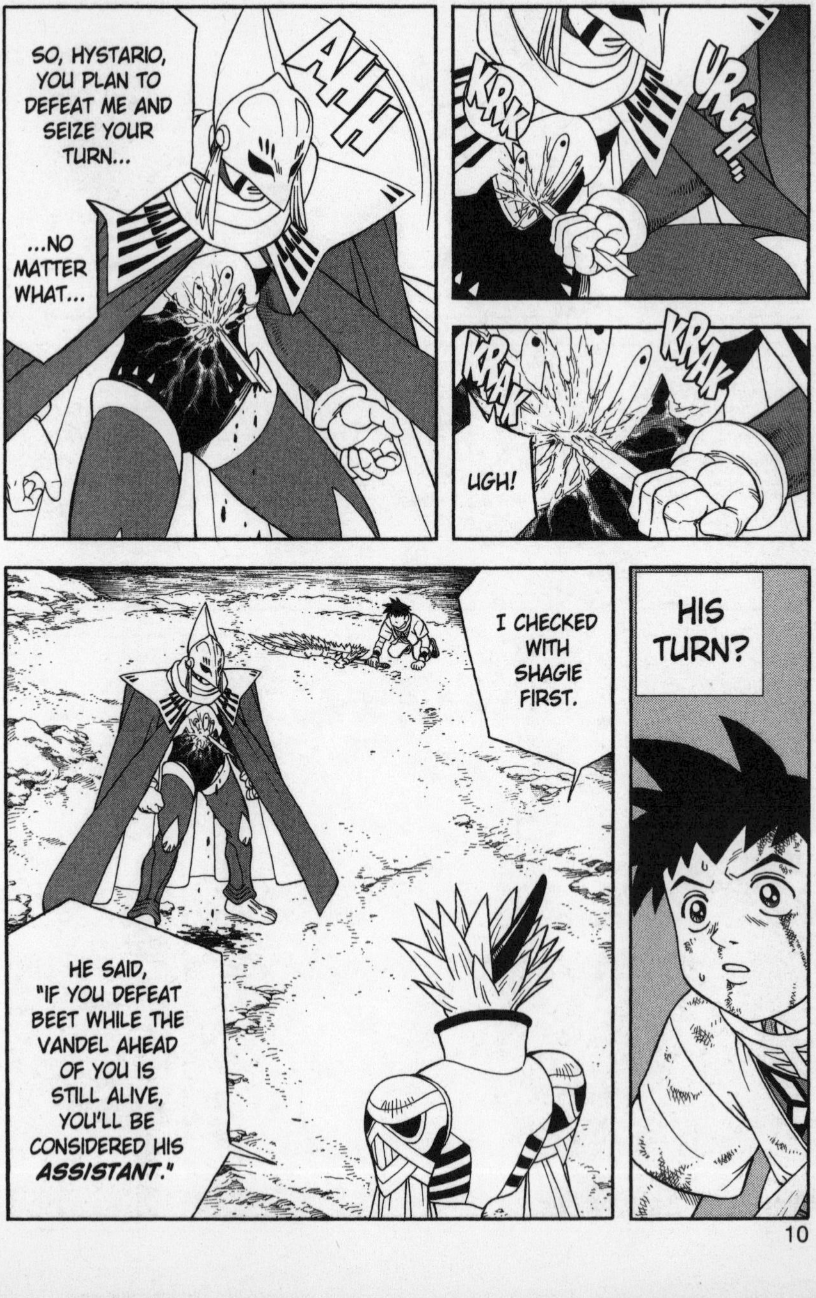

URGH...
KRK
KRAK
KRAK
UGH!
AHH
SO, HYSTARIO, YOU PLAN TO DEFEAT ME AND SEIZE YOUR TURN...
...NO MATTER WHAT...
HIS TURN?
I CHECKED WITH SHAGIE FIRST.
HE SAID, "IF YOU DEFEAT BEET WHILE THE VANDEL AHEAD OF YOU IS STILL ALIVE, YOU'LL BE CONSIDERED HIS *ASSISTANT*."

READ THIS WAY

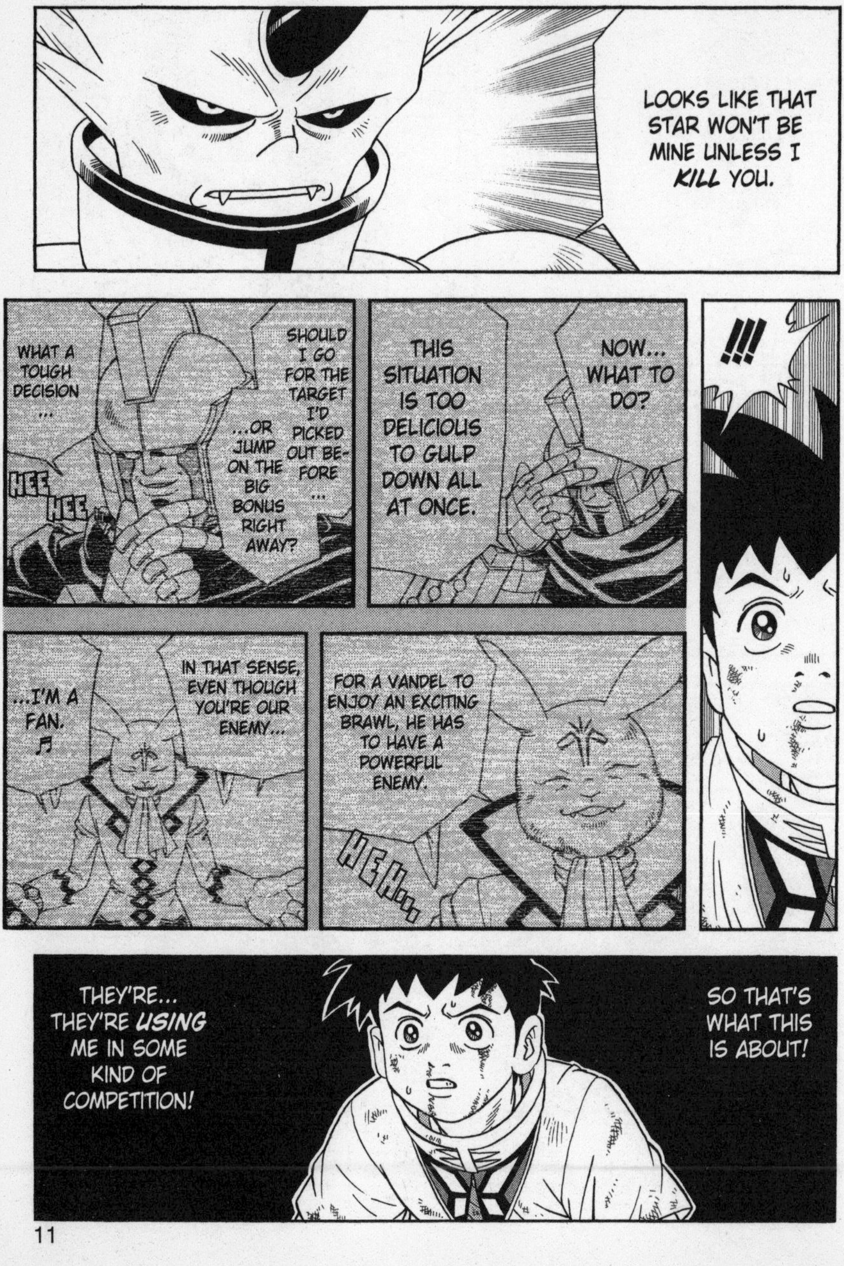

LOOKS LIKE THAT STAR WON'T BE MINE UNLESS I *KILL* YOU.
!!!
NOW... WHAT TO DO?
THIS SITUATION IS TOO DELICIOUS TO GULP DOWN ALL AT ONCE.
SHOULD I GO FOR THE TARGET I'D PICKED OUT BE-FORE...
...OR JUMP ON THE BIG BONUS RIGHT AWAY?
WHAT A TOUGH DECISION...
HEE HEE
FOR A VANDEL TO ENJOY AN EXCITING BRAWL, HE HAS TO HAVE A POWERFUL ENEMY.
IN THAT SENSE, EVEN THOUGH YOU'RE OUR ENEMY...
...I'M A FAN. ♪
SO THAT'S WHAT THIS IS ABOUT!
THEY'RE... THEY'RE *USING* ME IN SOME KIND OF COMPETITION!

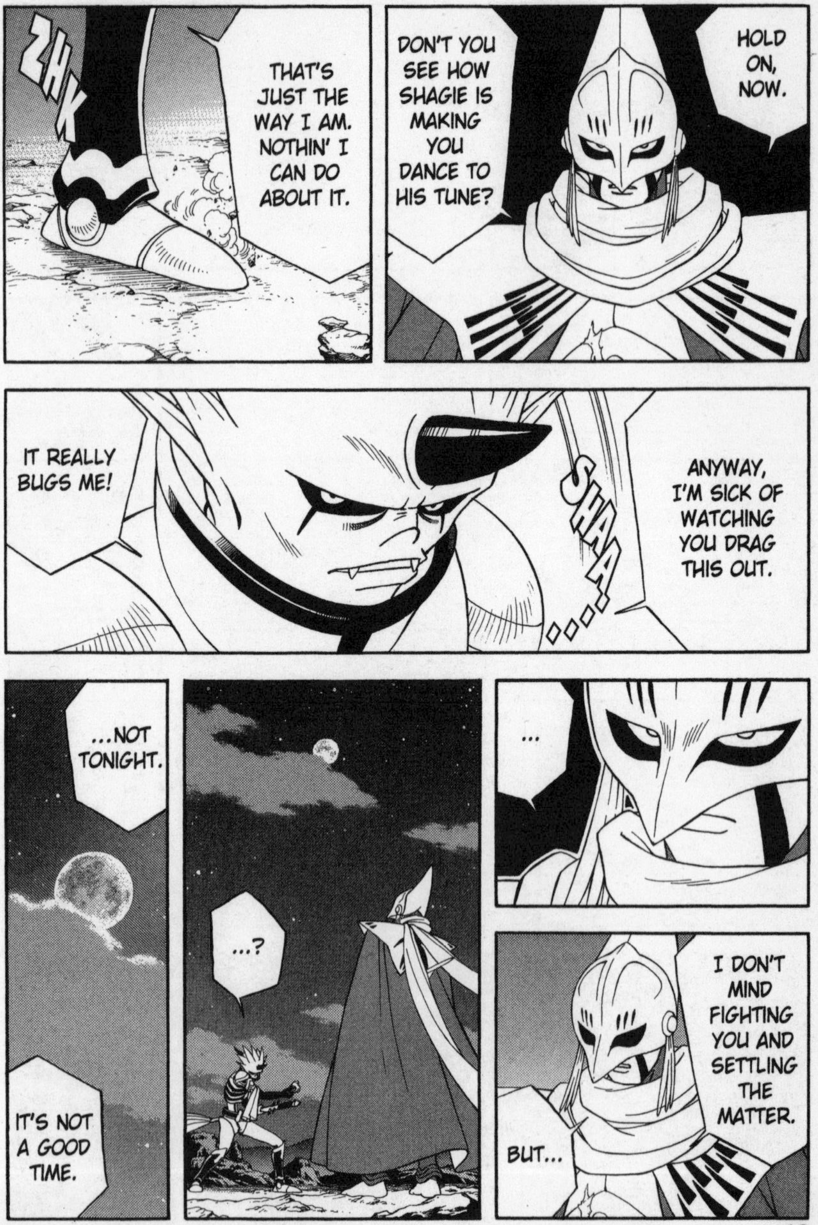
HOLD ON, NOW.
DON'T YOU SEE HOW SHAGIE IS MAKING YOU DANCE TO HIS TUNE?
ZHK
THAT'S JUST THE WAY I AM. NOTHIN' I CAN DO ABOUT IT.
ANYWAY, I'M SICK OF WATCHING YOU DRAG THIS OUT.
SHAA...
IT REALLY BUGS ME!
...
I DON'T MIND FIGHTING YOU AND SETTLING THE MATTER.
BUT...
...?
...NOT TONIGHT.
IT'S NOT A GOOD TIME.

READ THIS WAY

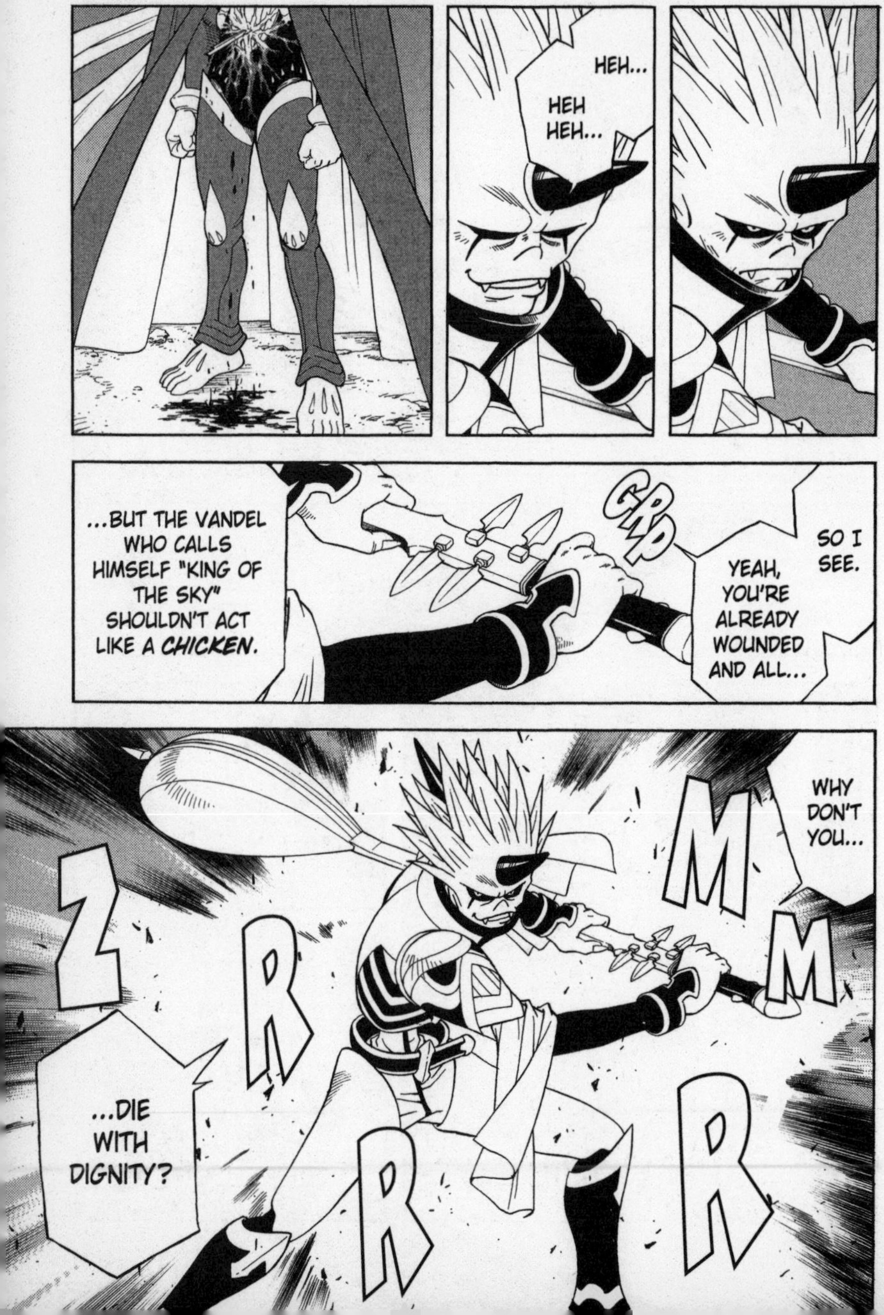
HEH...
HEH HEH...
SO I SEE.
YEAH, YOU'RE ALREADY WOUNDED AND ALL...
GRP
...BUT THE VANDEL WHO CALLS HIMSELF "KING OF THE SKY" SHOULDN'T ACT LIKE A *CHICKEN*.
WHY DON'T YOU...
MMM
ZRRRR
...DIE WITH DIGNITY?

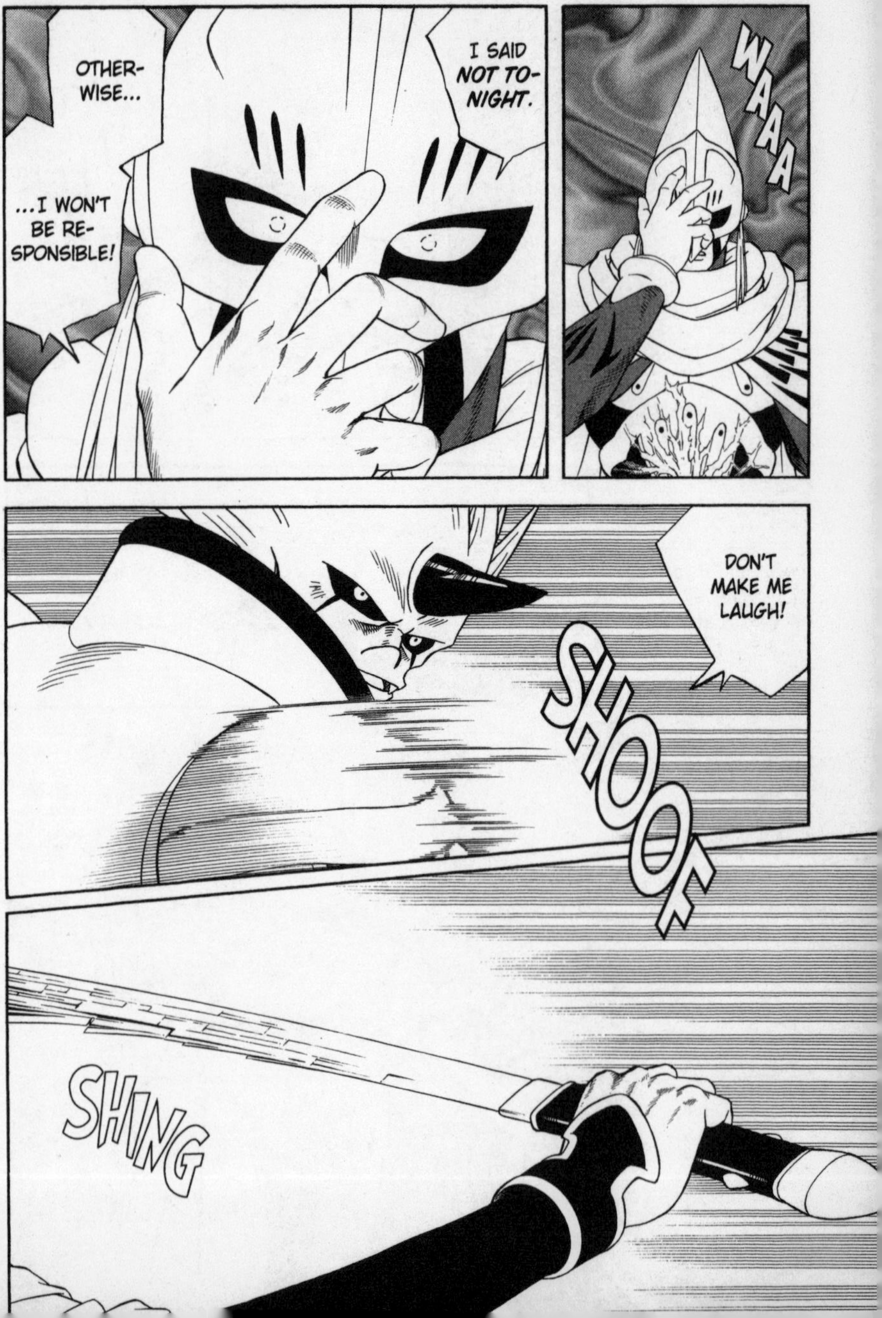
WAAAA
I SAID NOT TO-NIGHT.
OTHER-WISE...
...I WON'T BE RE-SPONSIBLE!
DON'T MAKE ME LAUGH!
SHOOF
SHING

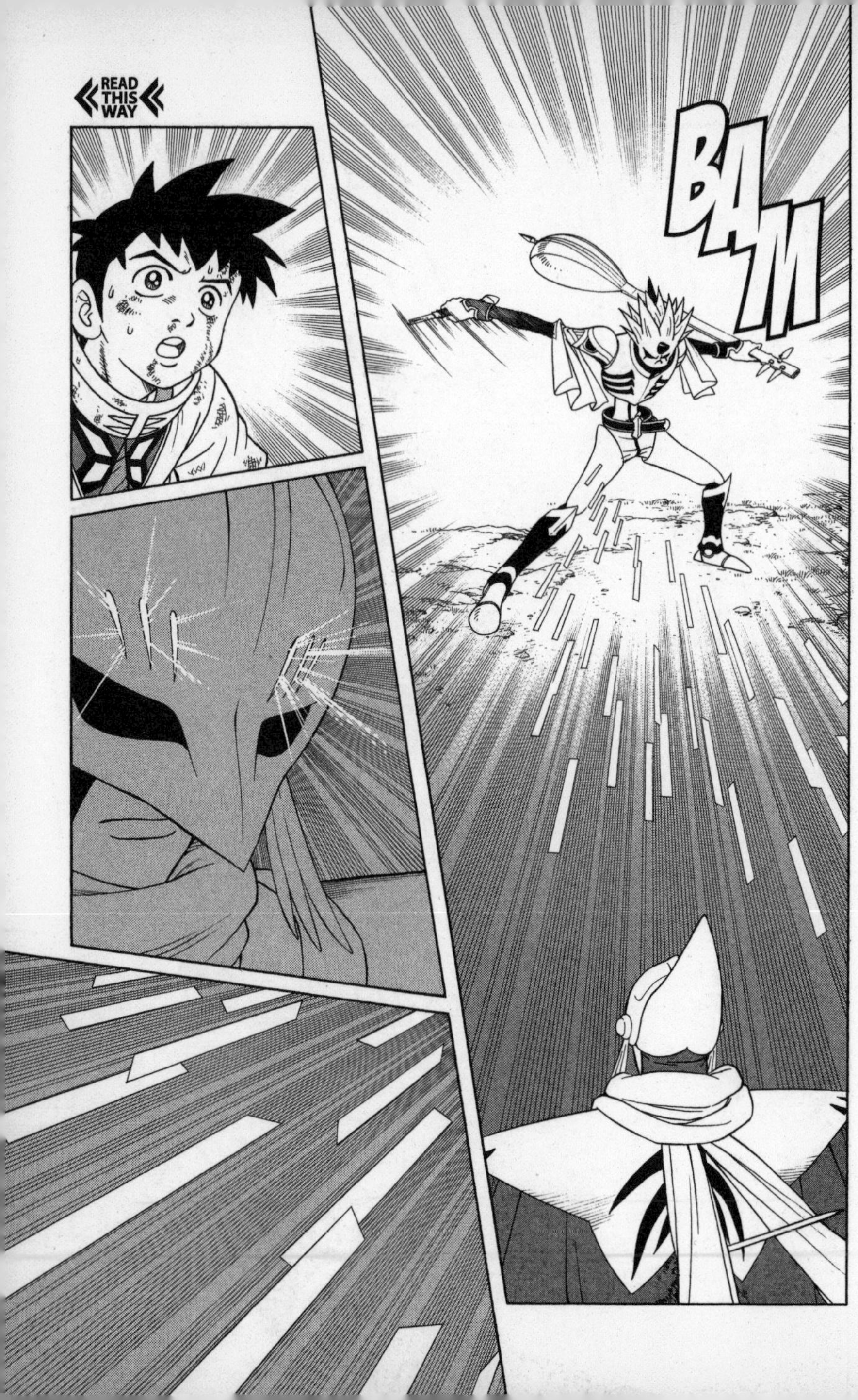
BAM
READ THIS WAY

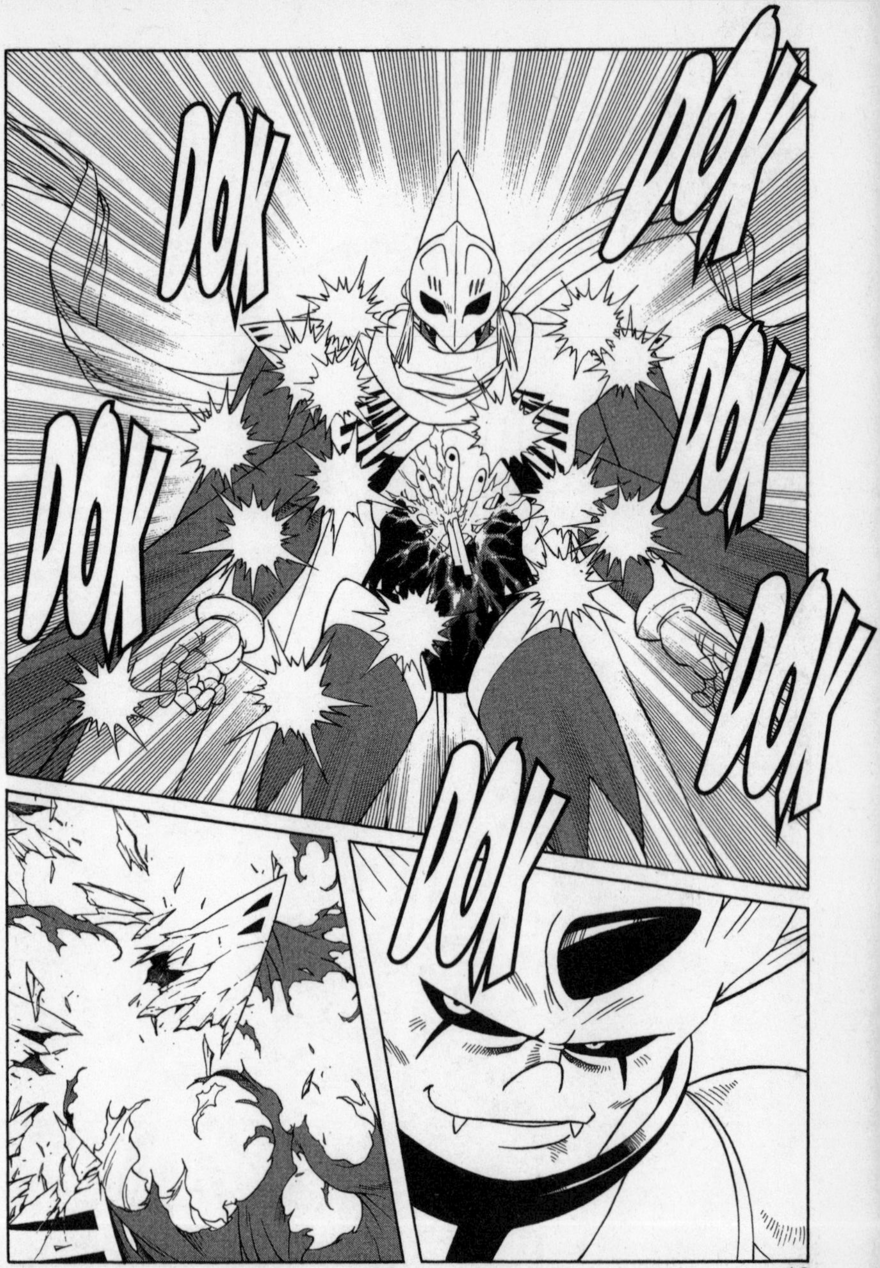
DOK
DOK
DOK
DOK
DOK
DOK

READ THIS WAY

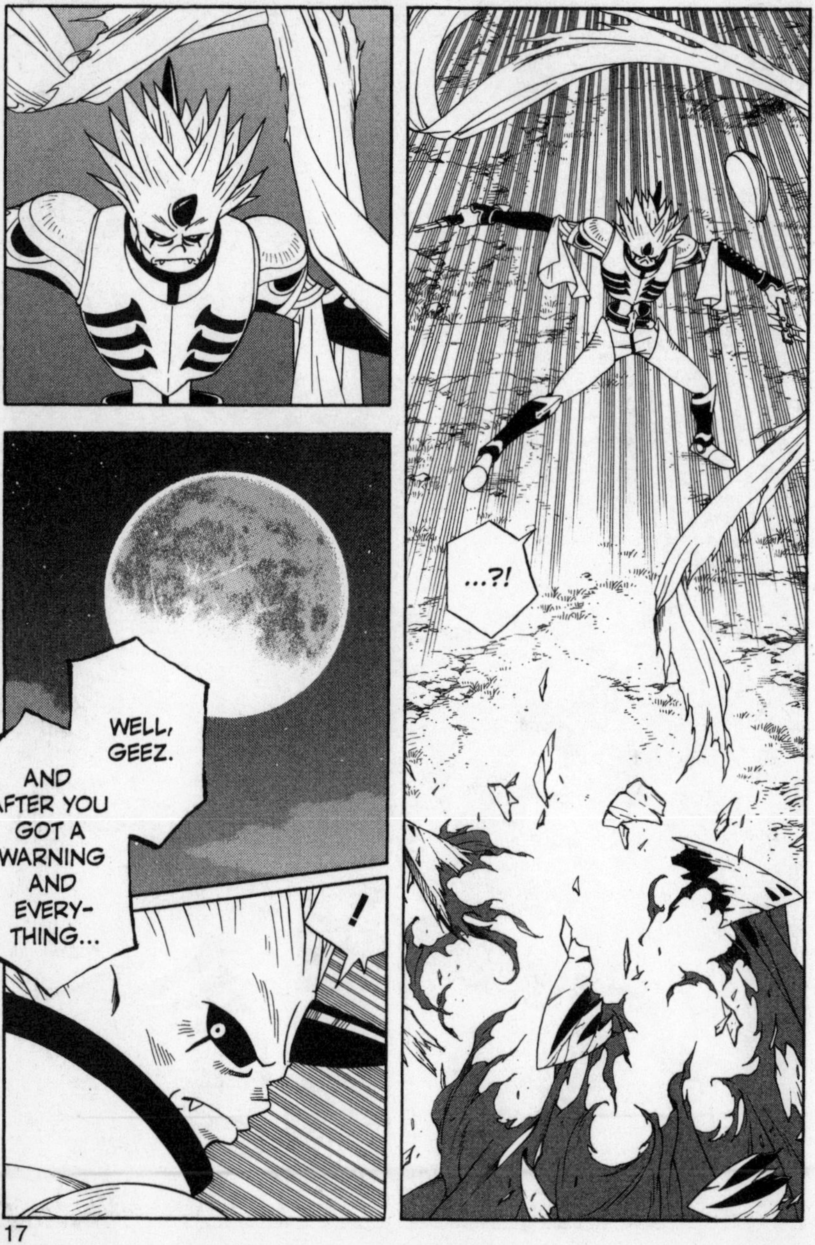
...?!
WELL, GEEZ.
AND AFTER YOU GOT A WARNING AND EVERYTHING...
!

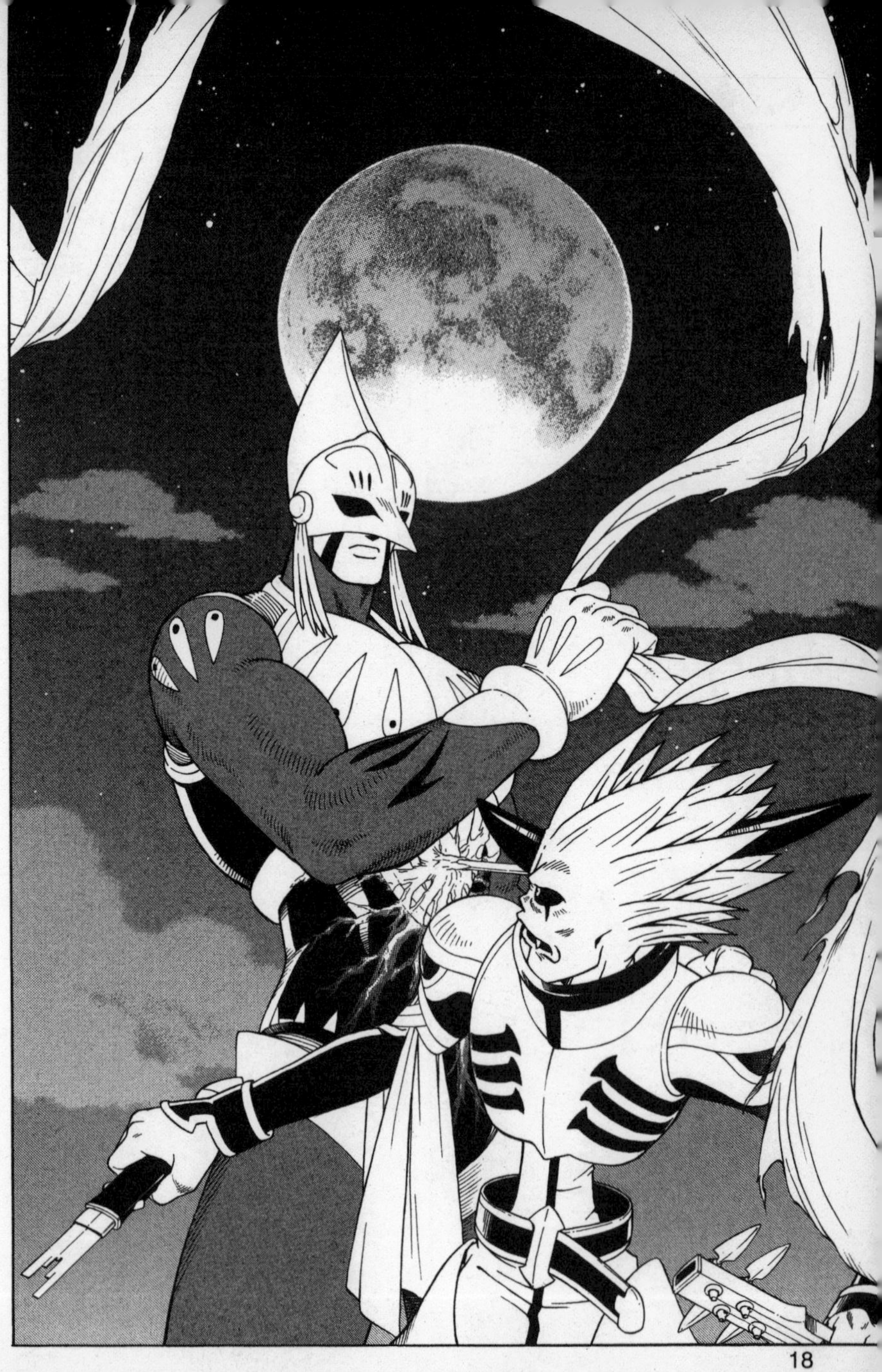

READ THIS WAY

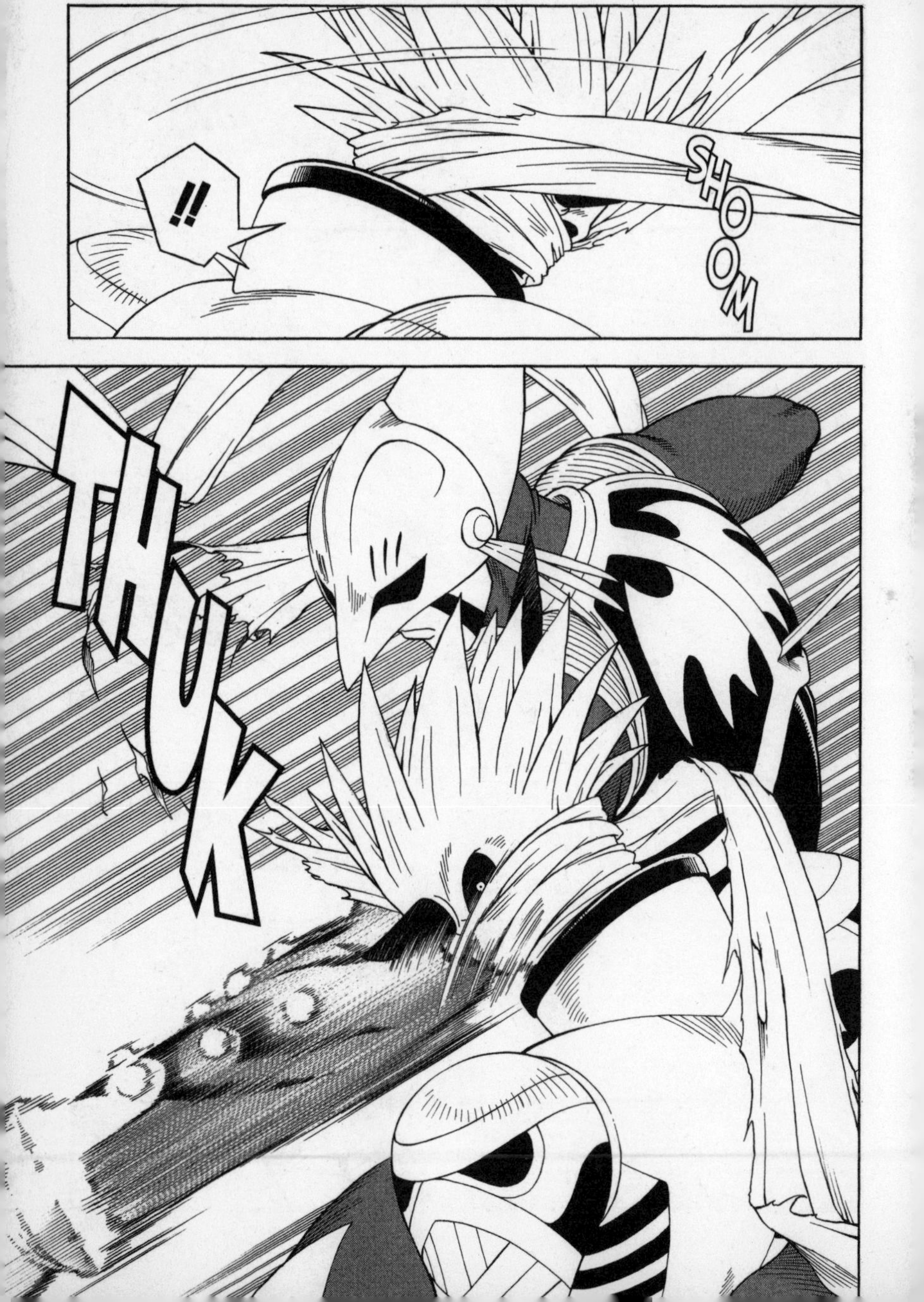
SHOOM
!!
THUK

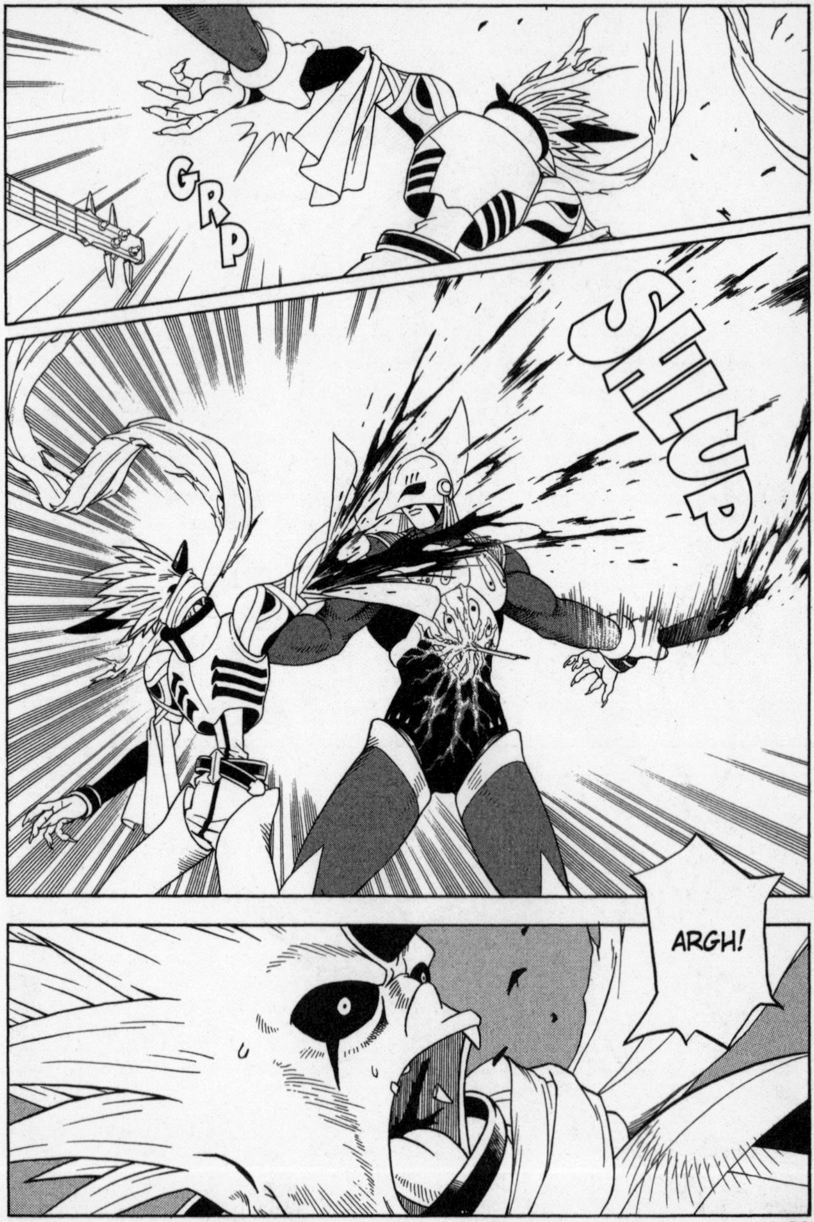
GRP
SHLUP
ARGH!

READ THIS WAY

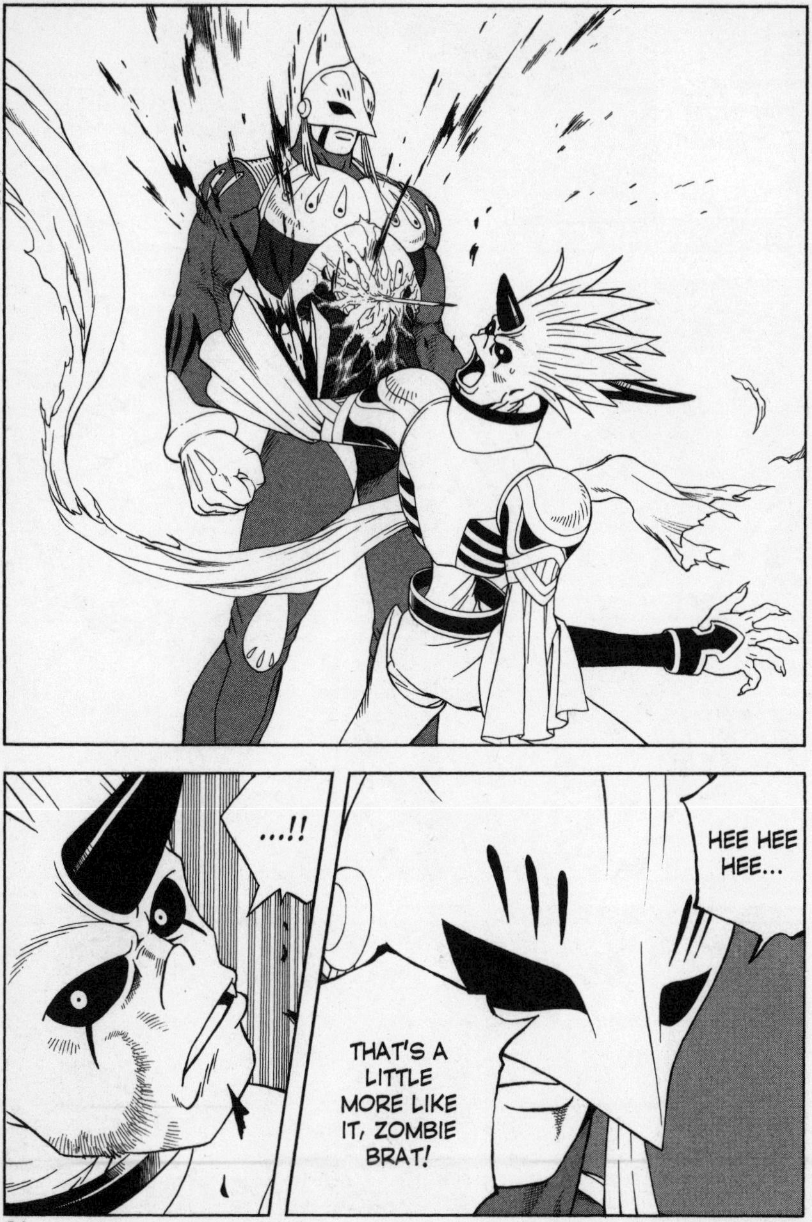
HEE HEE HEE...
THAT'S A LITTLE MORE LIKE IT, ZOMBIE BRAT!
...!!

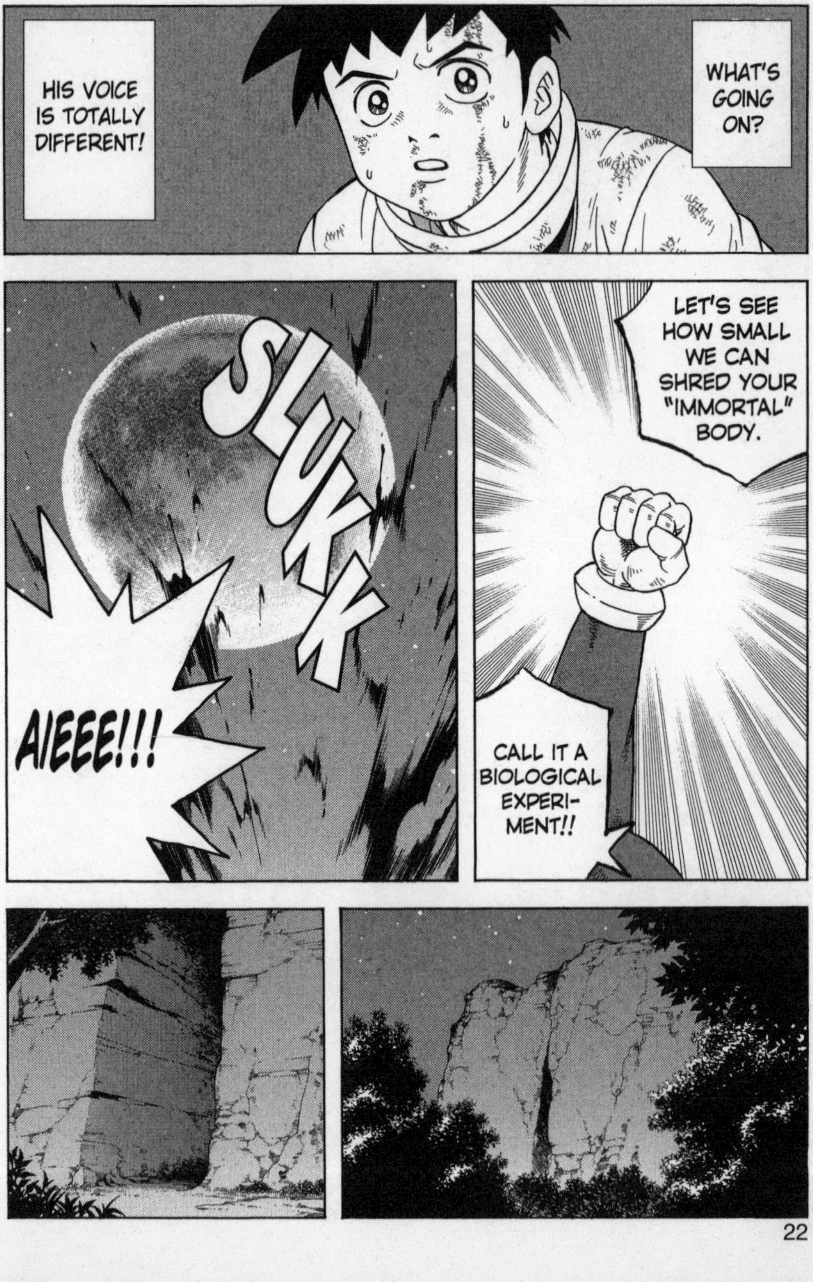
WHAT'S GOING ON?
HIS VOICE IS TOTALLY DIFFERENT!
LET'S SEE HOW SMALL WE CAN SHRED YOUR "IMMORTAL" BODY.
CALL IT A BIOLOGICAL EXPERI-MENT!!
SLUKK
AIEEE!!!

READ THIS WAY

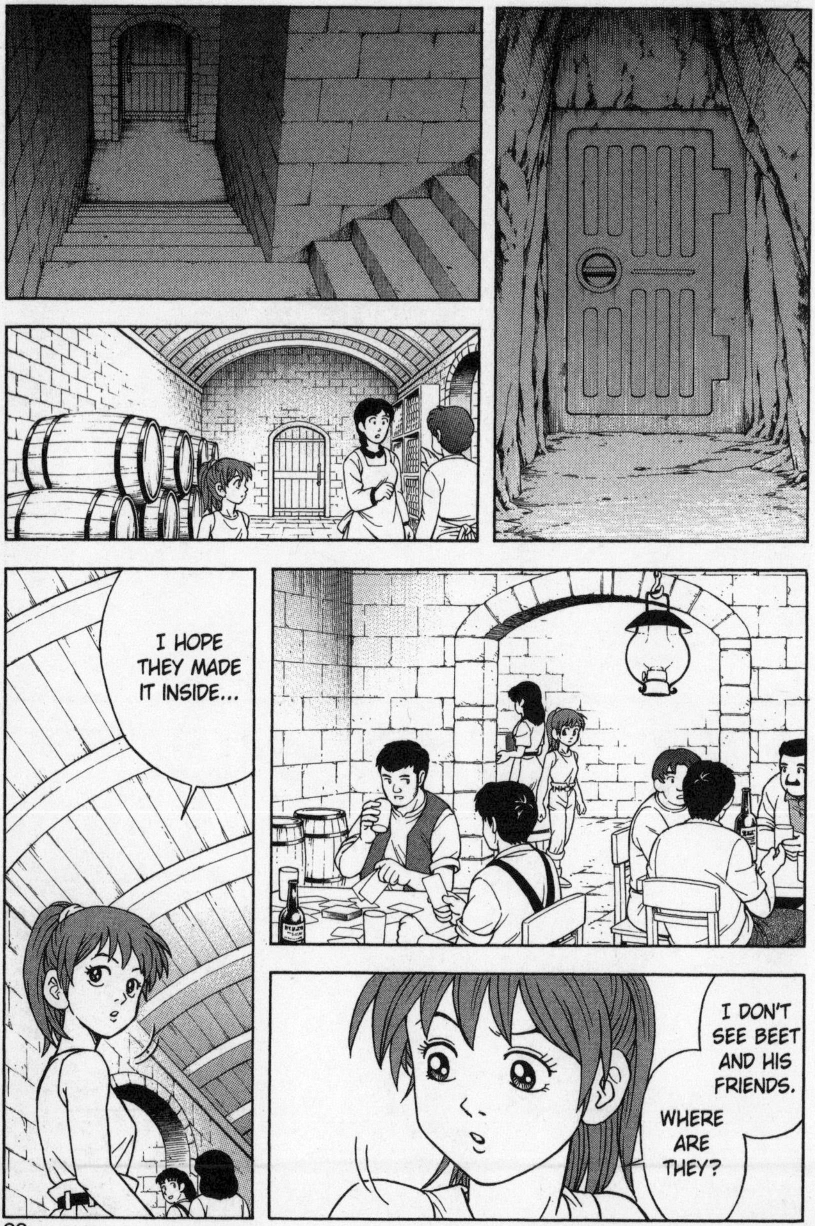
I DON'T SEE BEET AND HIS FRIENDS.
WHERE ARE THEY?
I HOPE THEY MADE IT INSIDE...

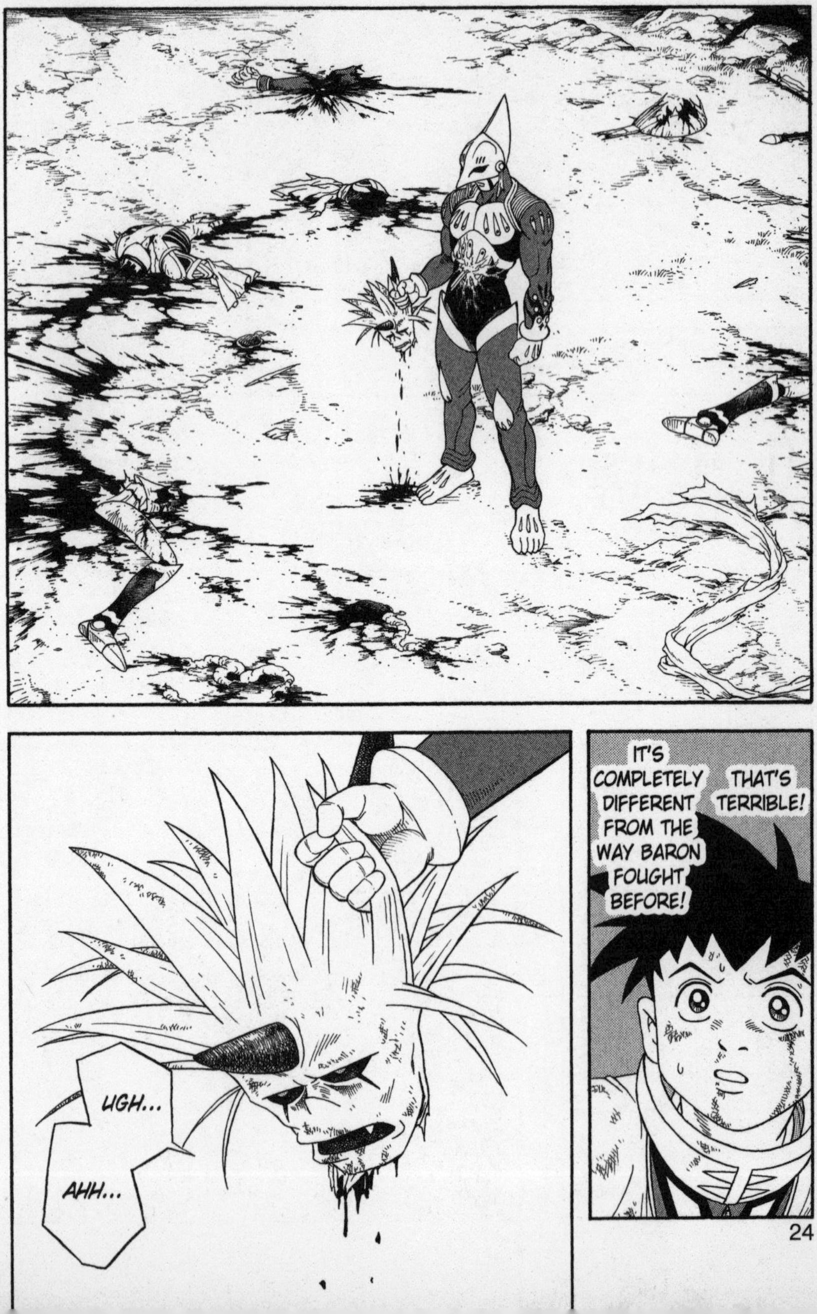
THAT'S TERRIBLE!
IT'S COMPLETELY DIFFERENT FROM THE WAY BARON FOUGHT BEFORE!
UGH...
AHH...

READ THIS WAY

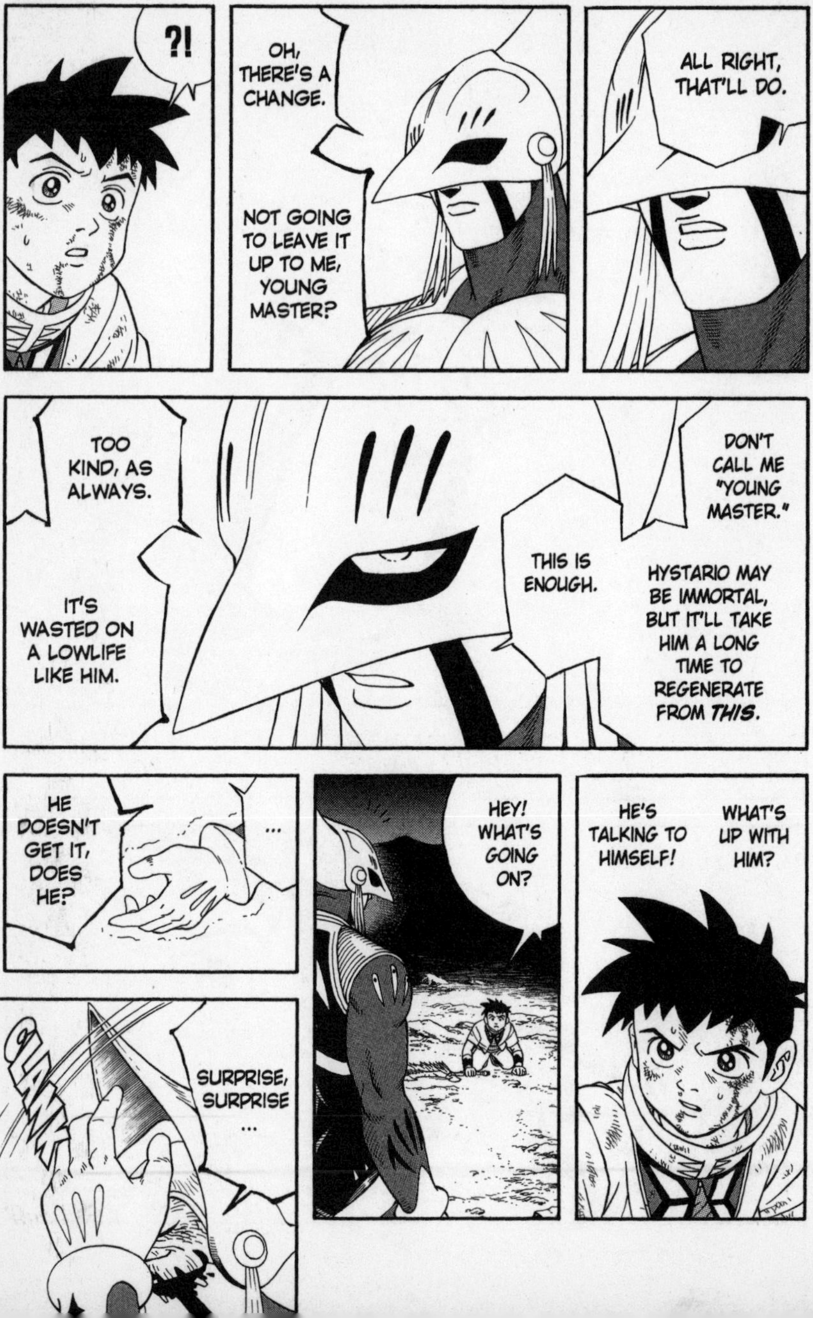
ALL RIGHT, THAT'LL DO.
OH, THERE'S A CHANGE.
NOT GOING TO LEAVE IT UP TO ME, YOUNG MASTER?
?!
DON'T CALL ME "YOUNG MASTER."
HYSTARIO MAY BE IMMORTAL, BUT IT'LL TAKE HIM A LONG TIME TO REGENERATE FROM *THIS*.
THIS IS ENOUGH.
TOO KIND, AS ALWAYS.
IT'S WASTED ON A LOWLIFE LIKE HIM.
WHAT'S UP WITH HIM?
HE'S TALKING TO HIMSELF!
HEY! WHAT'S GOING ON?
...
HE DOESN'T GET IT, DOES HE?
SURPRISE, SURPRISE ...
CLANK

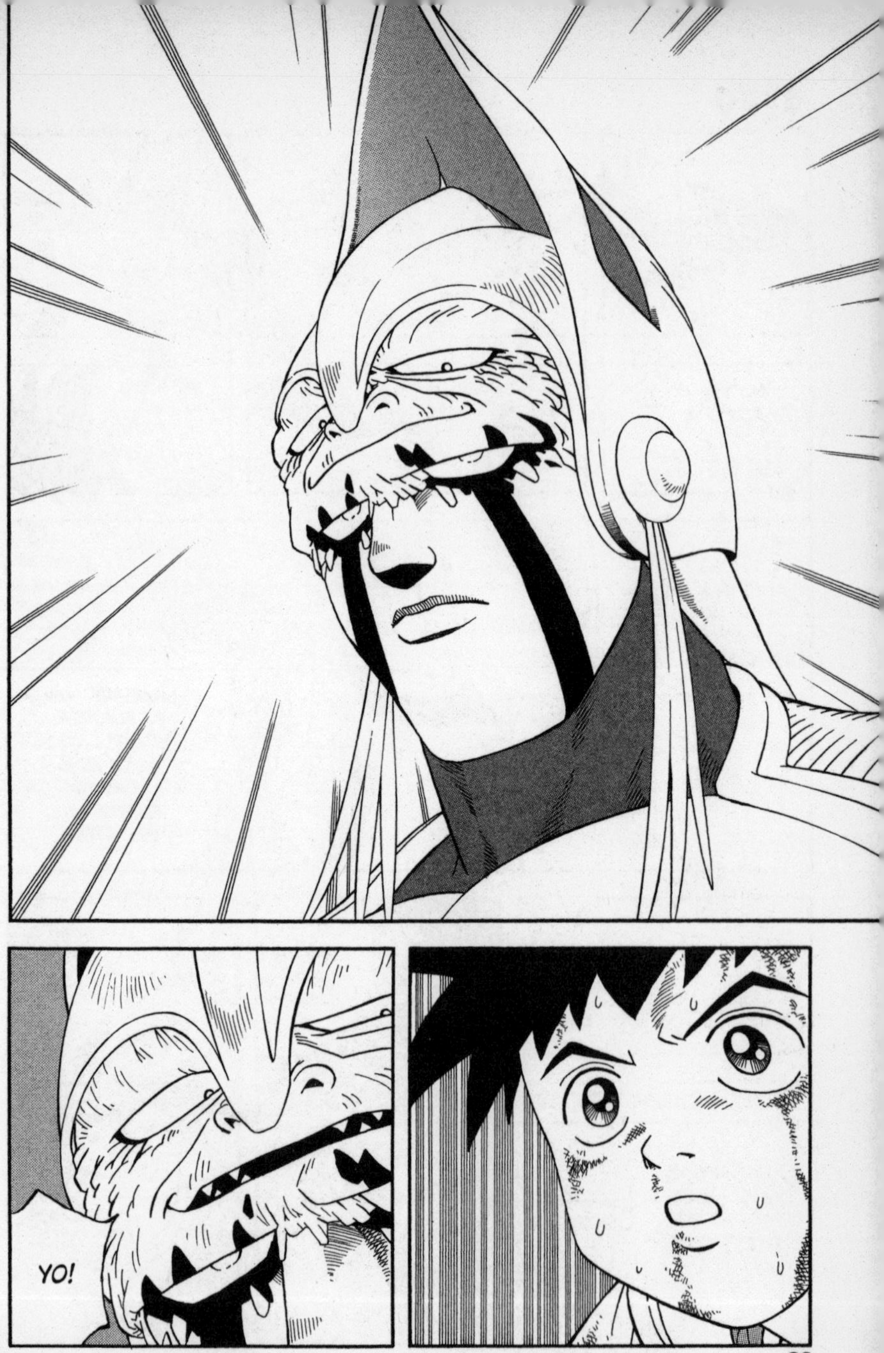
YO!

READ THIS WAY

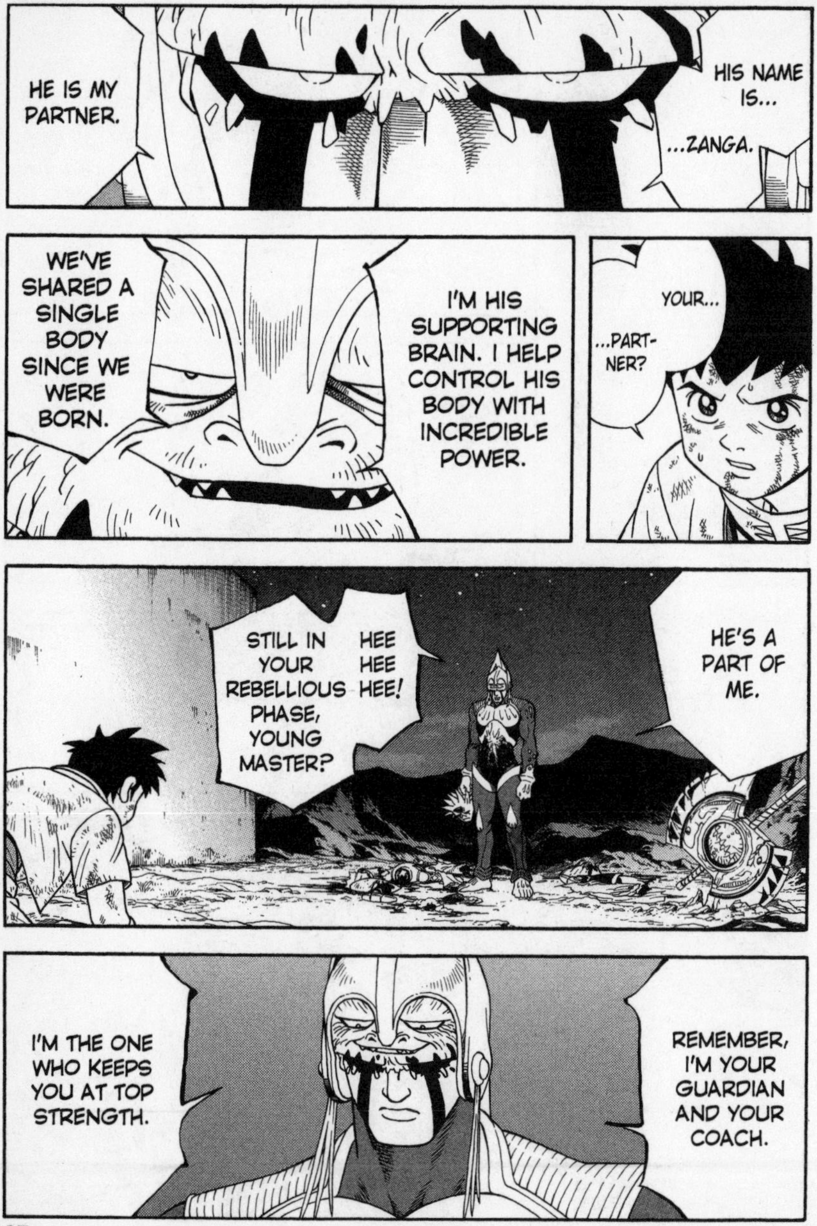

HIS NAME IS...
...ZANGA.
HE IS MY PARTNER.
YOUR...
...PART-NER?
I'M HIS SUPPORTING BRAIN. I HELP CONTROL HIS BODY WITH INCREDIBLE POWER.
WE'VE SHARED A SINGLE BODY SINCE WE WERE BORN.
HE'S A PART OF ME.
HEE HEE HEE!
STILL IN YOUR REBELLIOUS PHASE, YOUNG MASTER?
REMEMBER, I'M YOUR GUARDIAN AND YOUR COACH.
I'M THE ONE WHO KEEPS YOU AT TOP STRENGTH.

THUP

IT'S NOT THAT I DON'T APPRECI-ATE YOU

...ZANGA.

YOU'RE A GOOD BOY.

KLINK

HFF

...

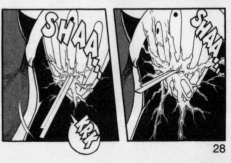

SHAA...!

SHAA...!

KRK

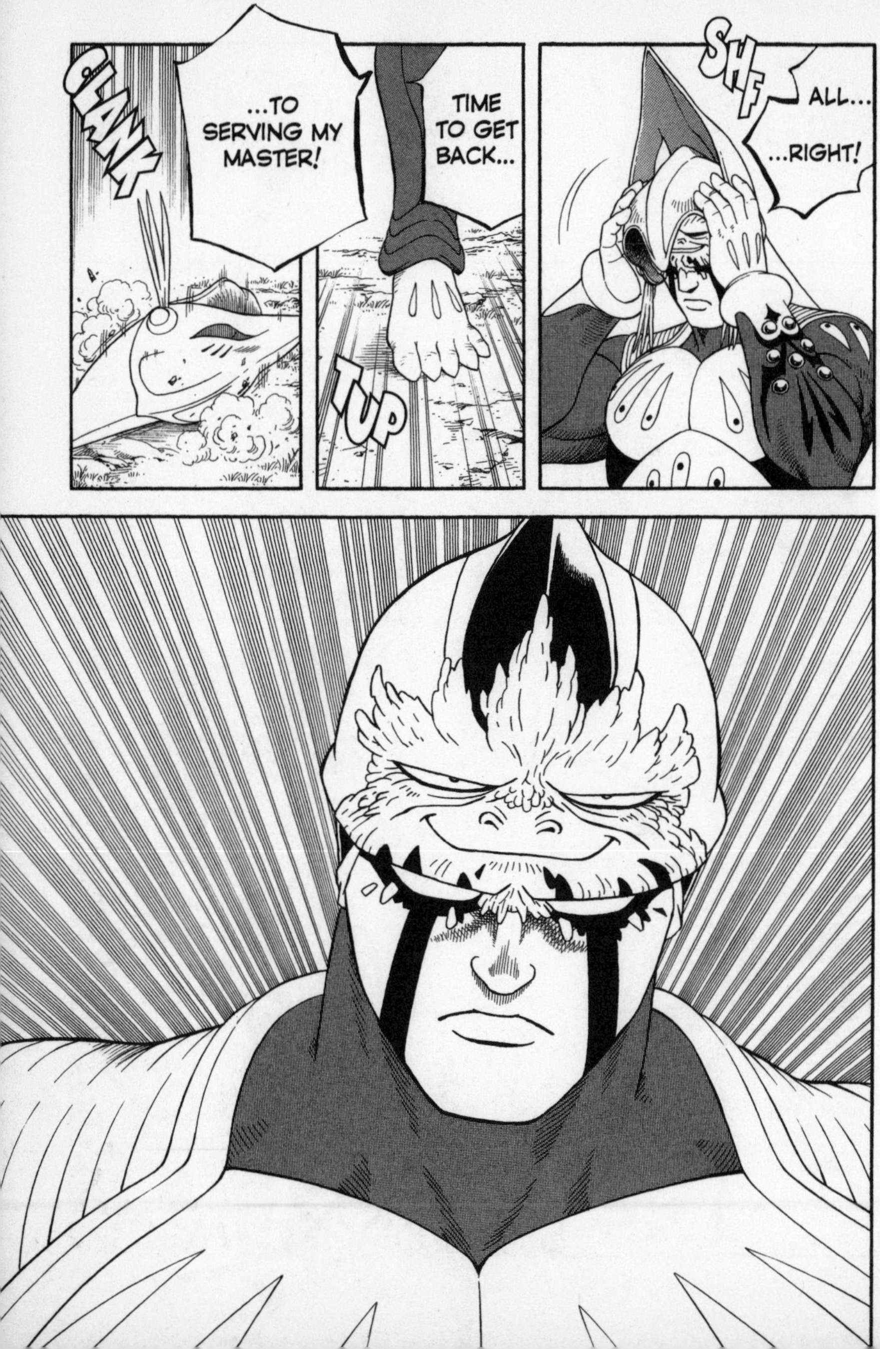
SHF
ALL...
...RIGHT!
TIME TO GET BACK...
TUP
...TO SERVING MY MASTER!
CLANK

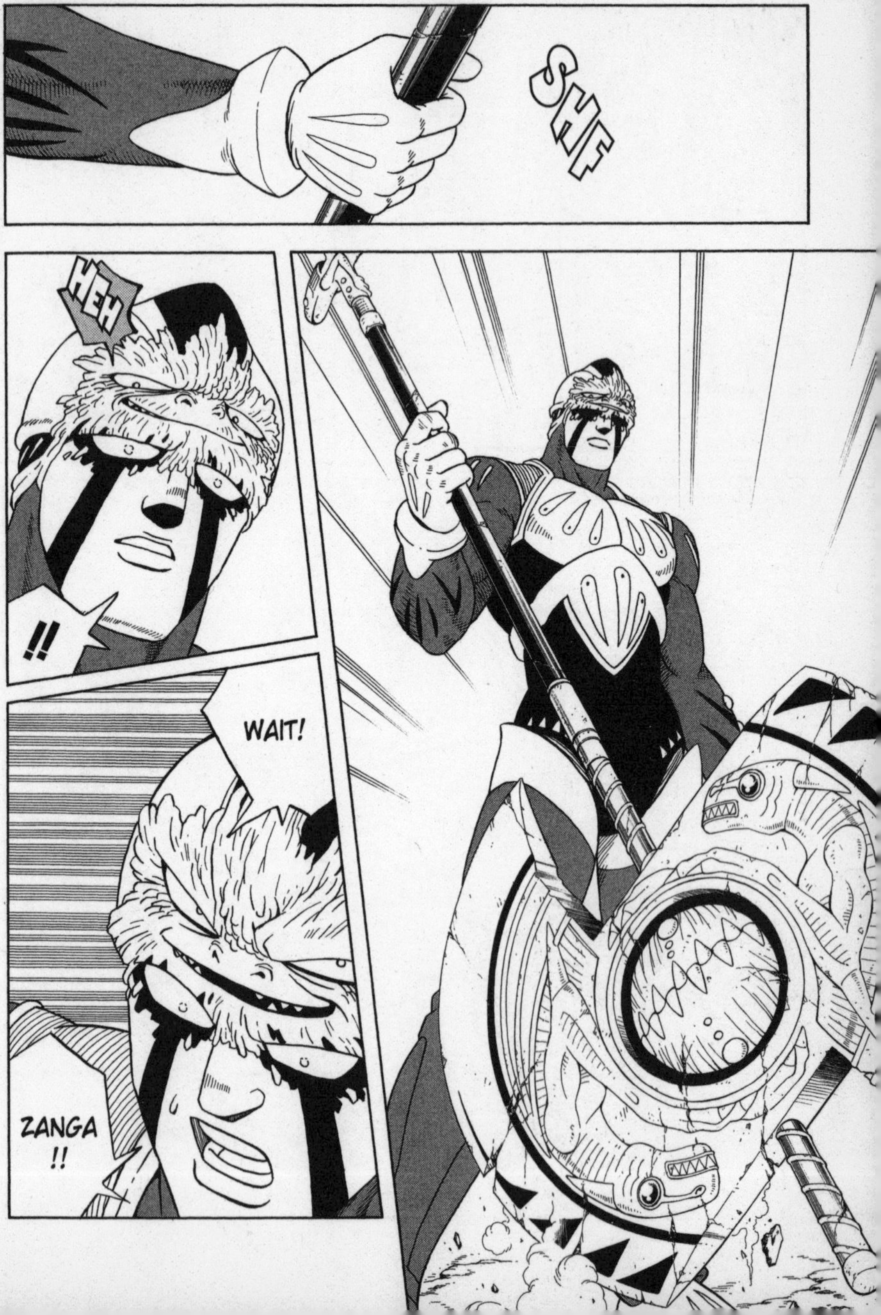
SHF
HEH
!!
WAIT!
ZANGA !!

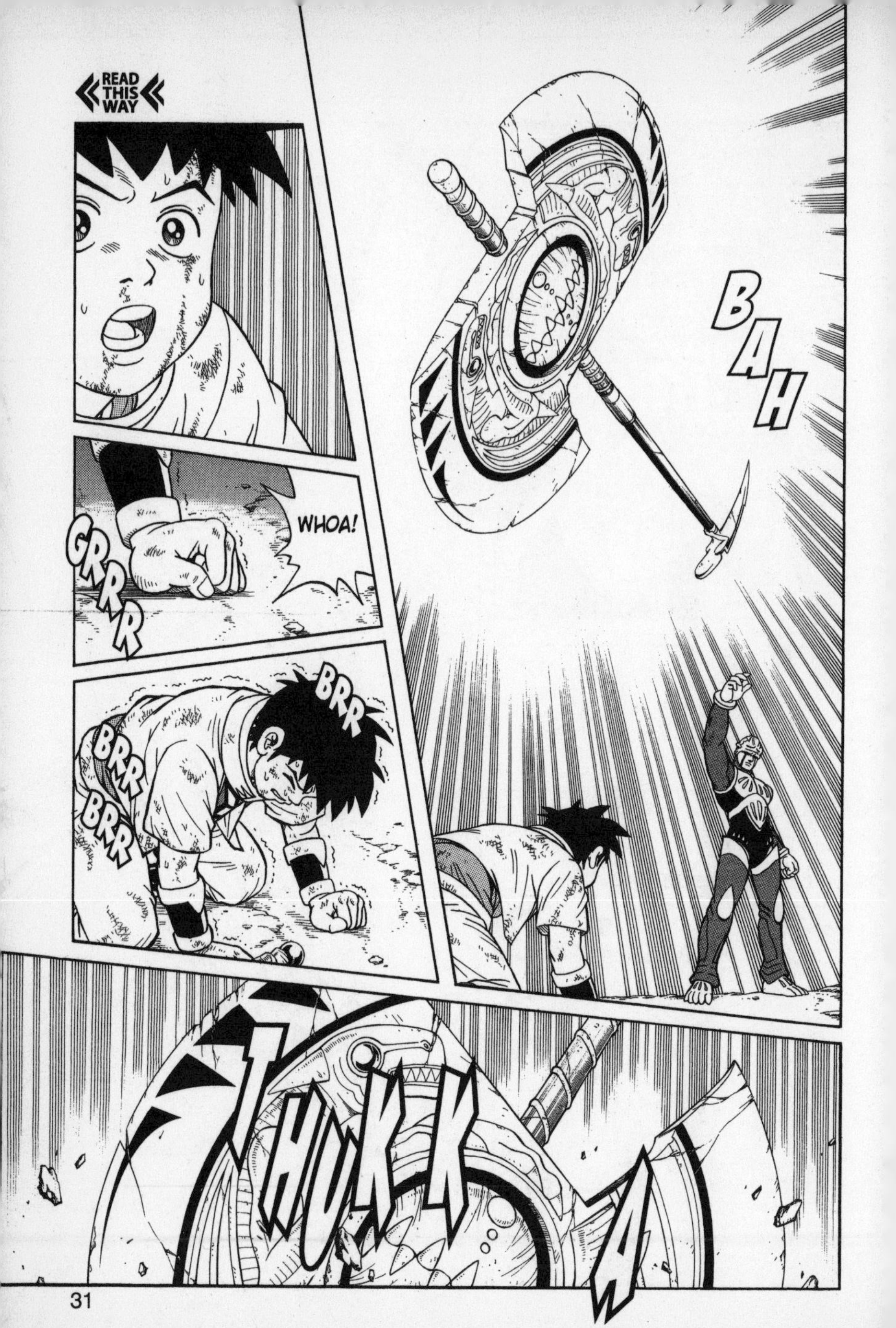
READ THIS WAY
BAH
WHOA!
GRRRR
BRRR
BRRR
BRRR
THUKKA

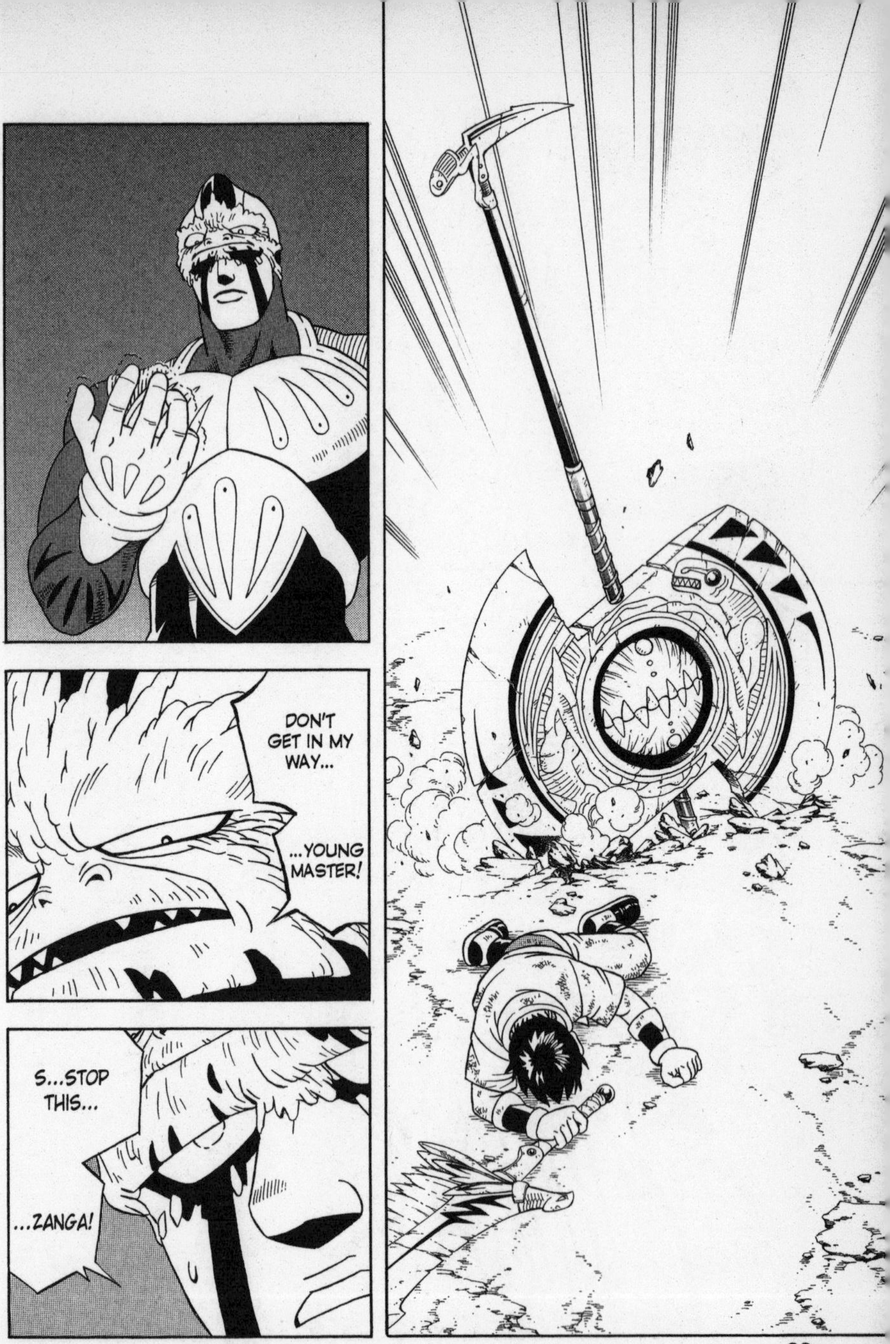
DON'T GET IN MY WAY...
...YOUNG MASTER!
S...STOP THIS...
...ZANGA!

READ THIS WAY

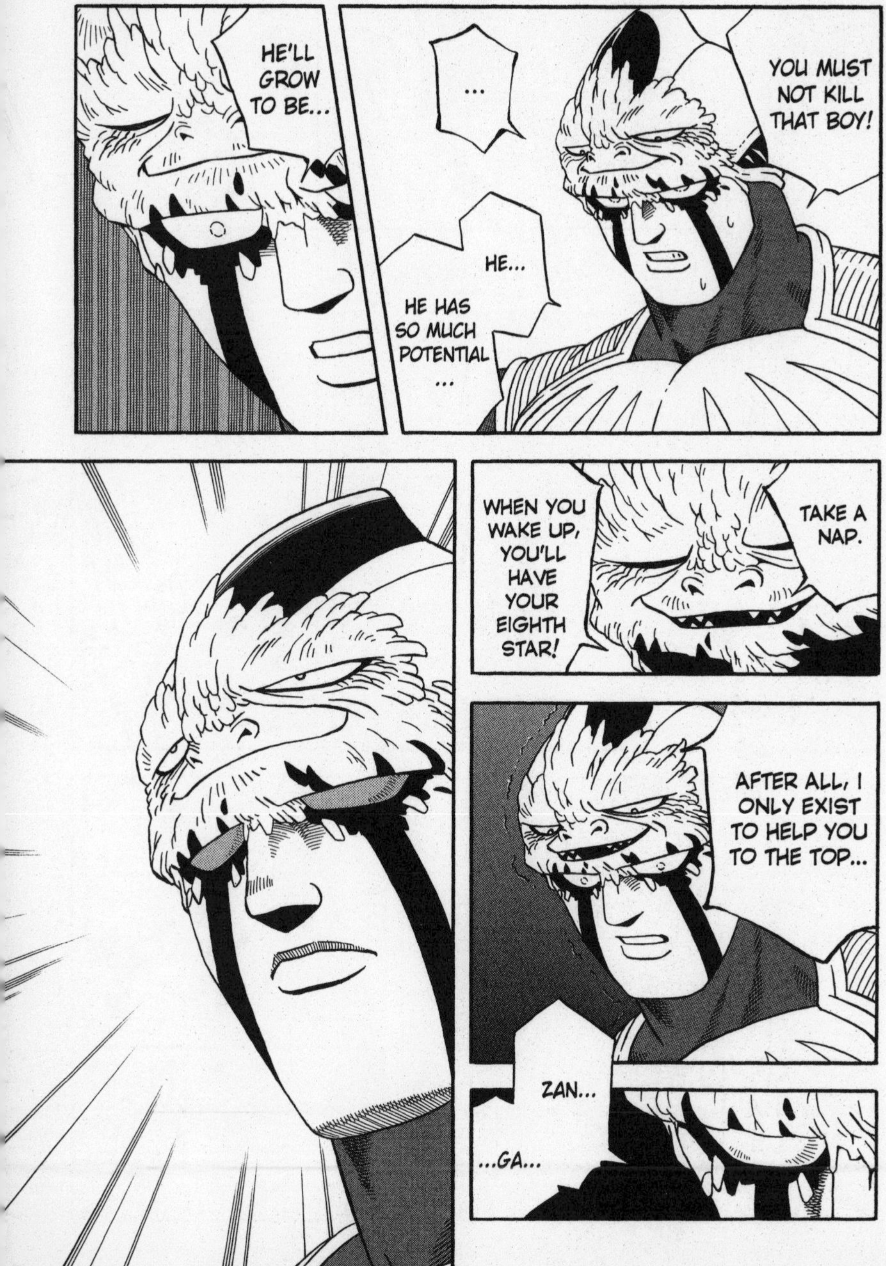

YOU MUST NOT KILL THAT BOY!
...
HE...
HE HAS SO MUCH POTENTIAL ...
HE'LL GROW TO BE...
TAKE A NAP.
WHEN YOU WAKE UP, YOU'LL HAVE YOUR EIGHTH STAR!
AFTER ALL, I ONLY EXIST TO HELP YOU TO THE TOP...
ZAN...
...GA...

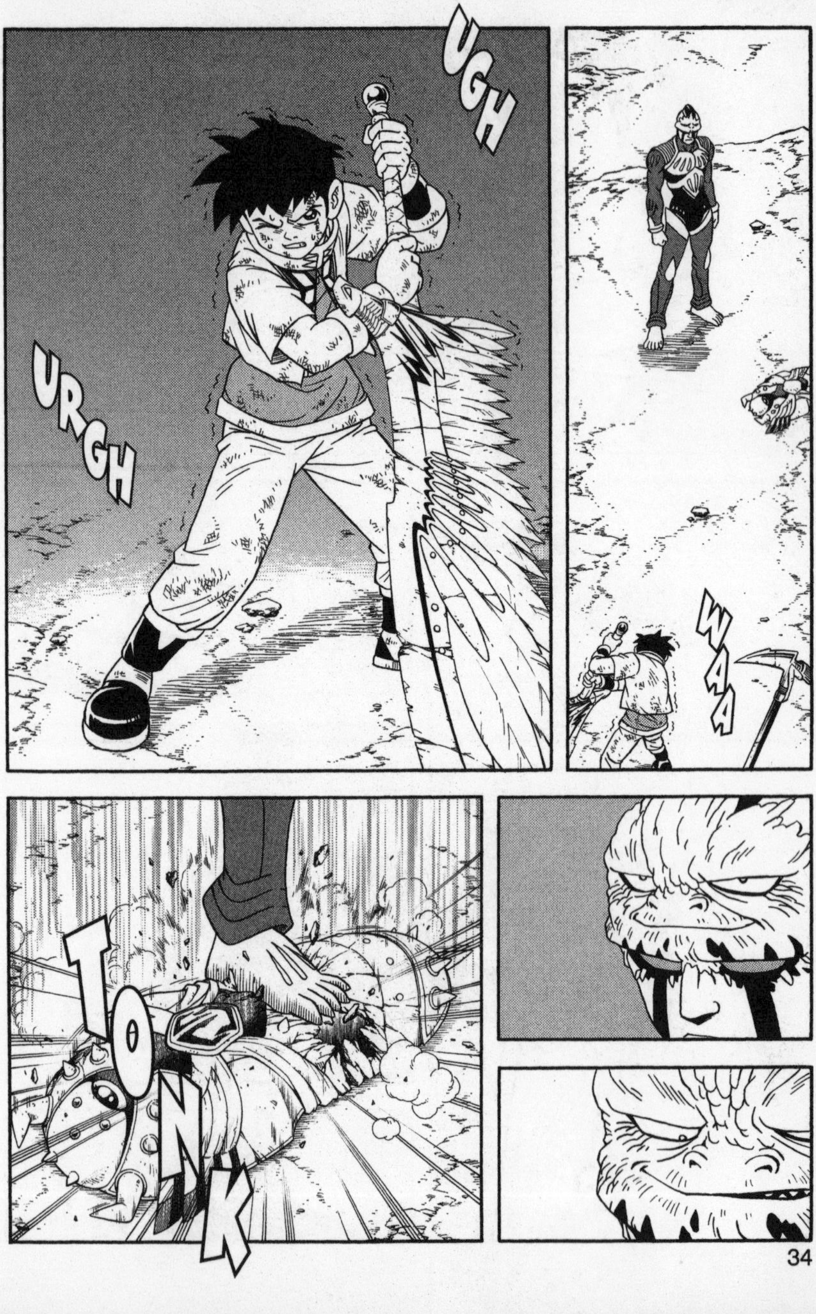
WAA
UGH
URGH
TONK

READ THIS WAY

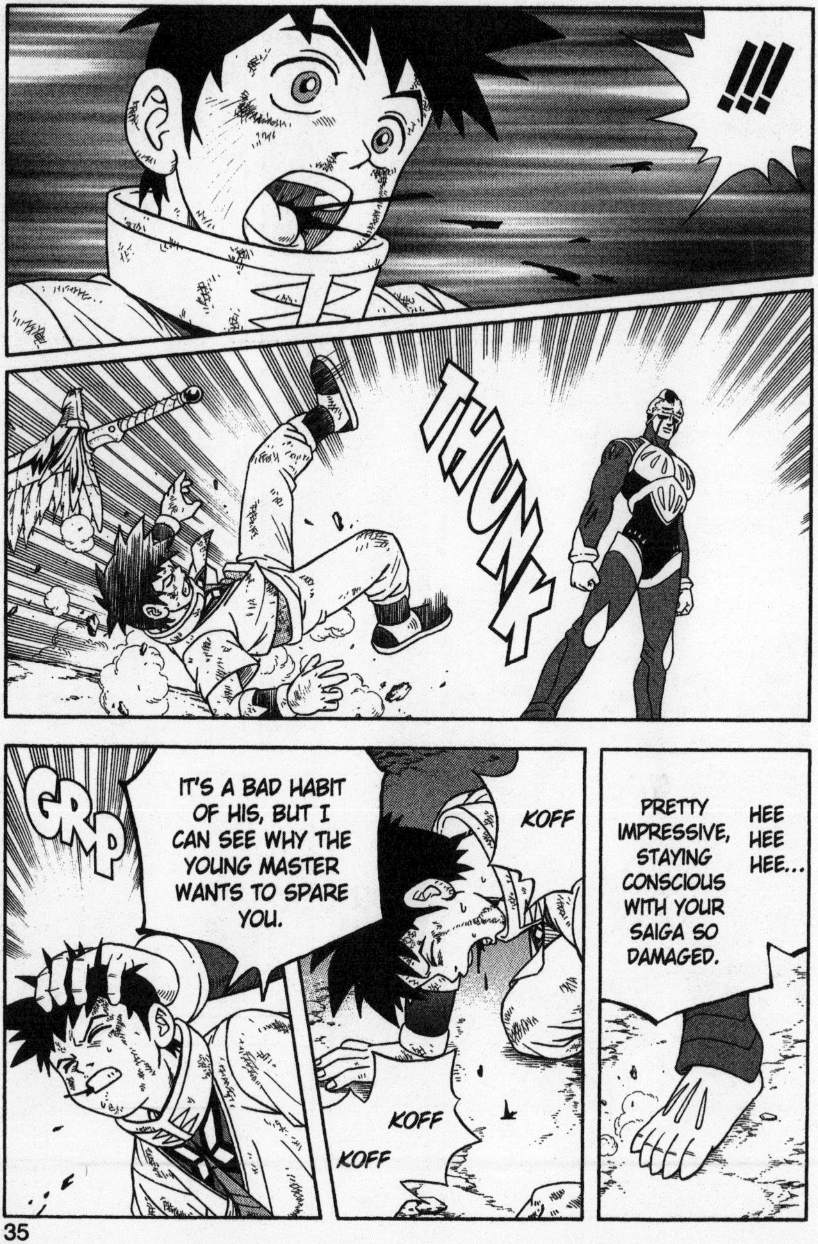
!!!!
THUNK
HEE HEE HEE...
PRETTY IMPRESSIVE, STAYING CONSCIOUS WITH YOUR SAIGA SO DAMAGED.
KOFF
IT'S A BAD HABIT OF HIS, BUT I CAN SEE WHY THE YOUNG MASTER WANTS TO SPARE YOU.
GRP
KOFF
KOFF

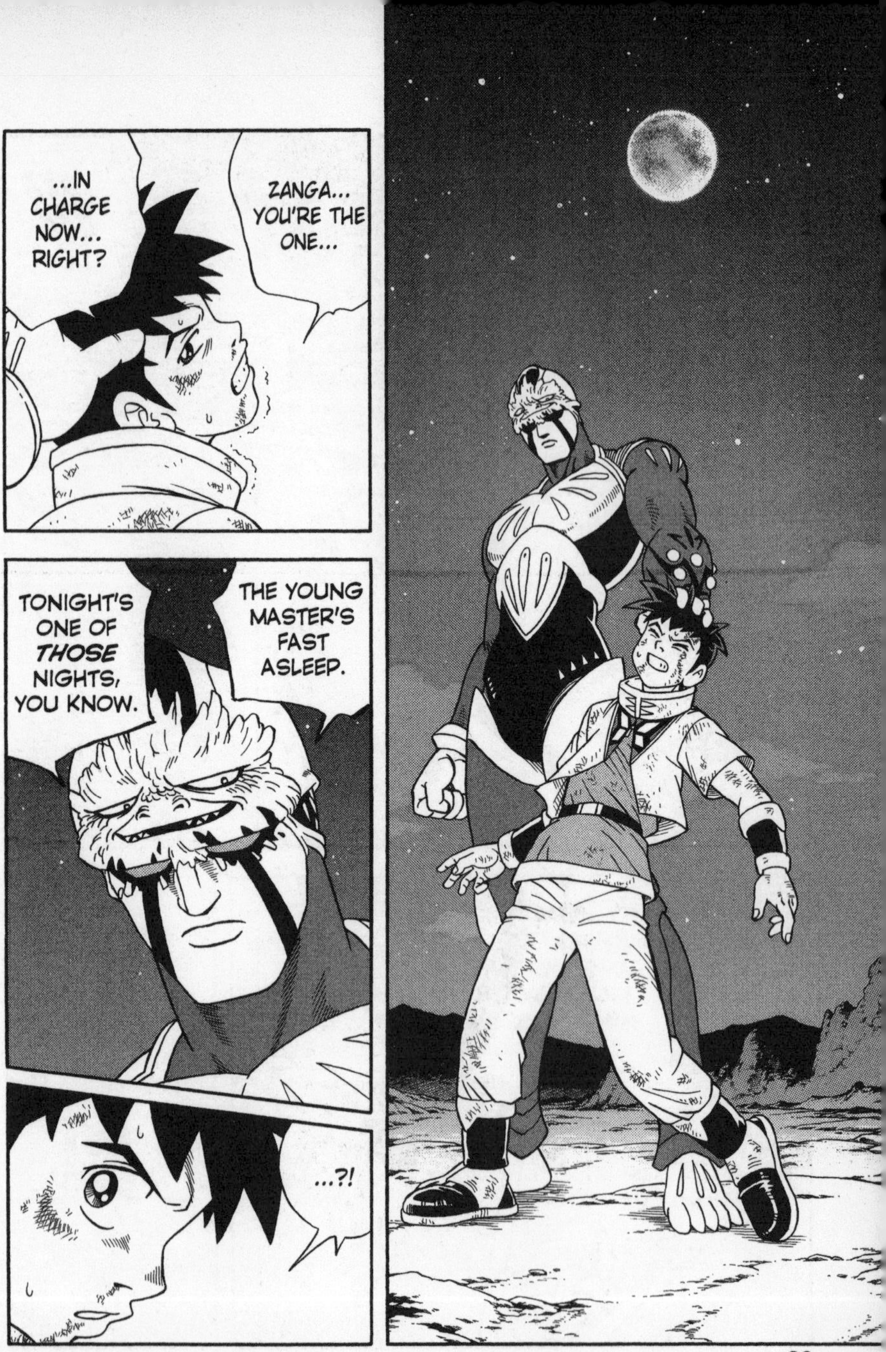
ZANGA... YOU'RE THE ONE...
...IN CHARGE NOW... RIGHT?
THE YOUNG MASTER'S FAST ASLEEP.
TONIGHT'S ONE OF *THOSE* NIGHTS, YOU KNOW.
...?!

READ THIS WAY

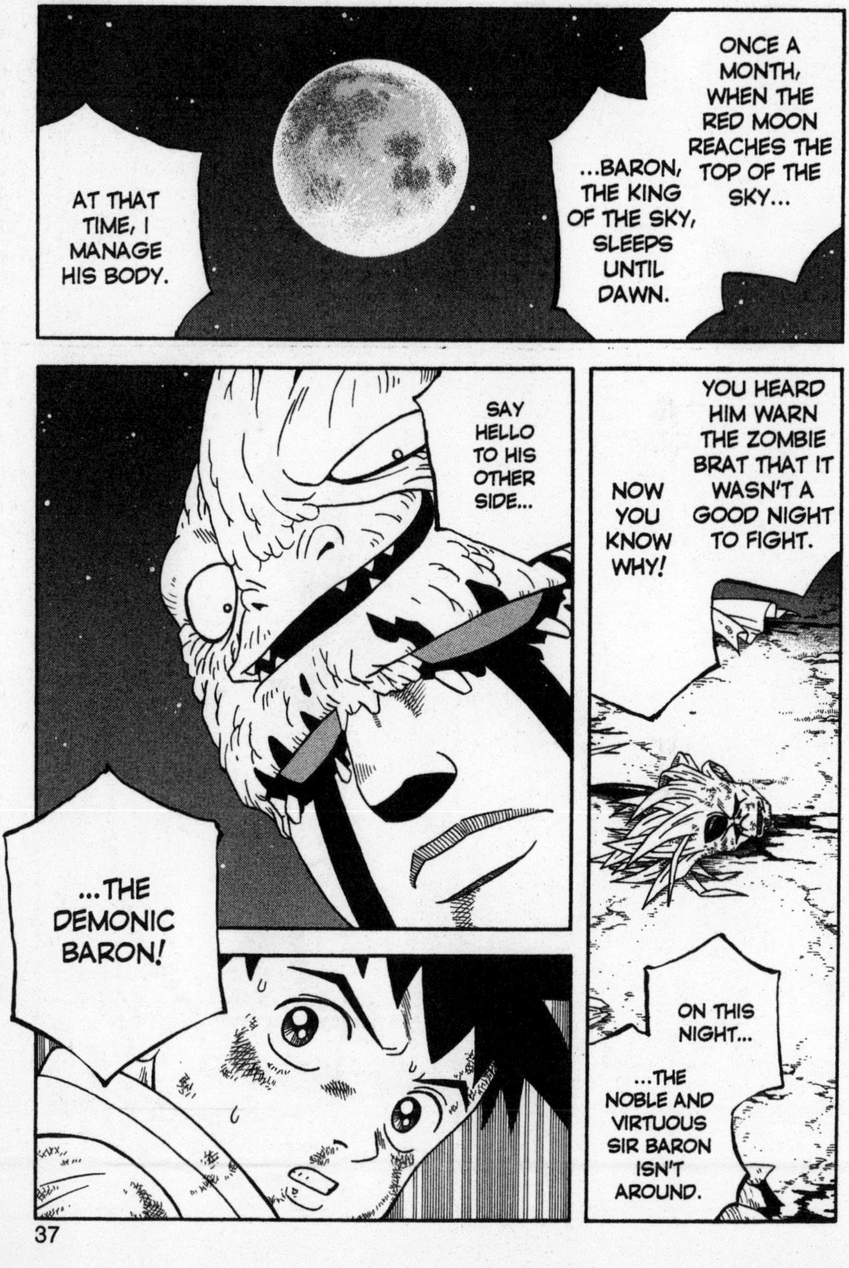
ONCE A MONTH, WHEN THE RED MOON REACHES THE TOP OF THE SKY...
...BARON, THE KING OF THE SKY, SLEEPS UNTIL DAWN.
AT THAT TIME, I MANAGE HIS BODY.
YOU HEARD HIM WARN THE ZOMBIE BRAT THAT IT WASN'T A GOOD NIGHT TO FIGHT.
NOW YOU KNOW WHY!
ON THIS NIGHT...
...THE NOBLE AND VIRTUOUS SIR BARON ISN'T AROUND.
SAY HELLO TO HIS OTHER SIDE...
...THE DEMONIC BARON!

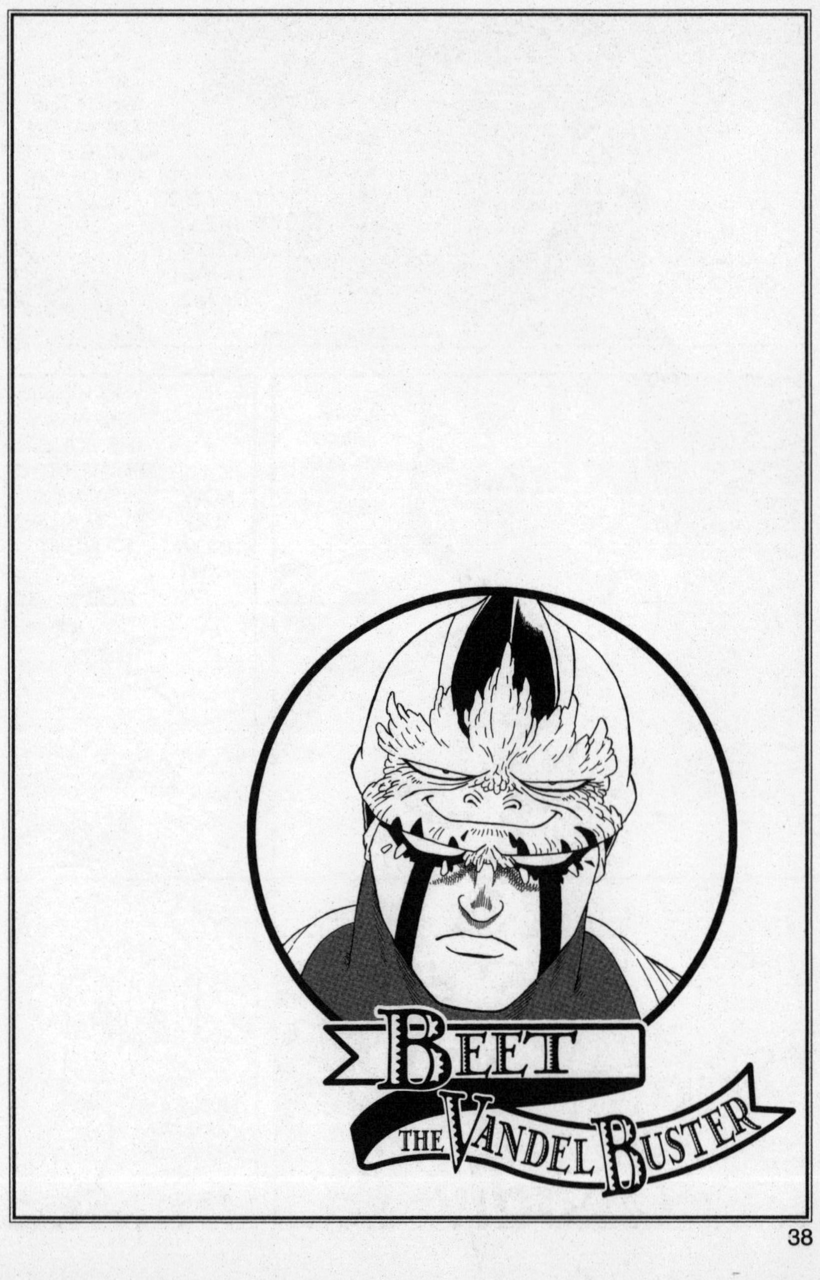
BEET
THE VANDEL BUSTER

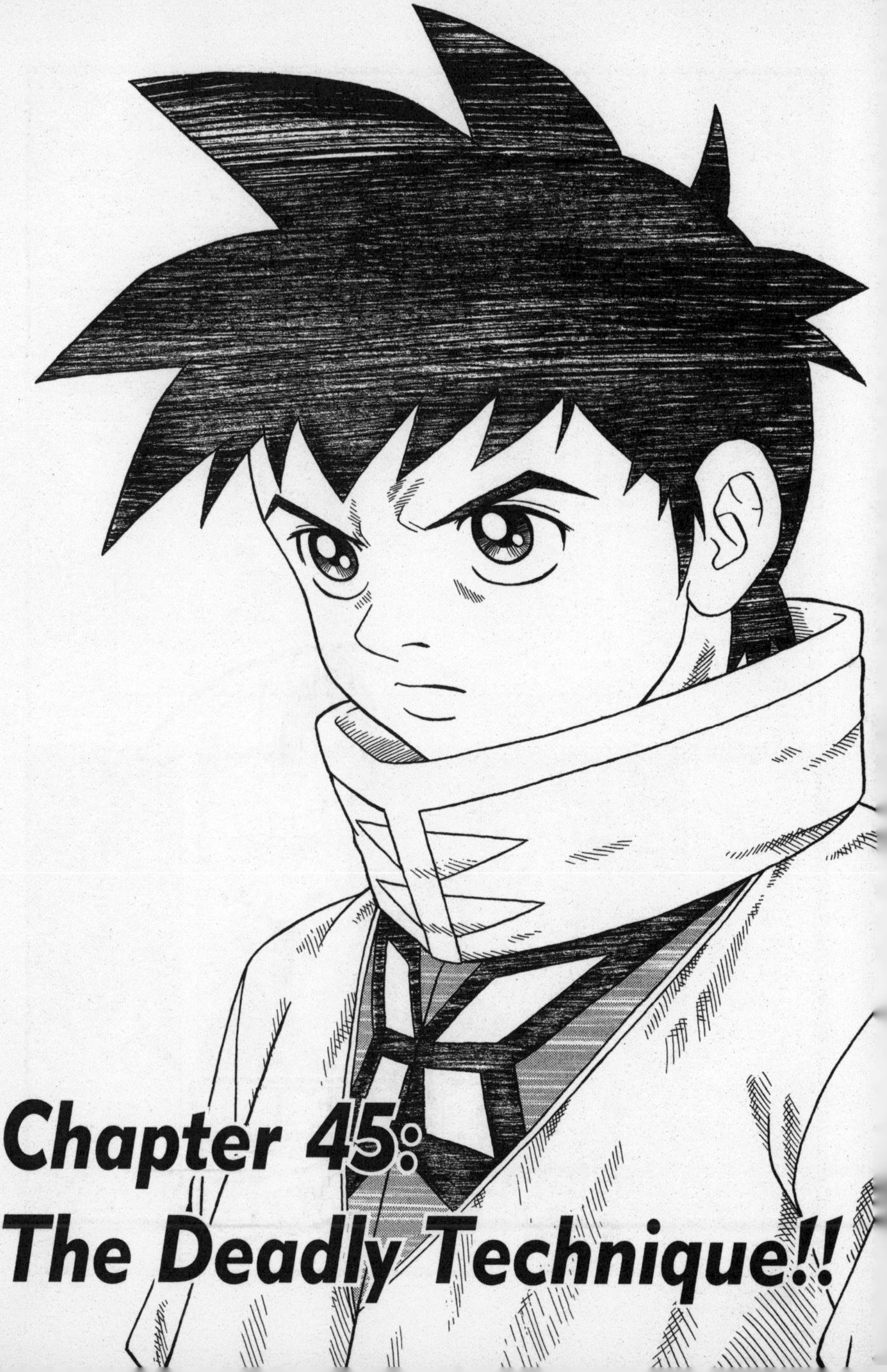
Chapter 45:
The Deadly Technique!!

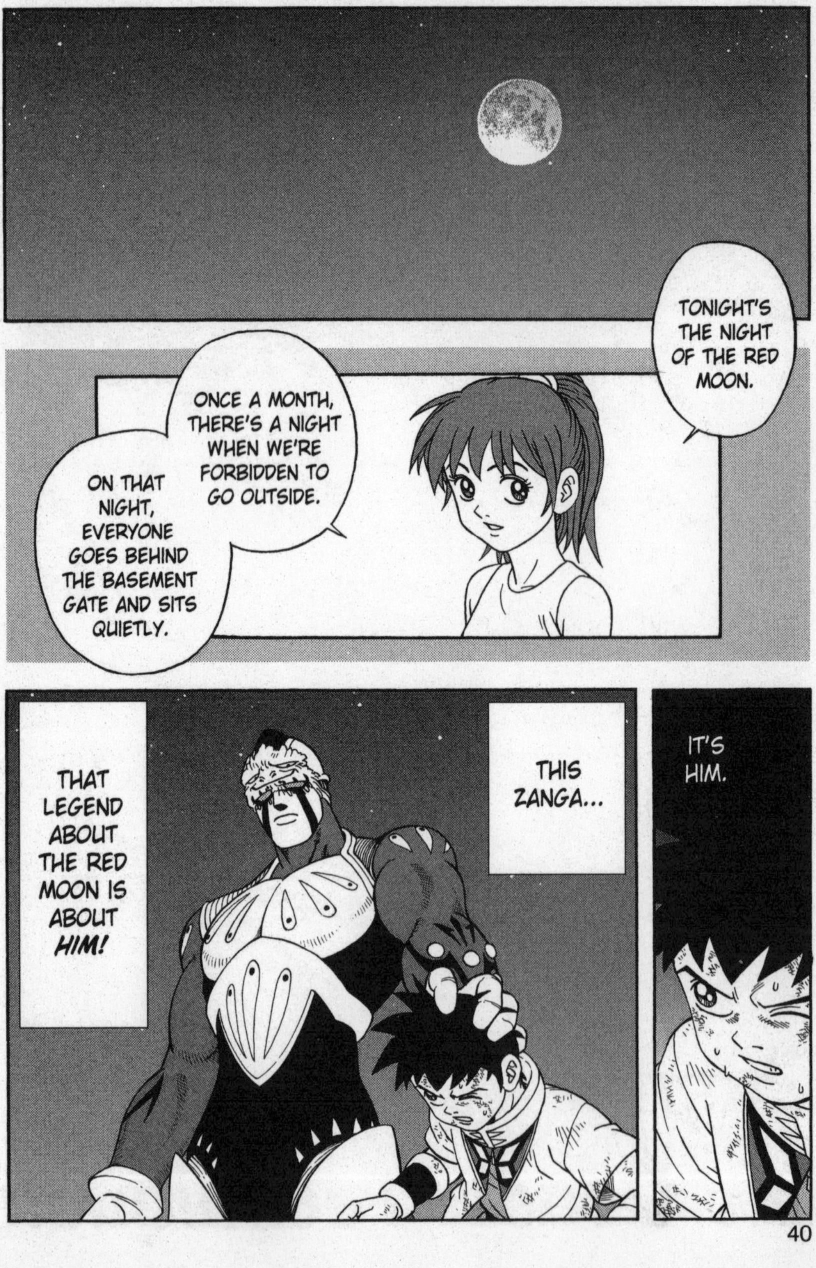
TONIGHT'S THE NIGHT OF THE RED MOON.
ONCE A MONTH, THERE'S A NIGHT WHEN WE'RE FORBIDDEN TO GO OUTSIDE.
ON THAT NIGHT, EVERYONE GOES BEHIND THE BASEMENT GATE AND SITS QUIETLY.
IT'S HIM.
THIS ZANGA...
THAT LEGEND ABOUT THE RED MOON IS ABOUT *HIM!*

READ THIS WAY

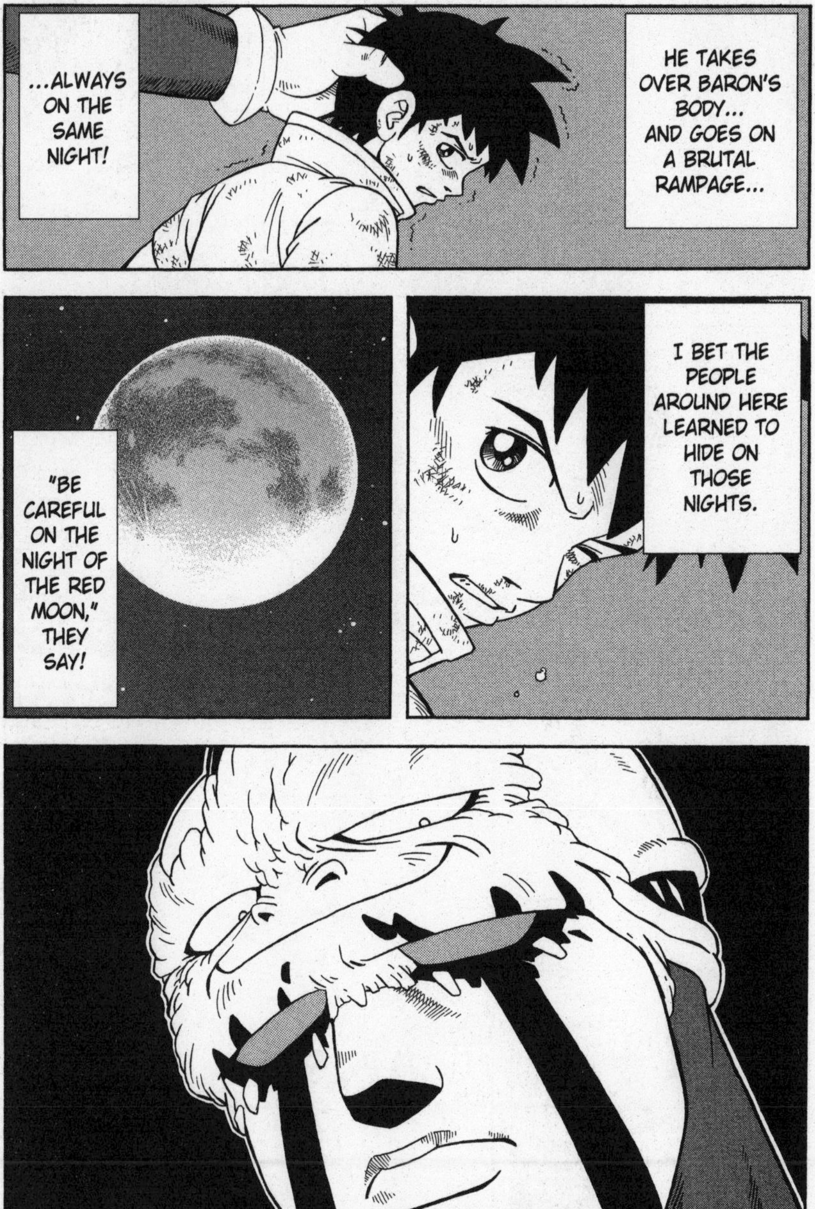
HE TAKES OVER BARON'S BODY... AND GOES ON A BRUTAL RAMPAGE...
...ALWAYS ON THE SAME NIGHT!
I BET THE PEOPLE AROUND HERE LEARNED TO HIDE ON THOSE NIGHTS.
"BE CAREFUL ON THE NIGHT OF THE RED MOON," THEY SAY!

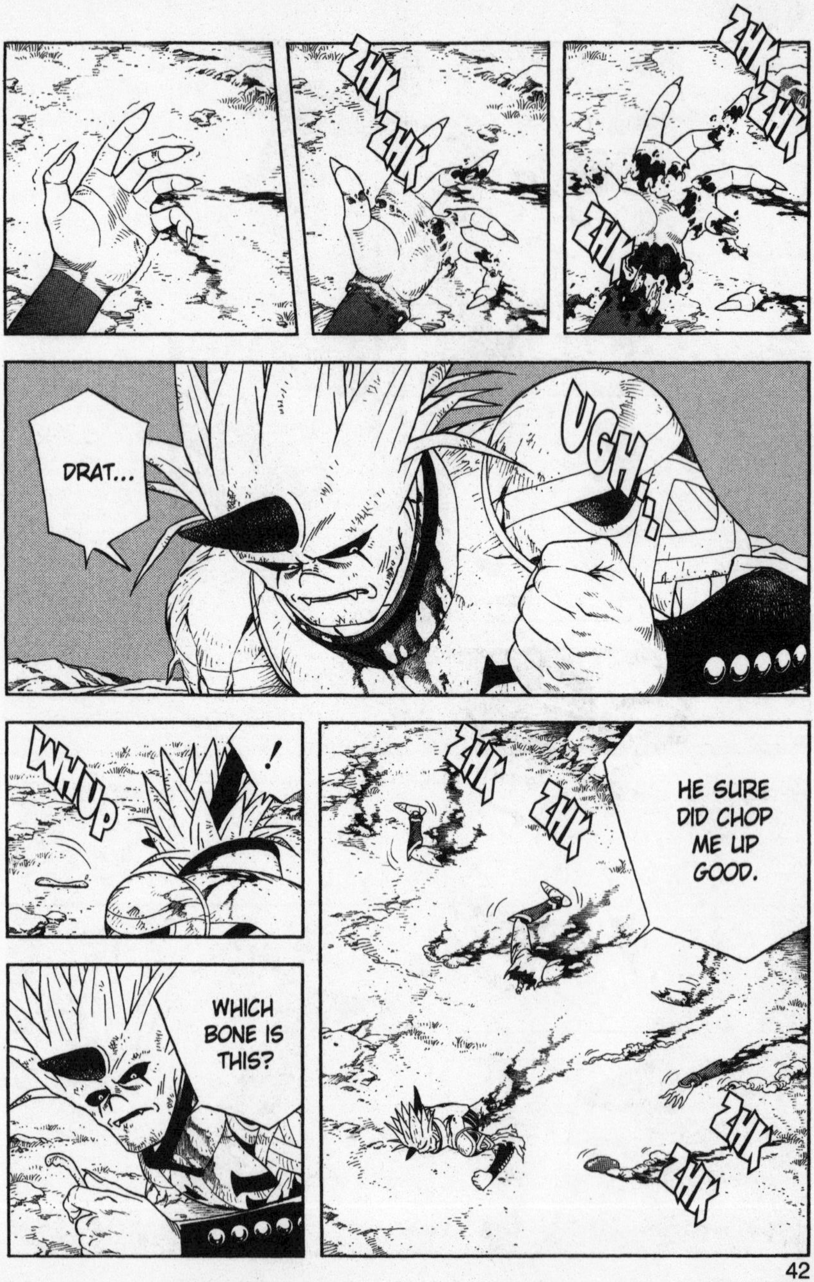
ZHK
ZHK
ZHK
ZHK
ZHK
ZHK
DRAT...
UGH...
ZHK
ZHK
HE SURE DID CHOP ME UP GOOD.
ZHK
ZHK
WHUP
!
WHICH BONE IS THIS?

READ THIS WAY

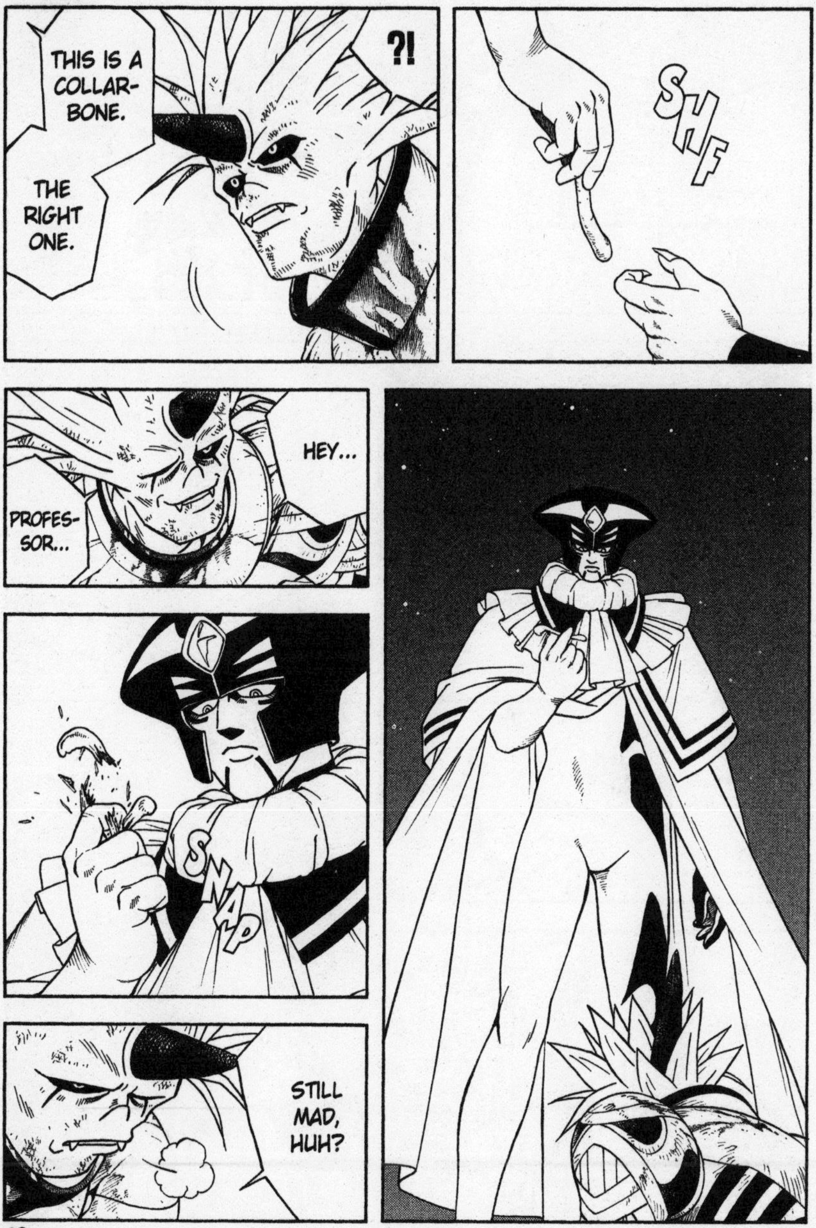
SHF
?!
THIS IS A COLLAR-BONE.
THE RIGHT ONE.
HEY...
PROFES-SOR...
SNAP
STILL MAD, HUH?

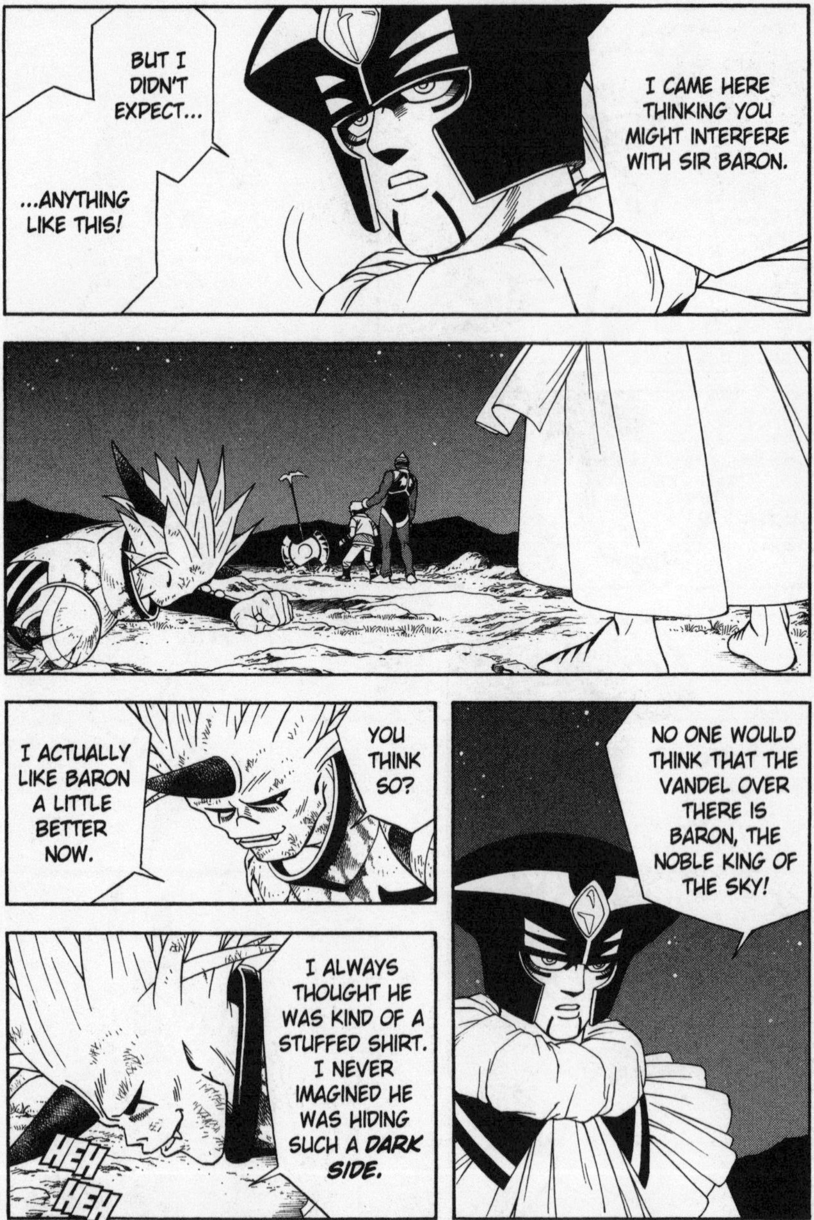
I CAME HERE THINKING YOU MIGHT INTERFERE WITH SIR BARON.
BUT I DIDN'T EXPECT...
...ANYTHING LIKE THIS!
NO ONE WOULD THINK THAT THE VANDEL OVER THERE IS BARON, THE NOBLE KING OF THE SKY!
YOU THINK SO?
I ACTUALLY LIKE BARON A LITTLE BETTER NOW.
I ALWAYS THOUGHT HE WAS KIND OF A STUFFED SHIRT. I NEVER IMAGINED HE WAS HIDING SUCH A *DARK SIDE.*
HEH HEH

READ THIS WAY

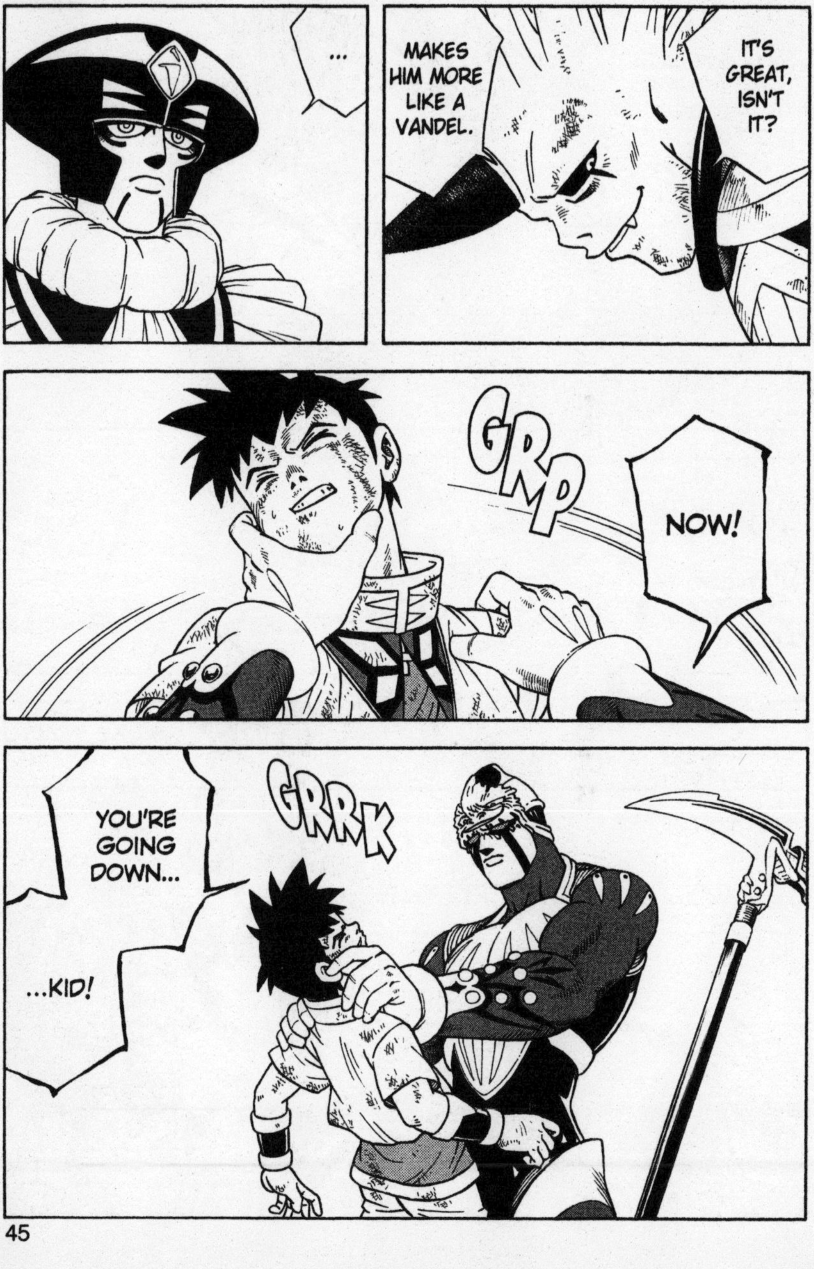
IT'S GREAT, ISN'T IT?
MAKES HIM MORE LIKE A VANDEL.
...
NOW!
GRP
GRRK
YOU'RE GOING DOWN...
...KID!

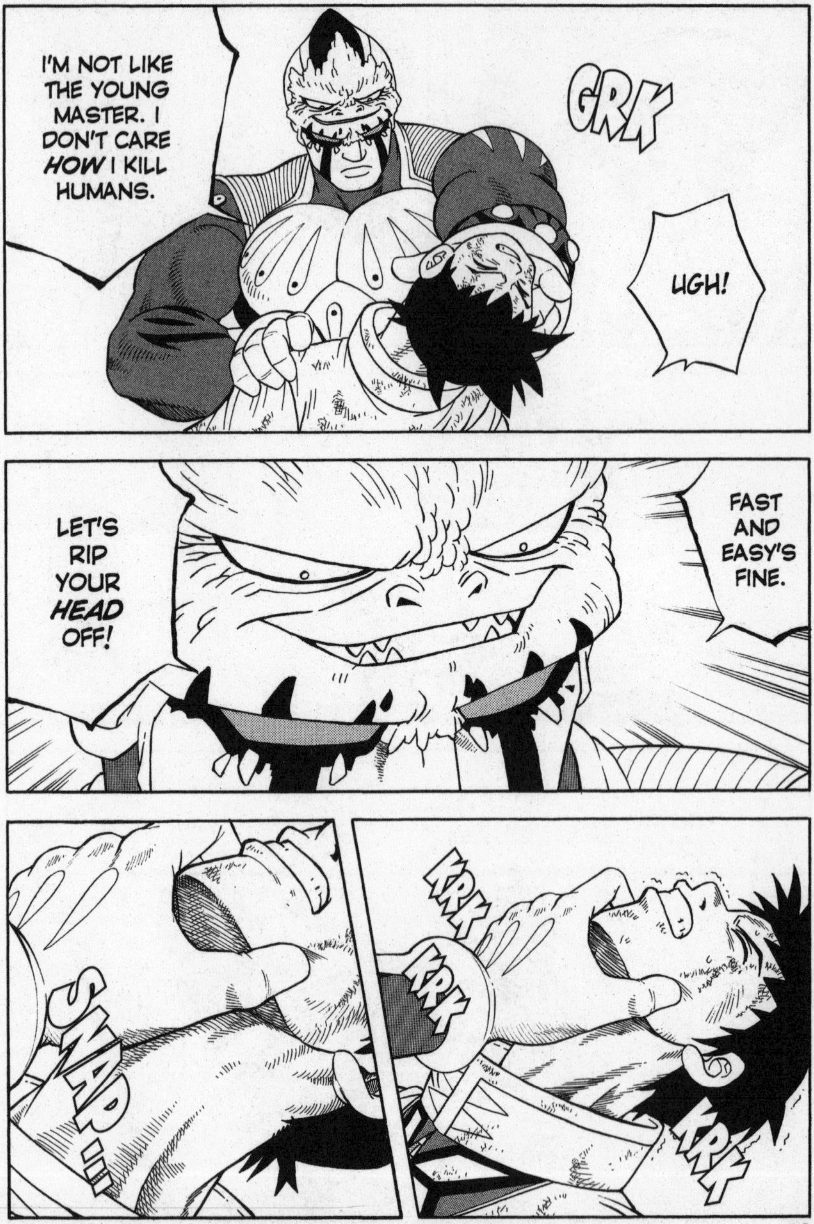
GRK
UGH!
I'M NOT LIKE THE YOUNG MASTER. I DON'T CARE *HOW* I KILL HUMANS.
FAST AND EASY'S FINE.
LET'S RIP YOUR *HEAD* OFF!
KRK
KRK
KRK
SNAP...!!

READ THIS WAY

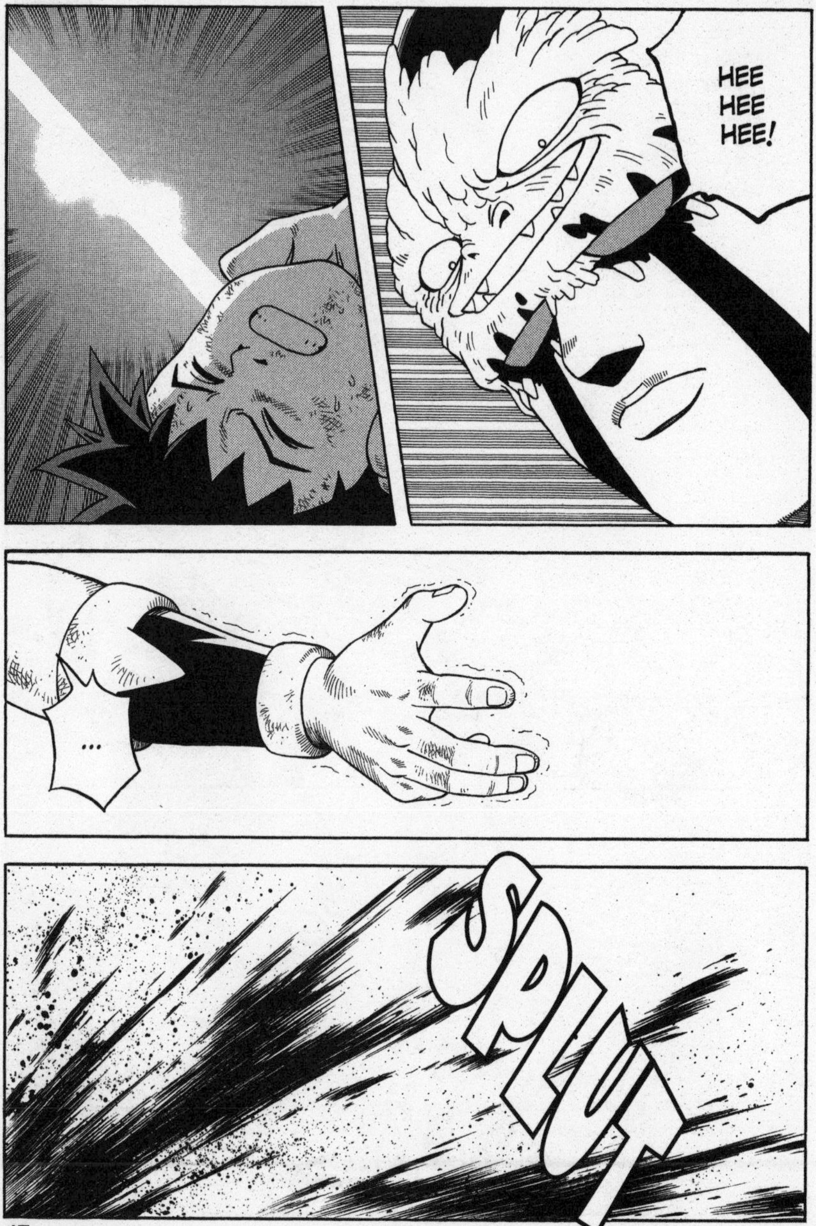
HEE HEE HEE!
...
SPLUT

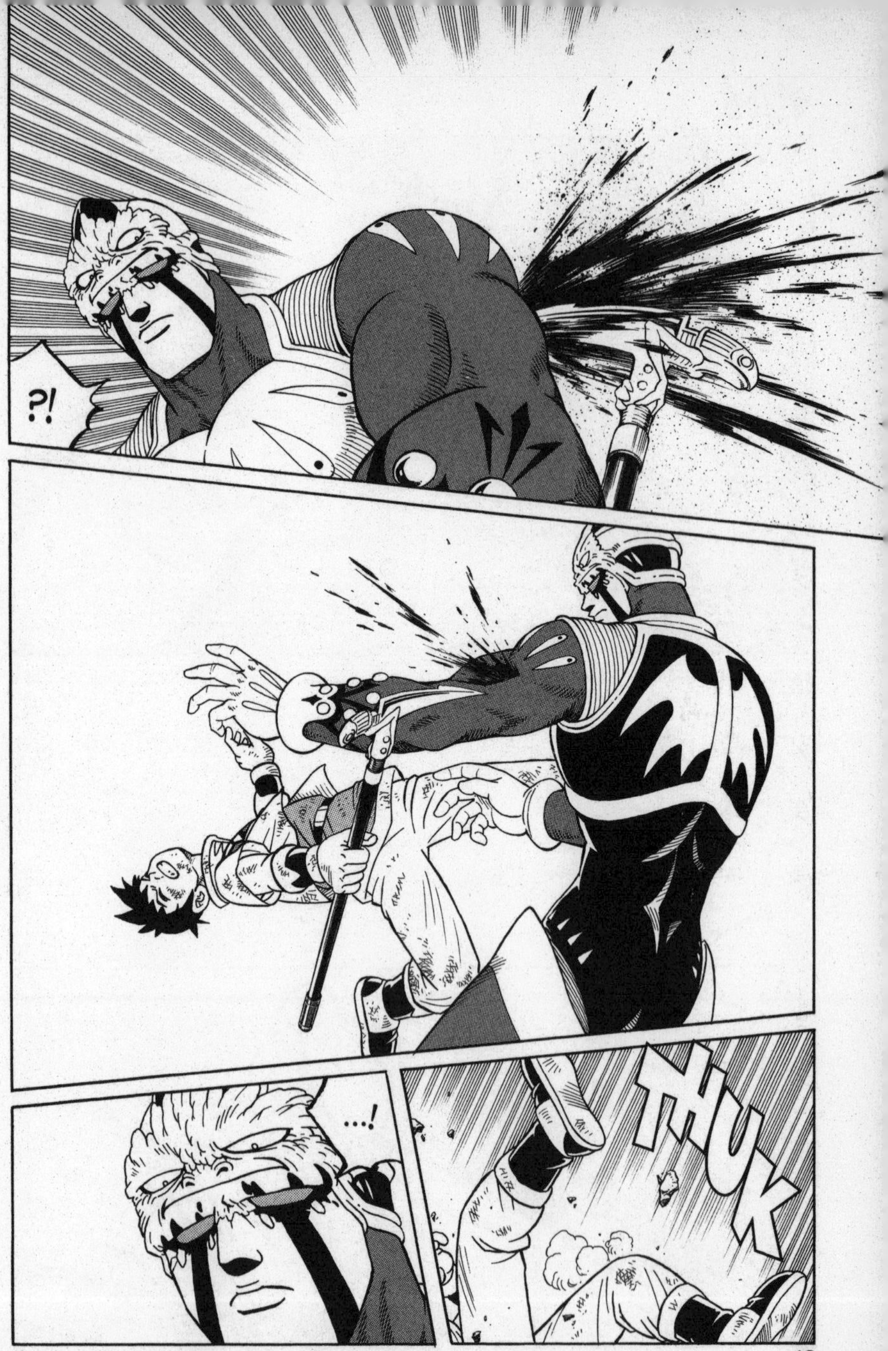
?!
THUK
...!

« READ THIS WAY «

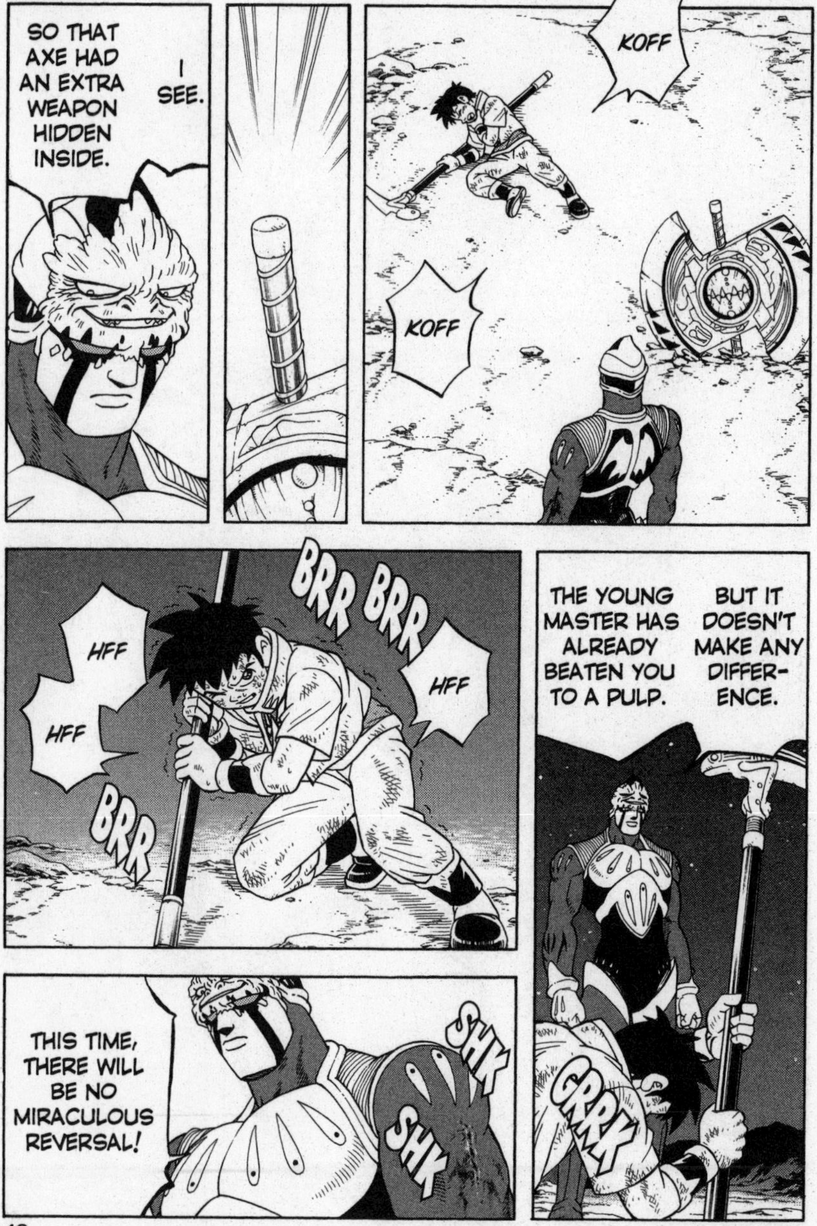

KOFF
KOFF
I SEE.
SO THAT AXE HAD AN EXTRA WEAPON HIDDEN INSIDE.
BUT IT DOESN'T MAKE ANY DIFFER-ENCE.
THE YOUNG MASTER HAS ALREADY BEATEN YOU TO A PULP.
GRRK
BRR BRR
HFF
HFF
HFF
BRR
SHK
SHK
THIS TIME, THERE WILL BE NO MIRACULOUS REVERSAL!

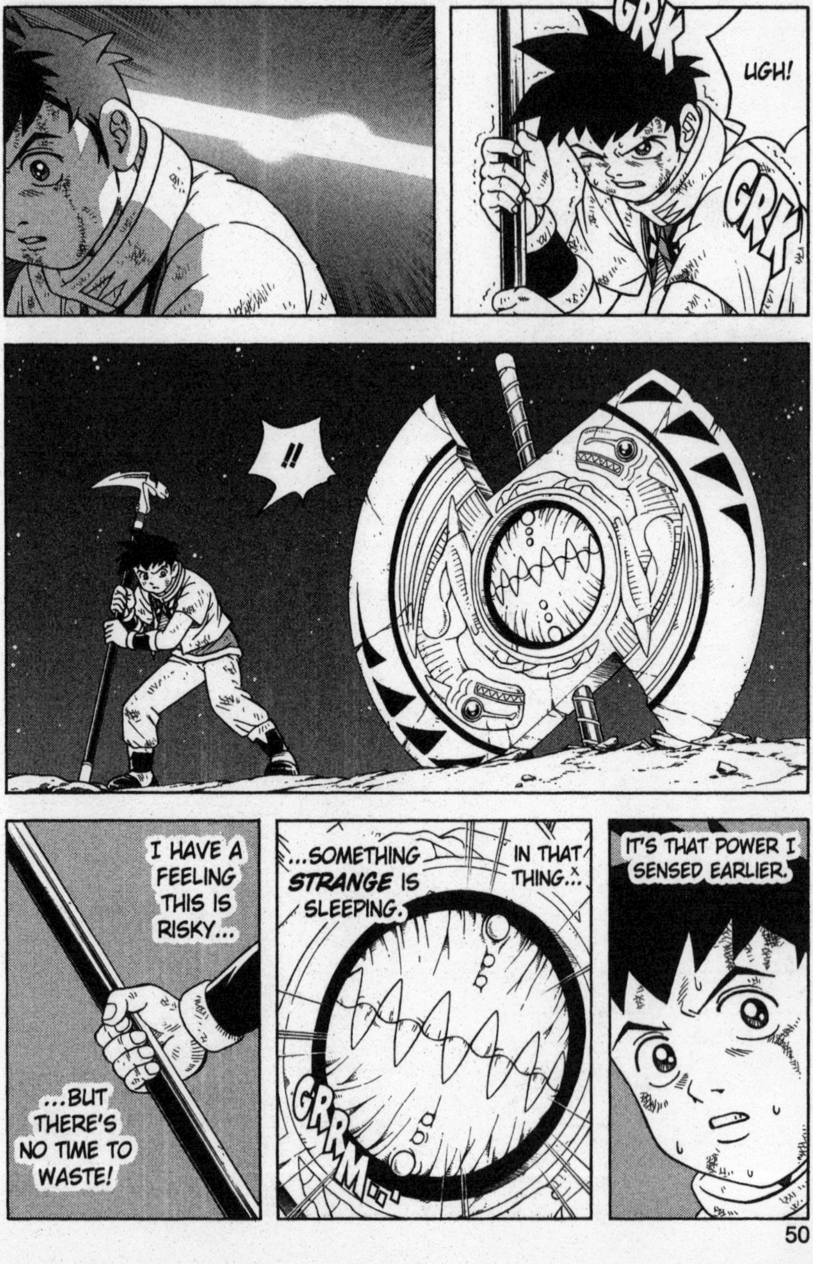
GRK
UGH!
GRK
!!
IT'S THAT POWER I SENSED EARLIER.
IN THAT THING...
...SOMETHING STRANGE IS SLEEPING.
GRRM
I HAVE A FEELING THIS IS RISKY...
...BUT THERE'S NO TIME TO WASTE!

READ THIS WAY

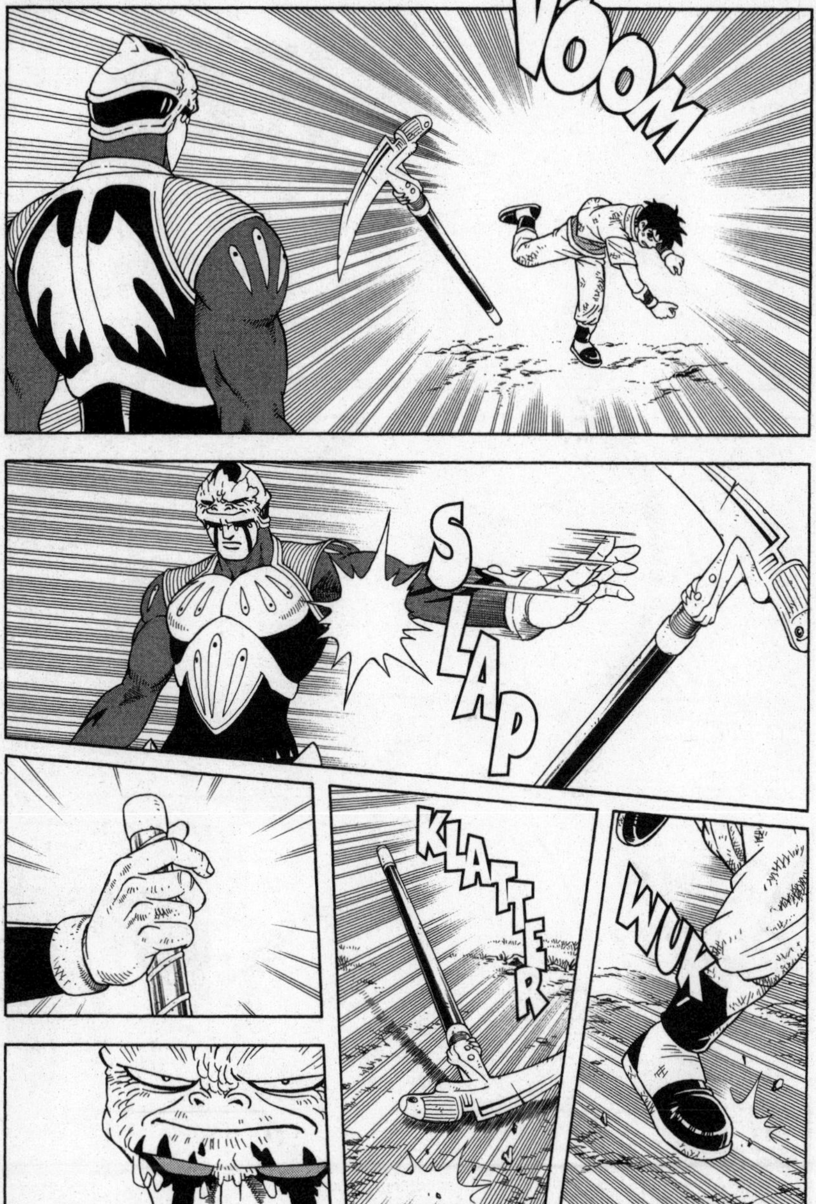
VOOM
SLAP
WUK
KLATTER

HFF

HFF

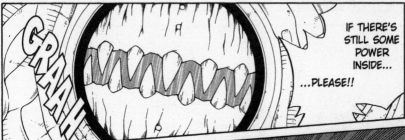

GRAAH

IF THERE'S STILL SOME POWER INSIDE...

...PLEASE!!

COME OUT!!!

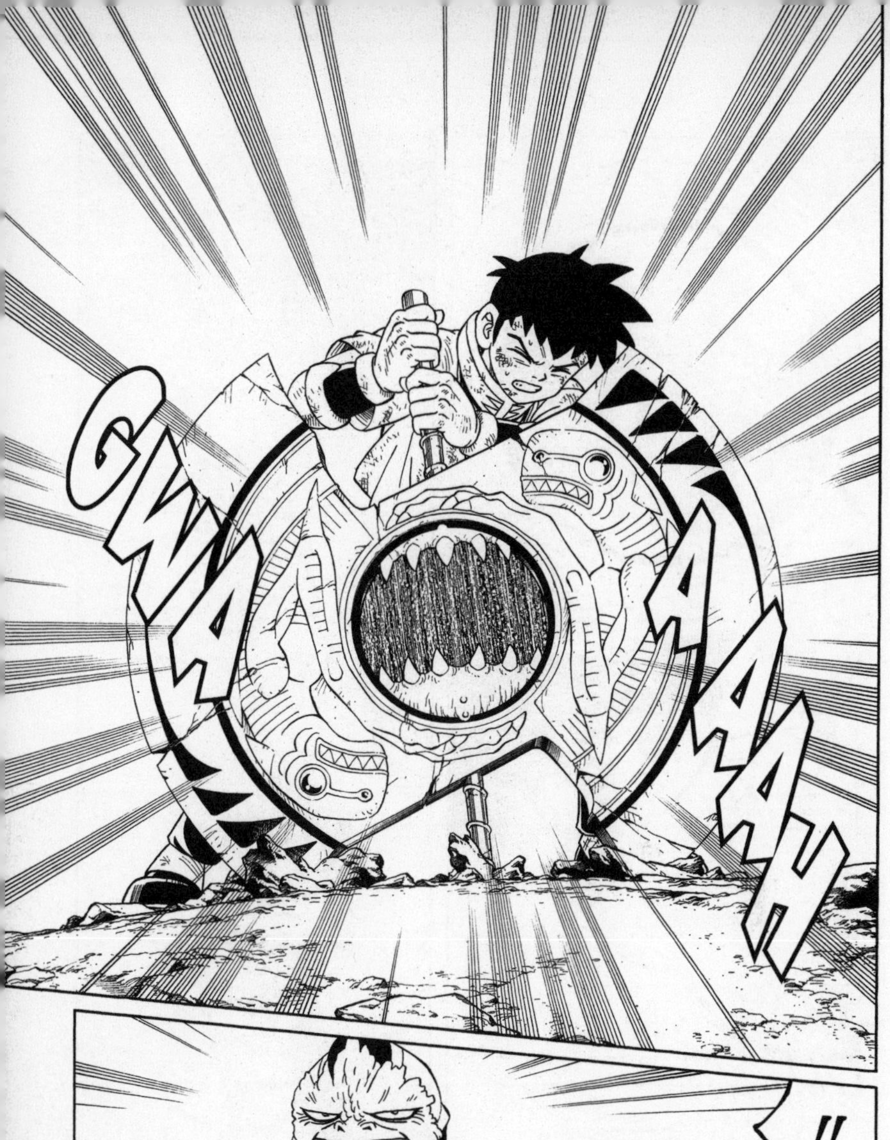
GWAAAAAH
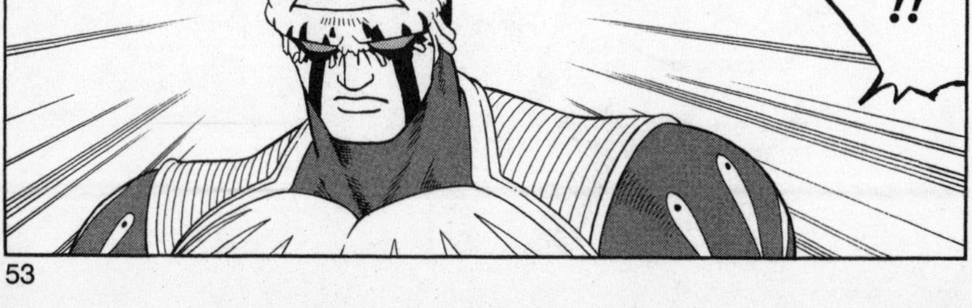
!!

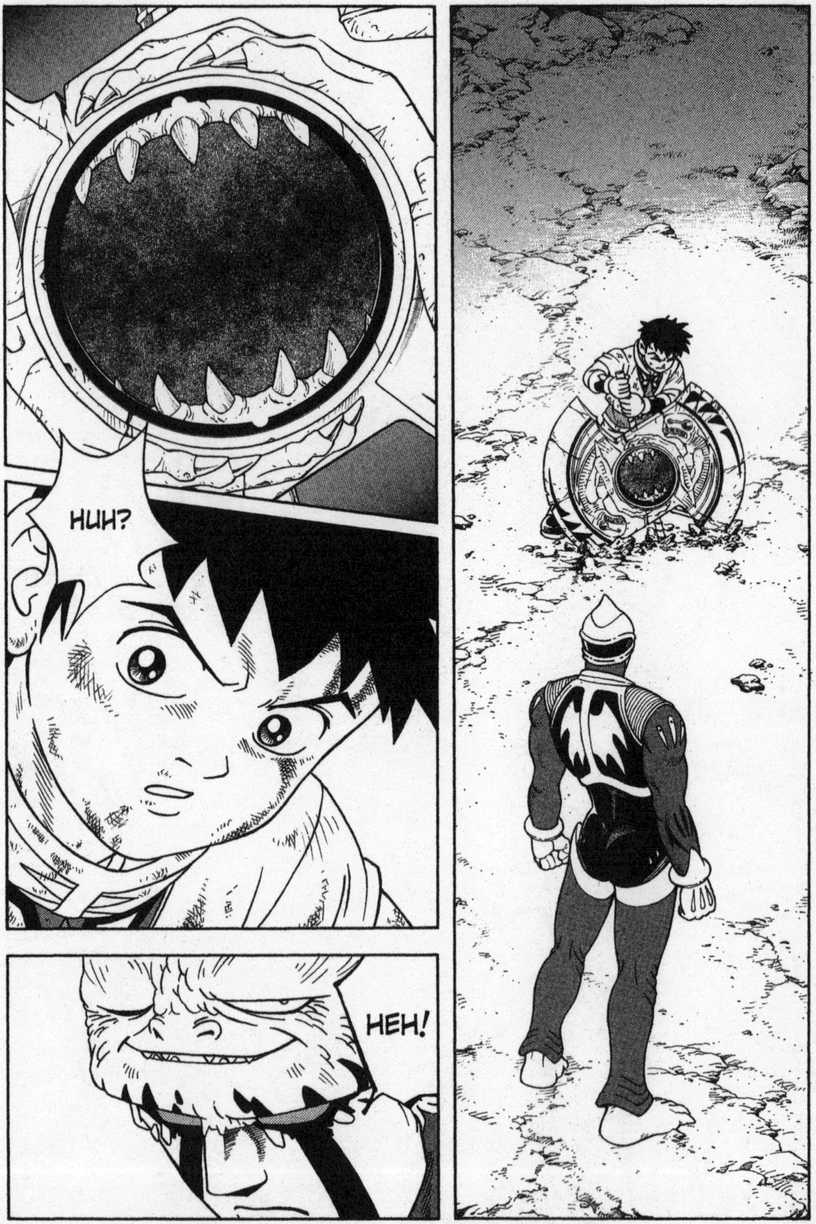
HUH?
HEH!

READ THIS WAY

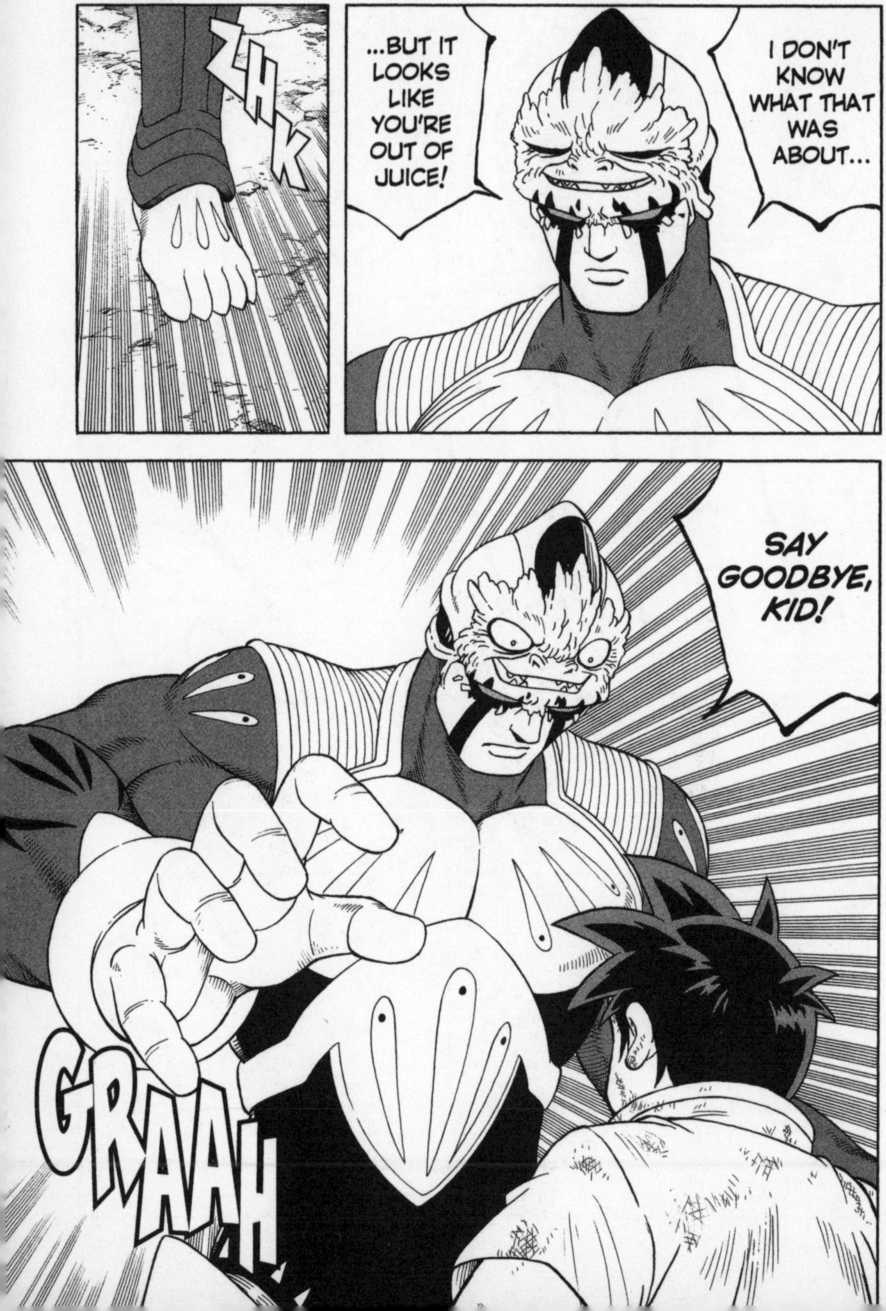
I DON'T KNOW WHAT THAT WAS ABOUT...
...BUT IT LOOKS LIKE YOU'RE OUT OF JUICE!
ZHK
SAY GOODBYE, KID!
GRAAAH

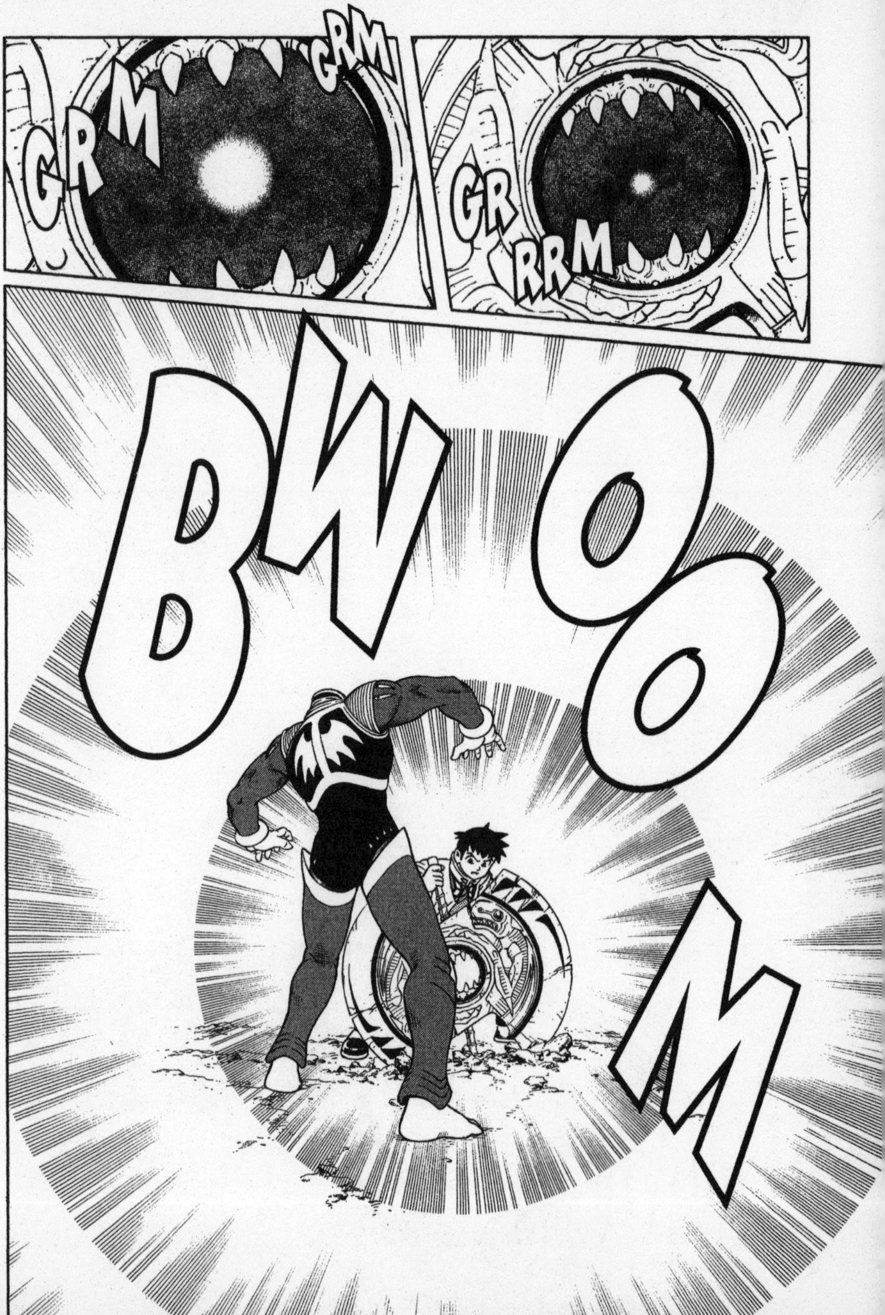
GRRRM
GRM
GRM
BWOOOM

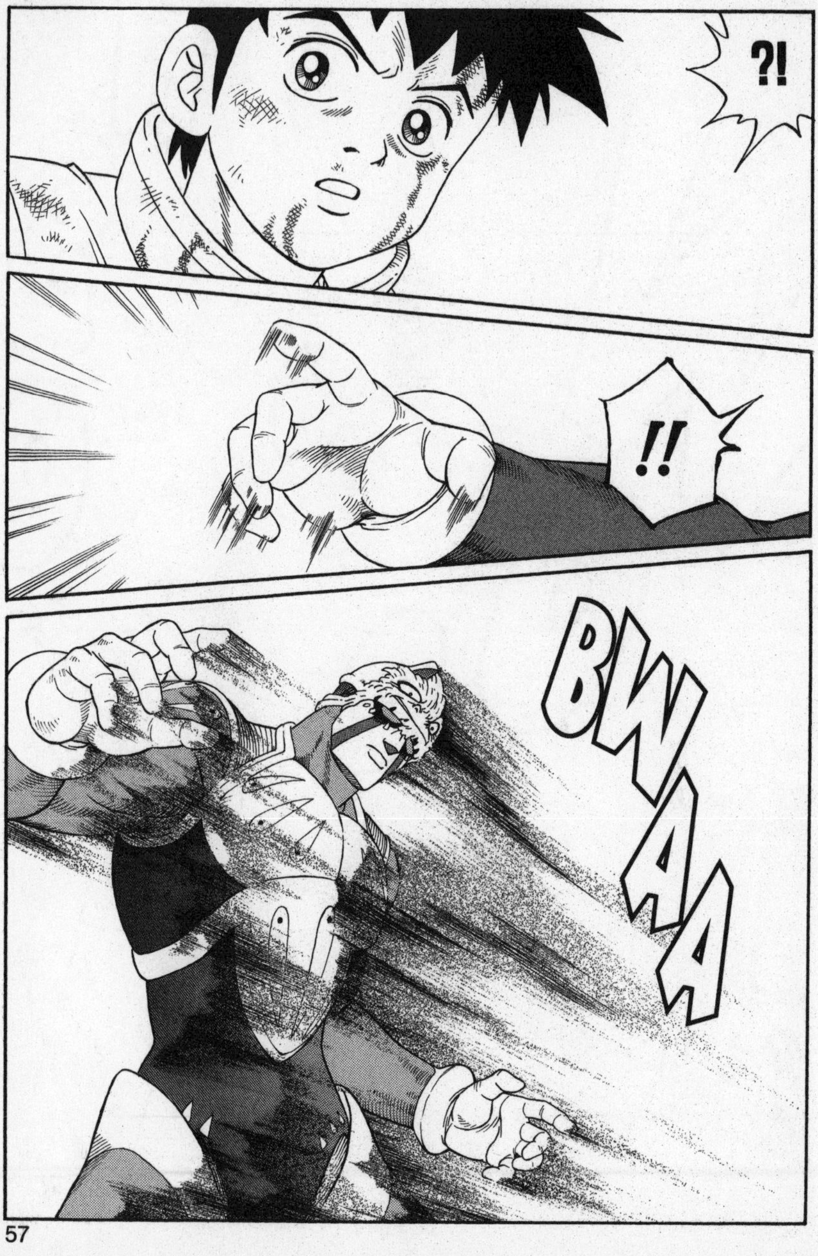
?!
!!
BWAA

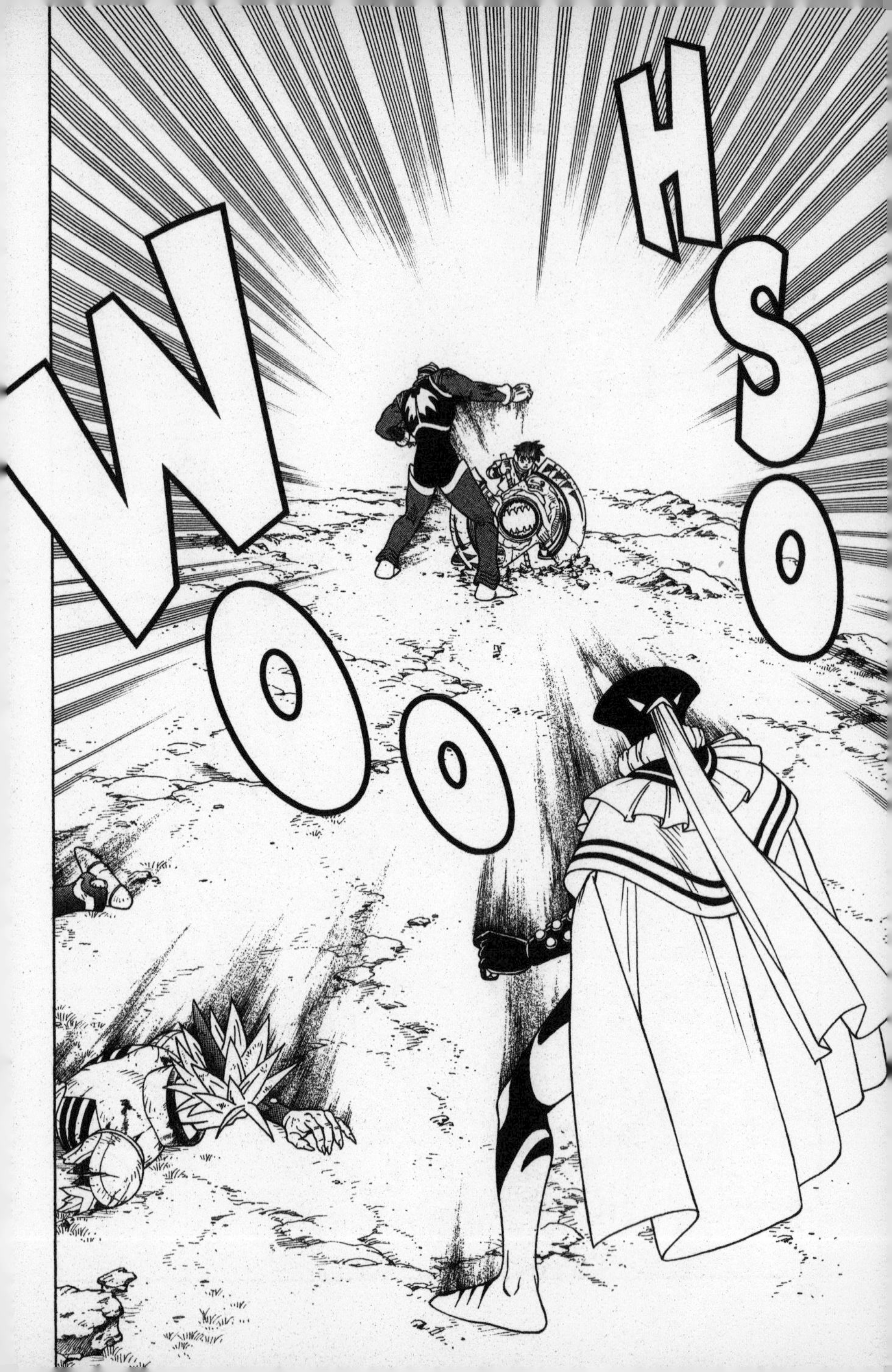
WOOOSH

READ THIS WAY

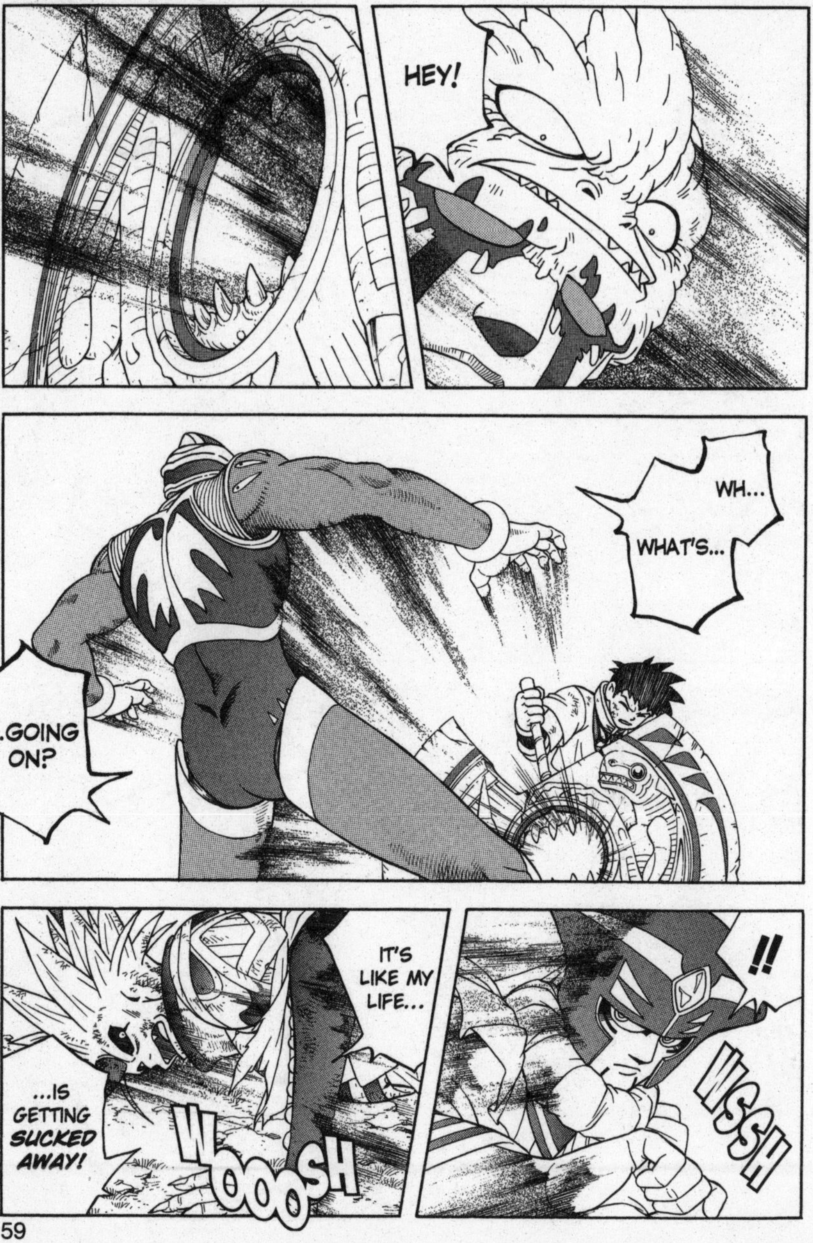
HEY!
WH... WHAT'S...
...GOING ON?
!!
WSSH
IT'S LIKE MY LIFE...
...IS GETTING SUCKED AWAY!
WOOOSH

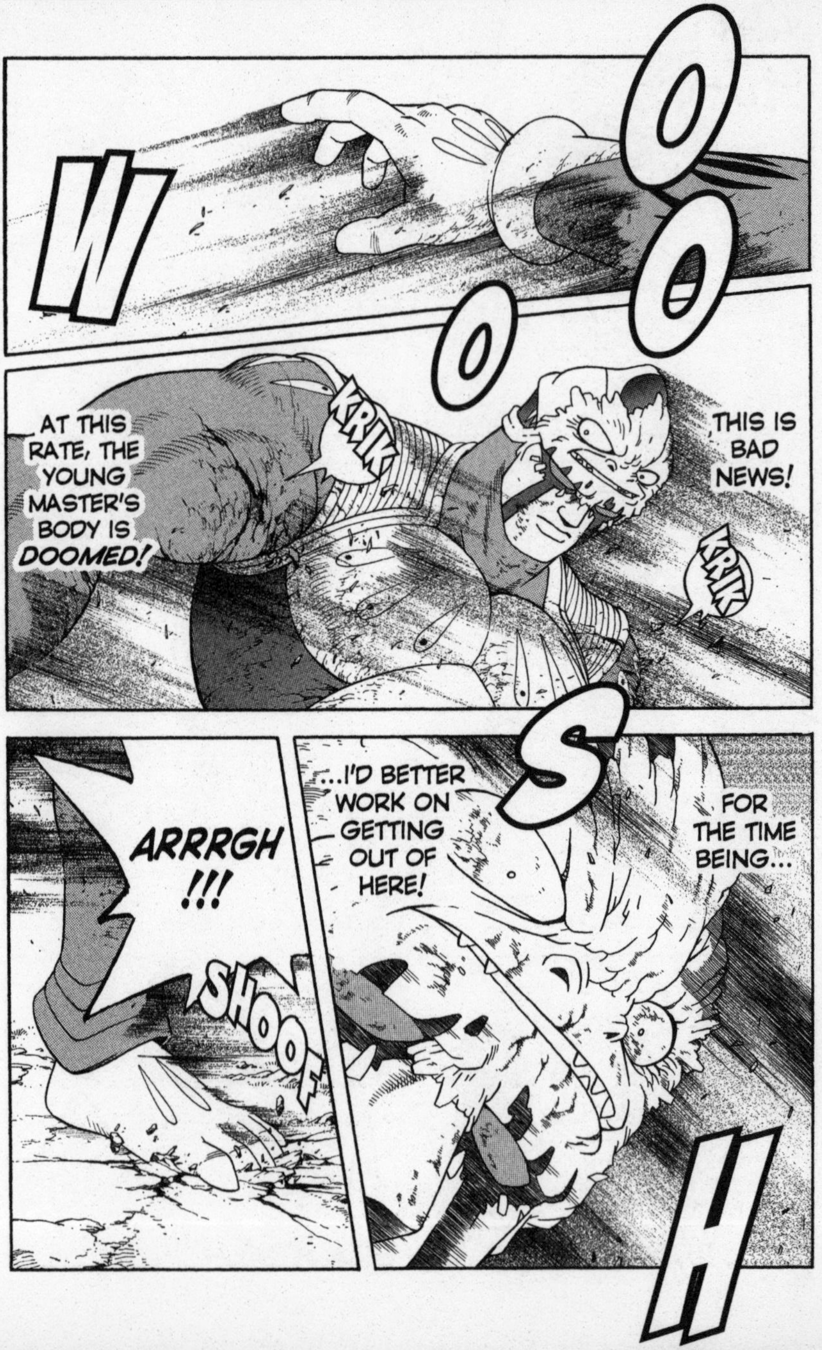
WOOOSH
THIS IS BAD NEWS!
KRIK
KRIK
AT THIS RATE, THE YOUNG MASTER'S BODY IS *DOOMED!*
FOR THE TIME BEING...
...I'D BETTER WORK ON GETTING OUT OF HERE!
SHOOF
ARRRGH !!!

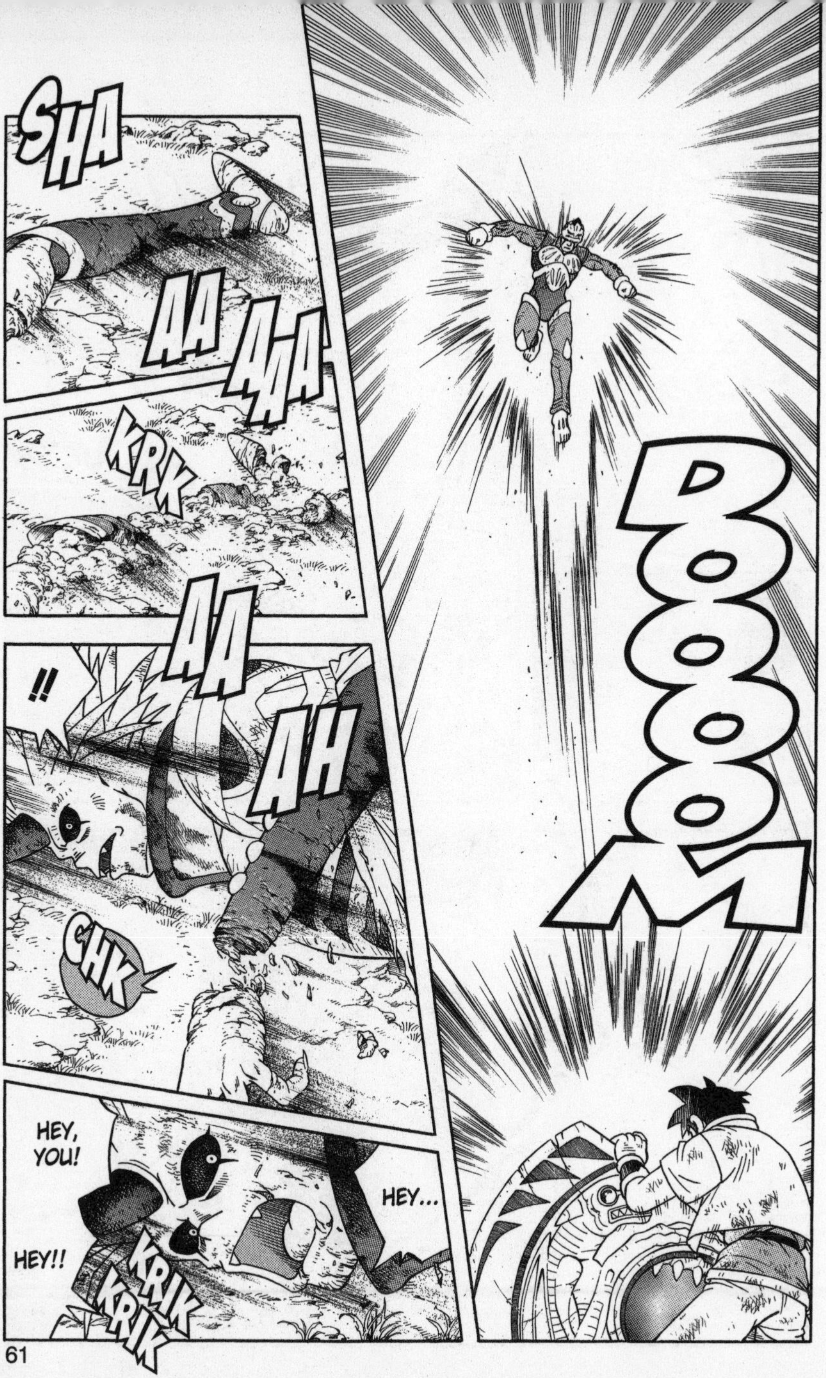
BOOOOOM
SHA
AA
AAAA
KRK
AA
AH
!!
CHK
HEY, YOU!
HEY...
HEY!!
KRIK
KRIK

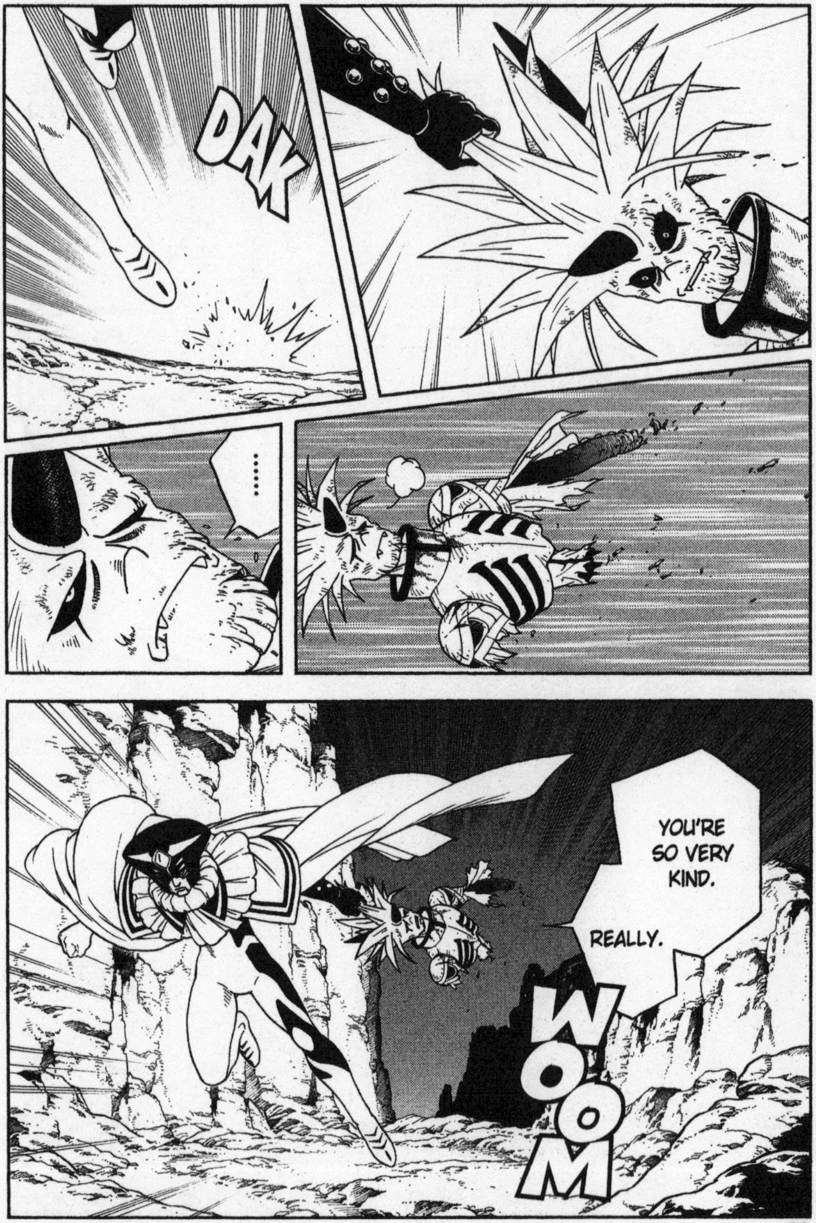
DAK
......
YOU'RE SO VERY KIND.
REALLY.
WOOOM

READ THIS WAY

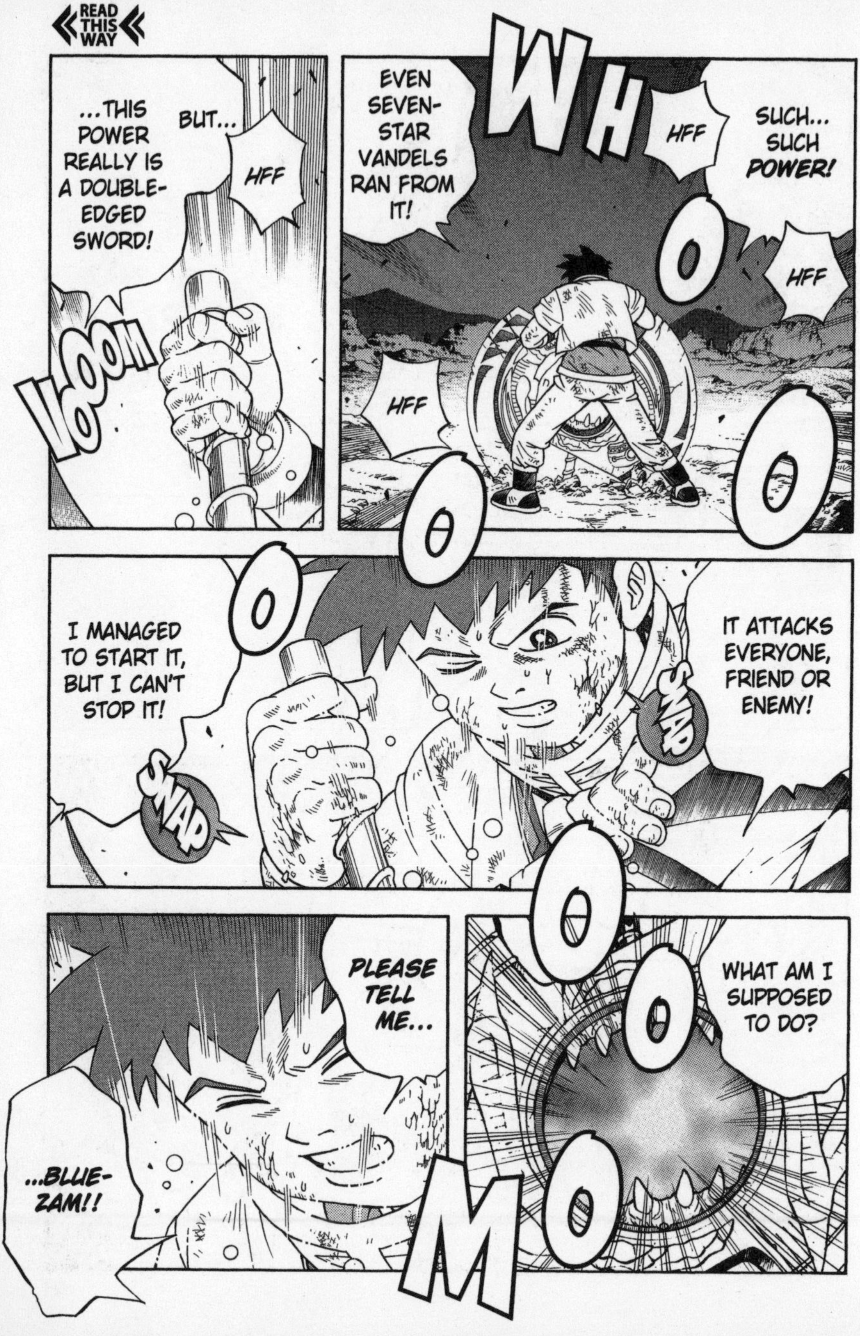
SUCH... SUCH POWER!
HFF
EVEN SEVEN-STAR VANDELS RAN FROM IT!
HFF
HFF
WHOOOOOOOOM
BUT...
...THIS POWER REALLY IS A DOUBLE-EDGED SWORD!
HFF
VOOOM
IT ATTACKS EVERYONE, FRIEND OR ENEMY!
SNAP
I MANAGED TO START IT, BUT I CAN'T STOP IT!
SNAP
WHAT AM I SUPPOSED TO DO?
PLEASE TELL ME...
...BLUE-ZAM!!

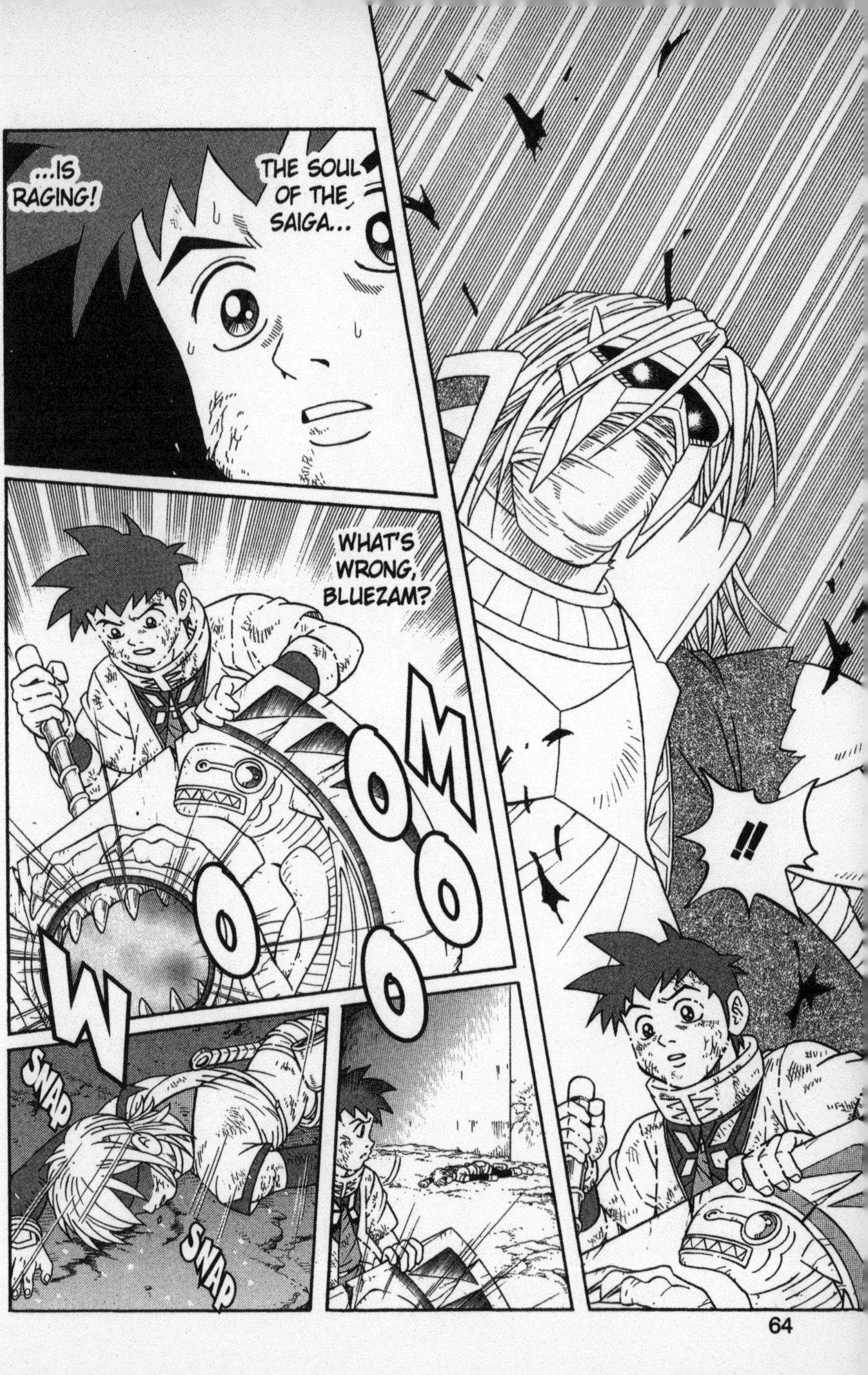
!!
THE SOUL OF THE SAIGA...
...IS RAGING!
WHAT'S WRONG, BLUEZAM?
WOOOOM
SNAP
SNAP

READ THIS WAY

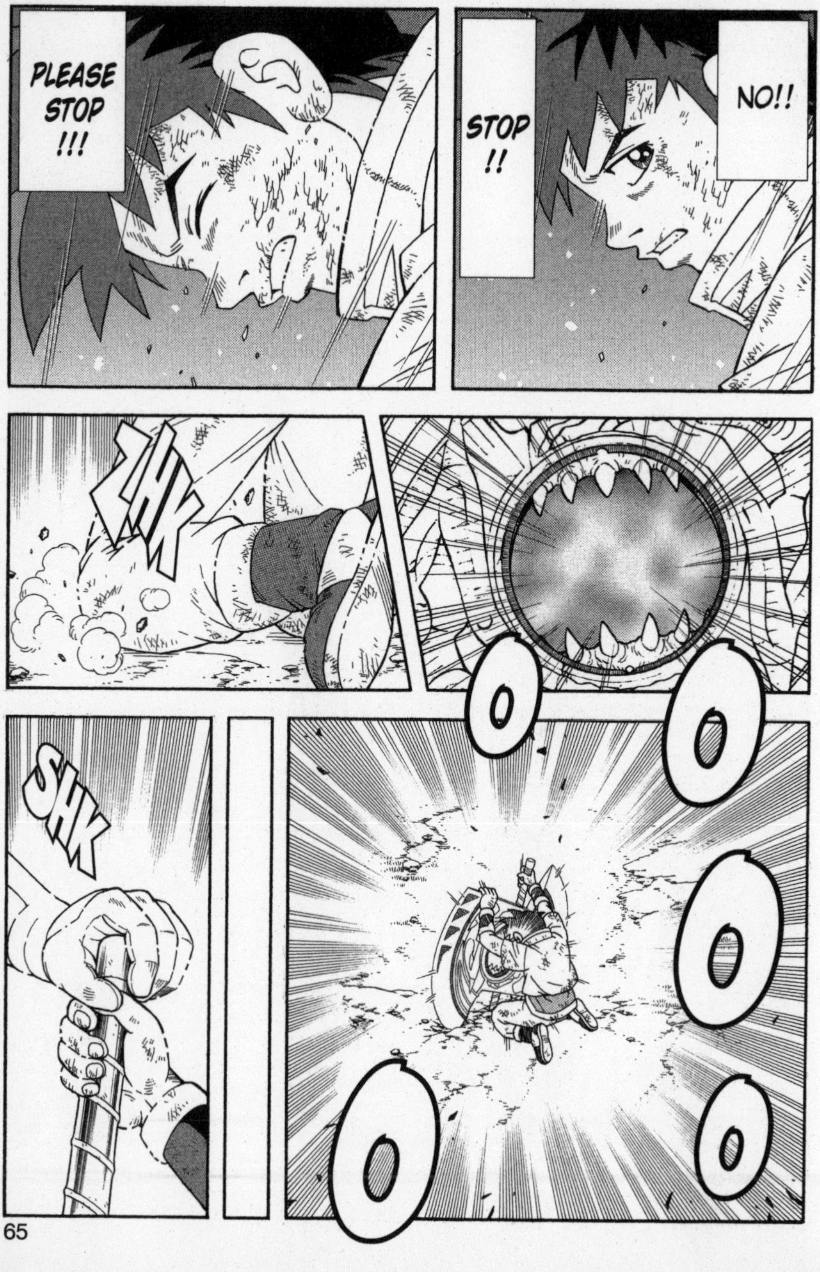
NO!!
STOP !!
PLEASE STOP !!!
ZHK
OOOOOO
SHK

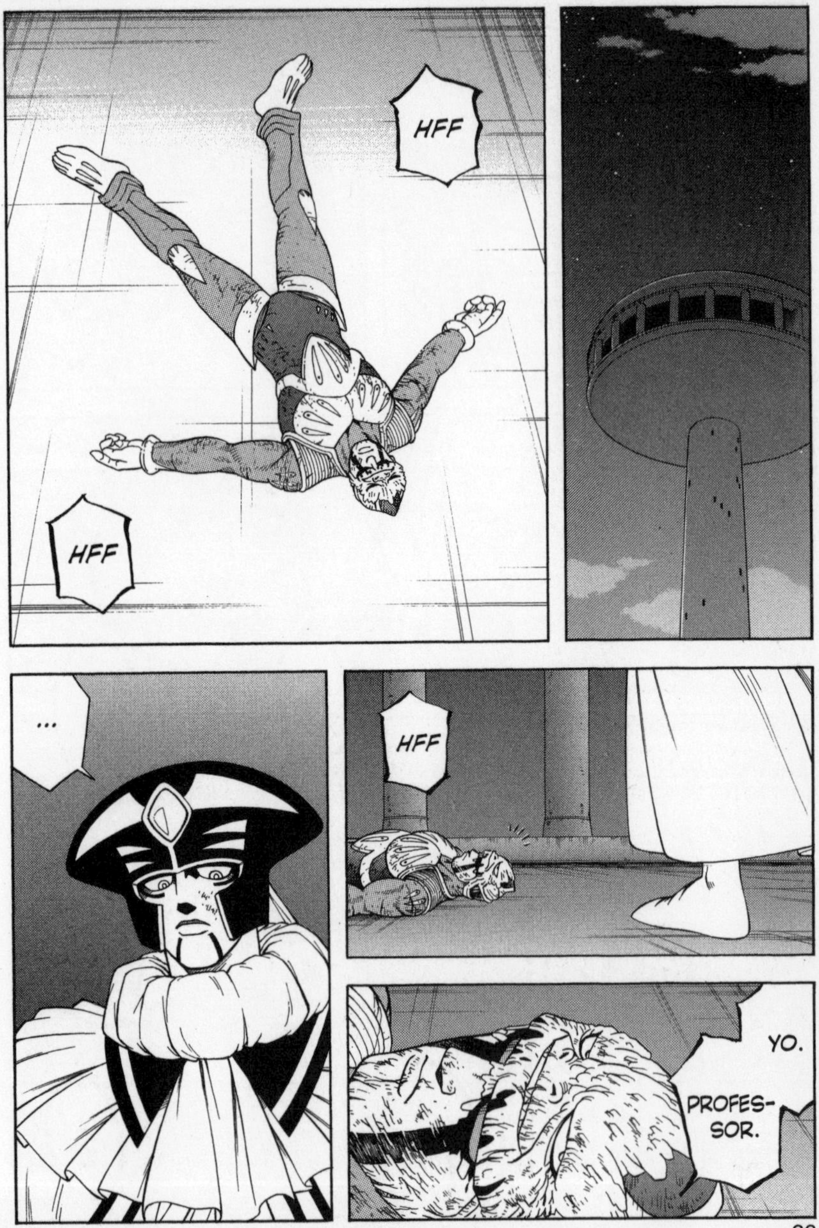
HFF
HFF
HFF
YO.
PROFES-SOR.
...

READ THIS WAY

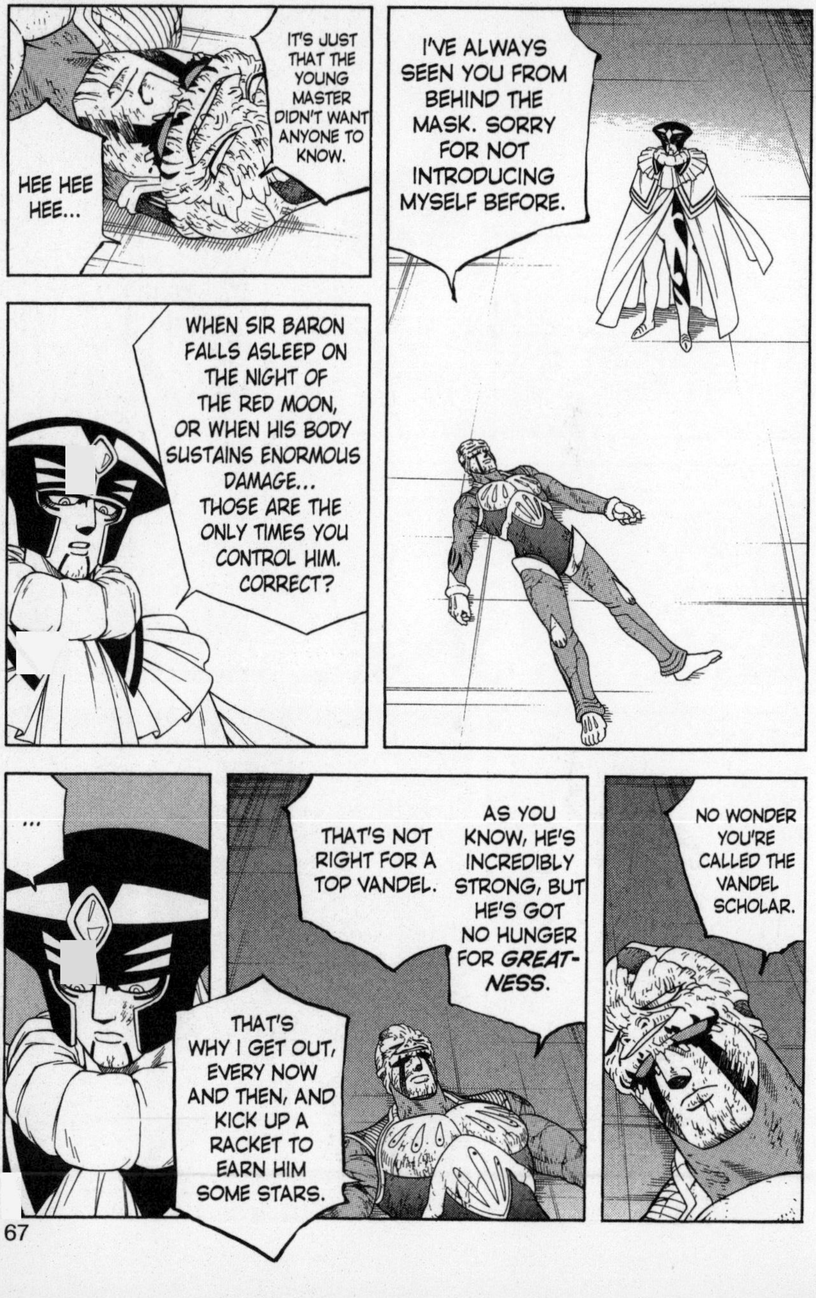
I'VE ALWAYS SEEN YOU FROM BEHIND THE MASK. SORRY FOR NOT INTRODUCING MYSELF BEFORE.
IT'S JUST THAT THE YOUNG MASTER DIDN'T WANT ANYONE TO KNOW.
HEE HEE HEE...
WHEN SIR BARON FALLS ASLEEP ON THE NIGHT OF THE RED MOON, OR WHEN HIS BODY SUSTAINS ENORMOUS DAMAGE... THOSE ARE THE ONLY TIMES YOU CONTROL HIM. CORRECT?
NO WONDER YOU'RE CALLED THE VANDEL SCHOLAR.
AS YOU KNOW, HE'S INCREDIBLY STRONG, BUT HE'S GOT NO HUNGER FOR *GREATNESS*.
THAT'S NOT RIGHT FOR A TOP VANDEL.
THAT'S WHY I GET OUT, EVERY NOW AND THEN, AND KICK UP A RACKET TO EARN HIM SOME STARS.
...

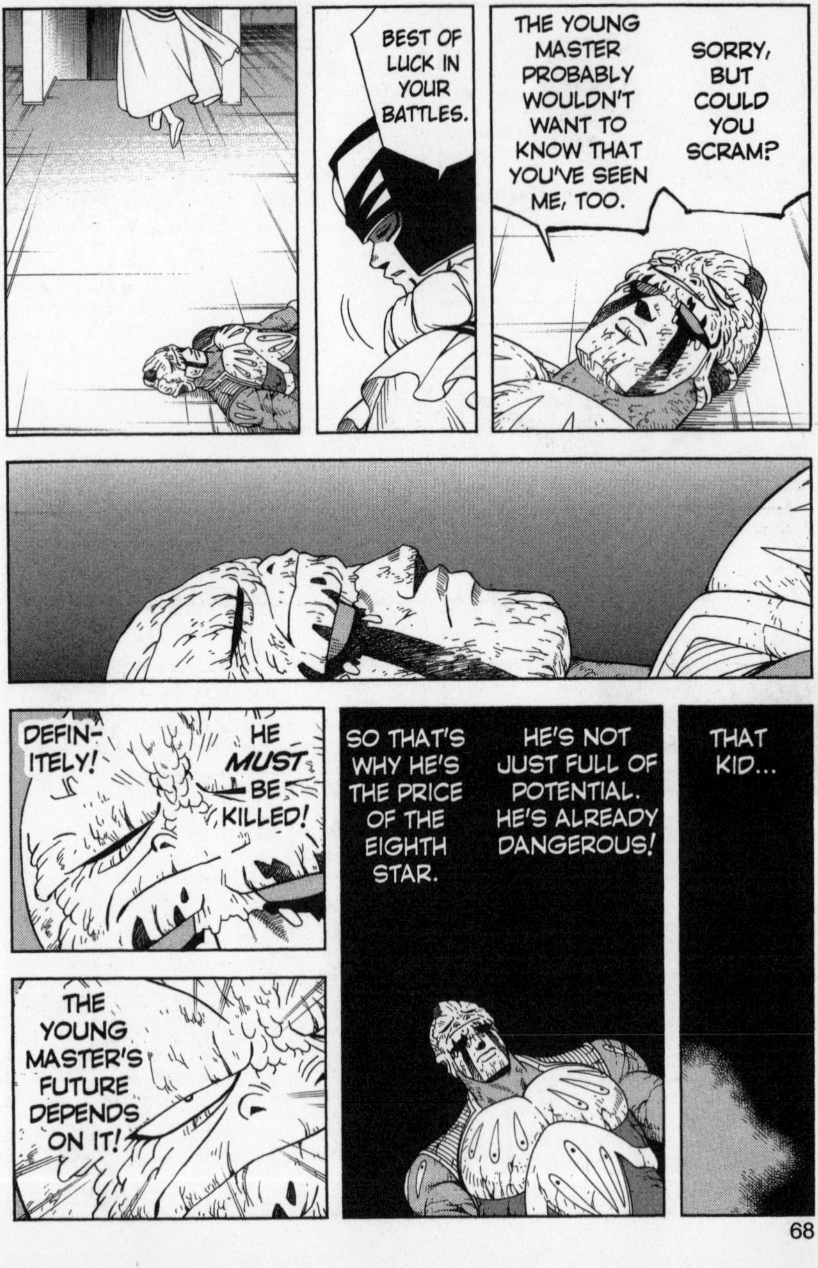
SORRY, BUT COULD YOU SCRAM?
THE YOUNG MASTER PROBABLY WOULDN'T WANT TO KNOW THAT YOU'VE SEEN ME, TOO.
BEST OF LUCK IN YOUR BATTLES.
THAT KID...
HE'S NOT JUST FULL OF POTENTIAL. HE'S ALREADY DANGEROUS!
SO THAT'S WHY HE'S THE PRICE OF THE EIGHTH STAR.
HE *MUST* BE KILLED!
DEFIN-ITELY!
THE YOUNG MASTER'S FUTURE DEPENDS ON IT!

READ THIS WAY

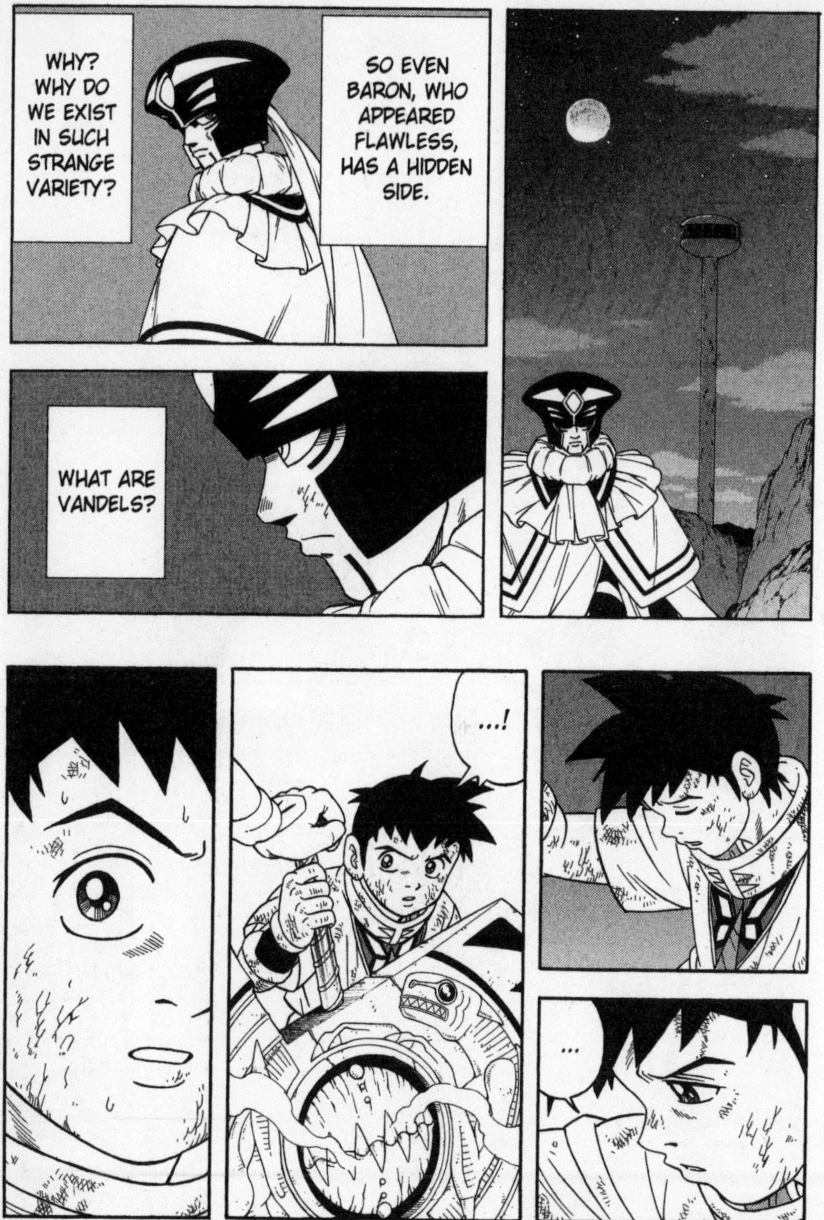

SO EVEN BARON, WHO APPEARED FLAWLESS, HAS A HIDDEN SIDE.
WHY? WHY DO WE EXIST IN SUCH STRANGE VARIETY?
WHAT ARE VANDELS?
...
...!

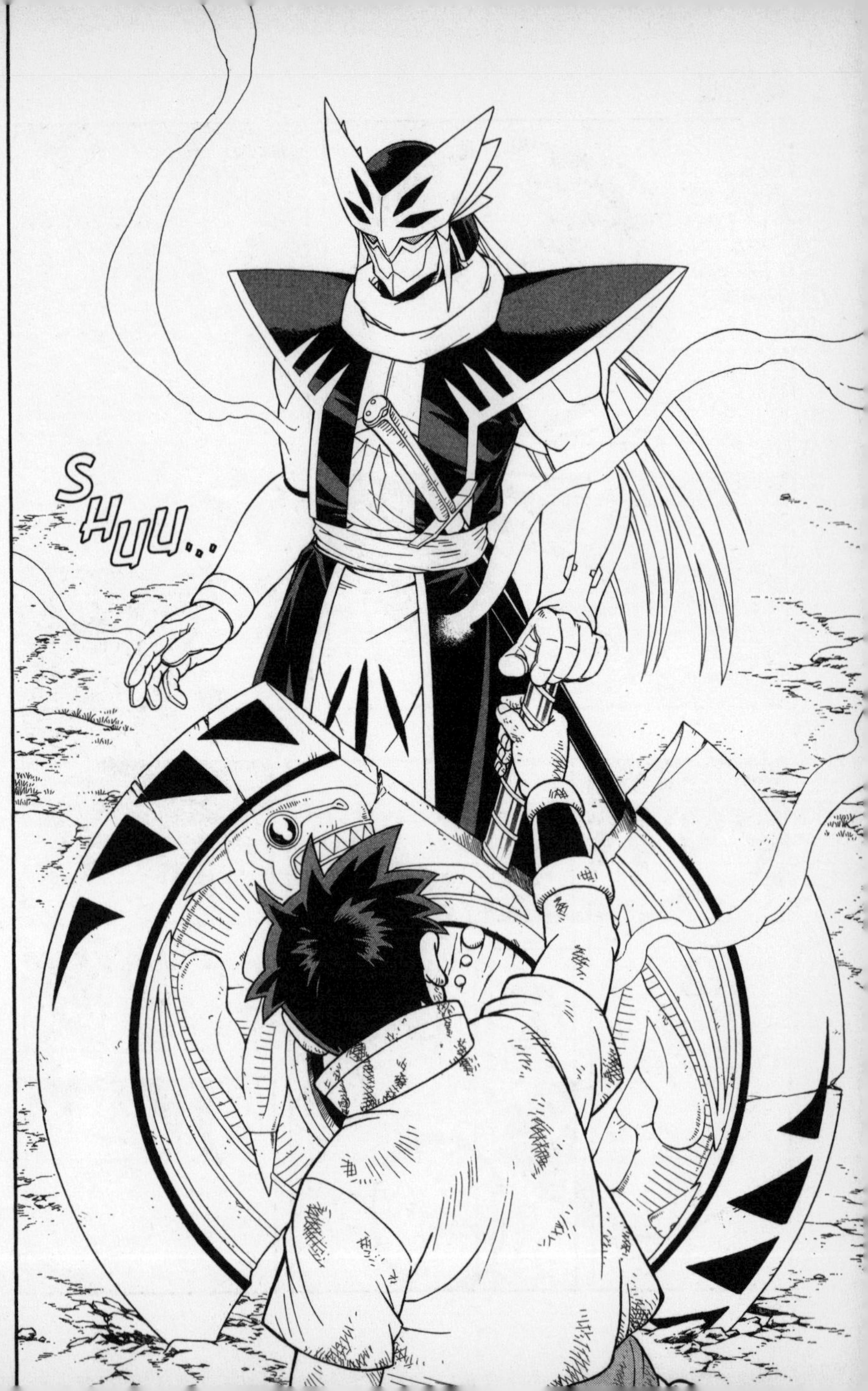
SHUU...

READ THIS WAY

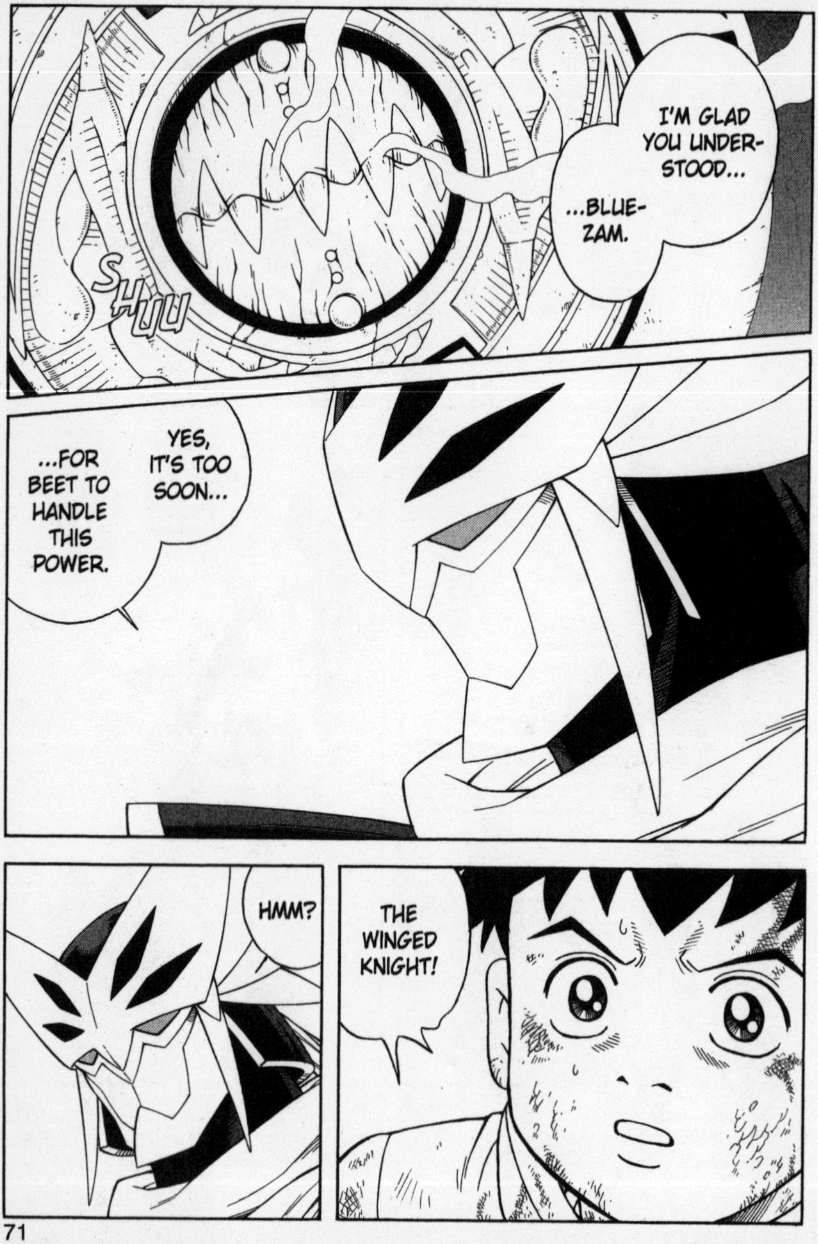
I'M GLAD YOU UNDER-STOOD...
...BLUE-ZAM.
SHUU
YES, IT'S TOO SOON...
...FOR BEET TO HANDLE THIS POWER.
THE WINGED KNIGHT!
HMM?

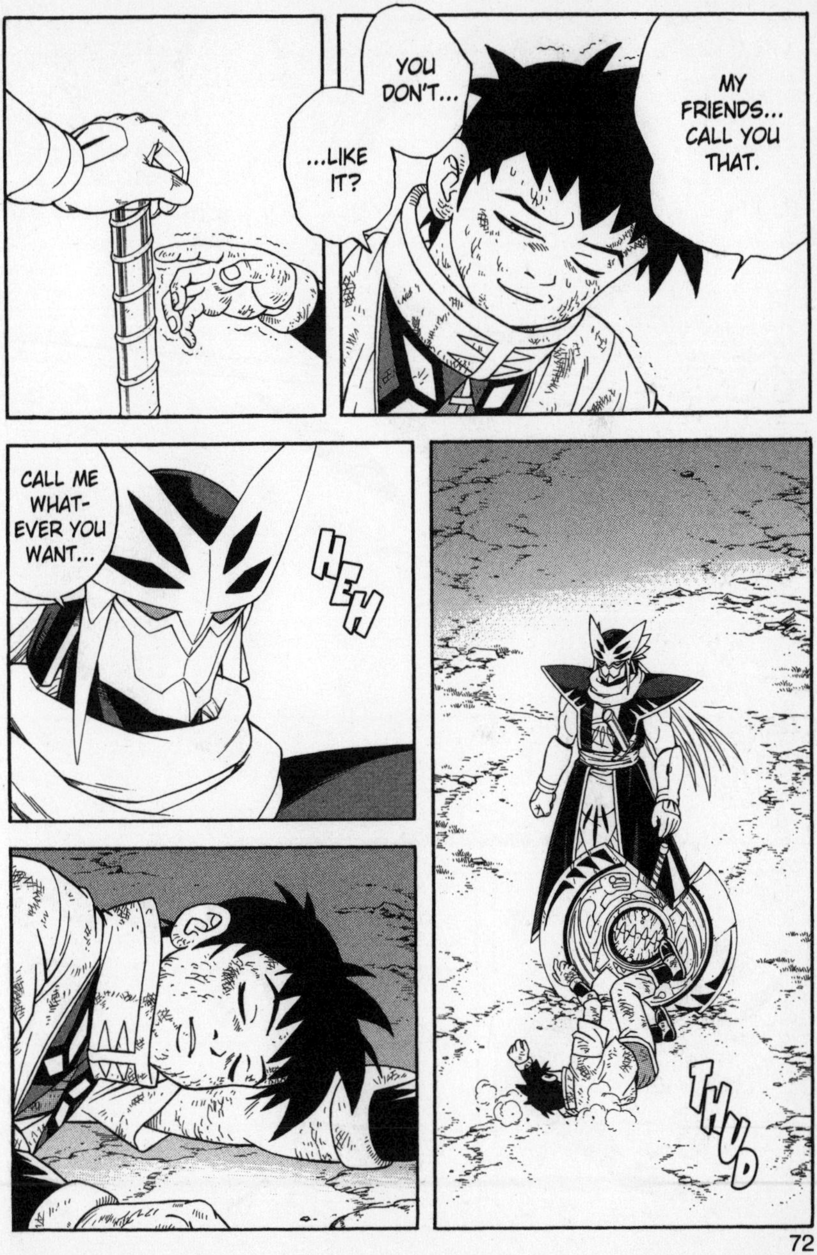
MY FRIENDS... CALL YOU THAT.
YOU DON'T...
...LIKE IT?
THUD
CALL ME WHAT-EVER YOU WANT...
HEH

READ THIS WAY

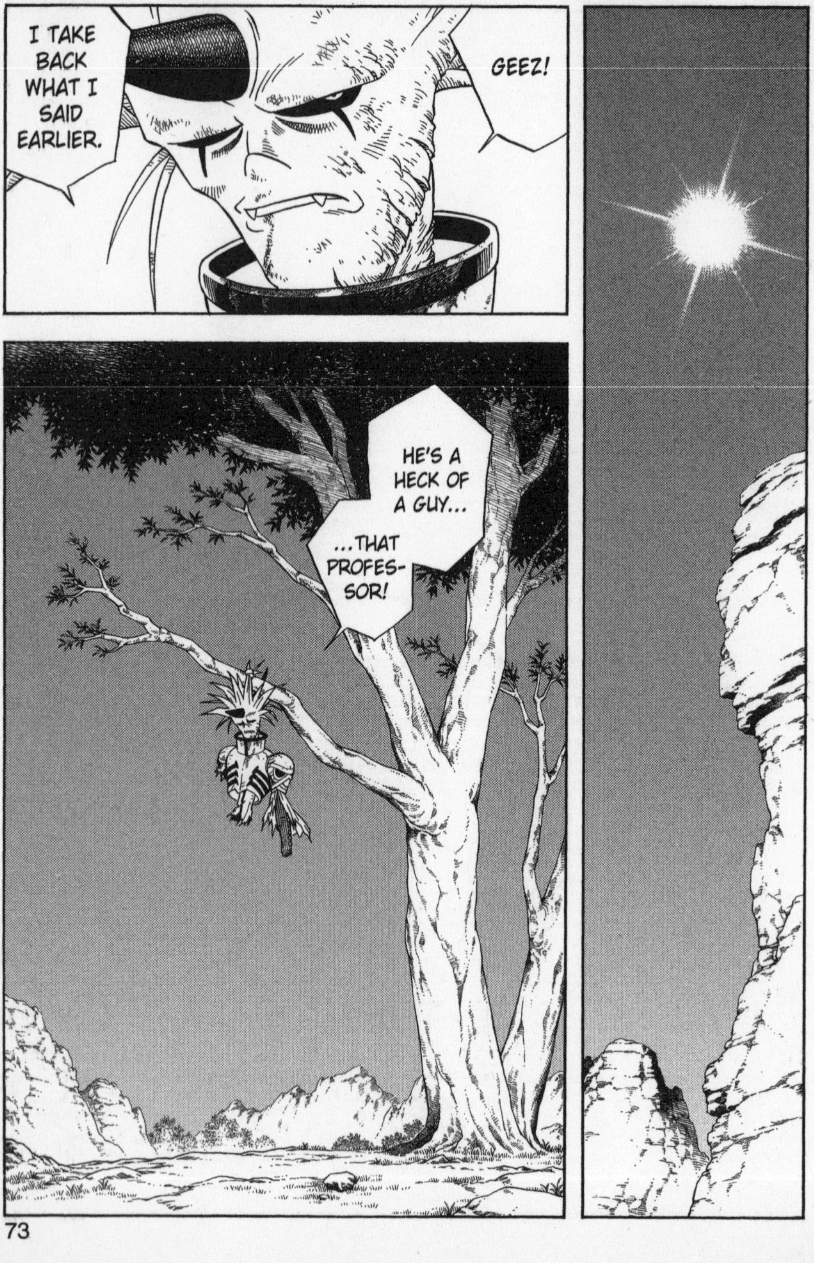
GEEZ!
I TAKE BACK WHAT I SAID EARLIER.
HE'S A HECK OF A GUY...
...THAT PROFES-SOR!

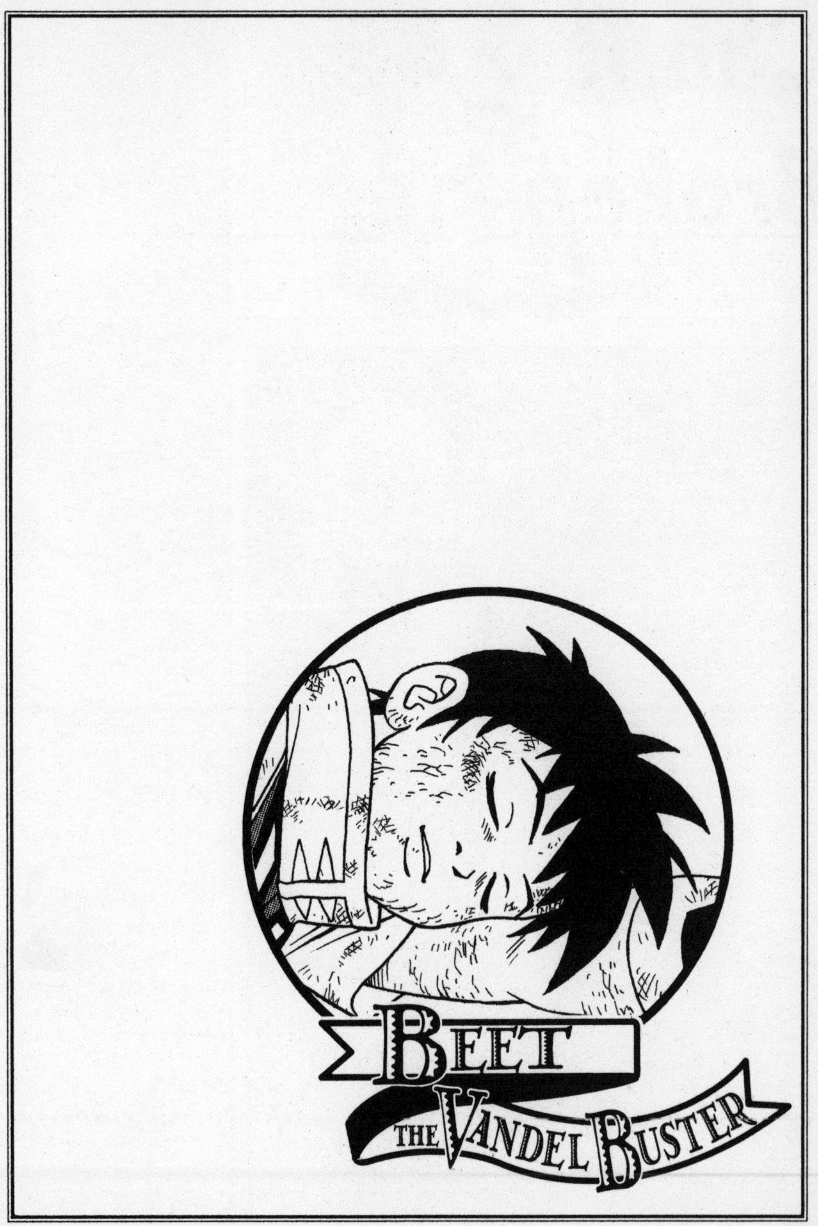
BEET
THE VANDEL BUSTER

Chapter 46: Broken Heart!

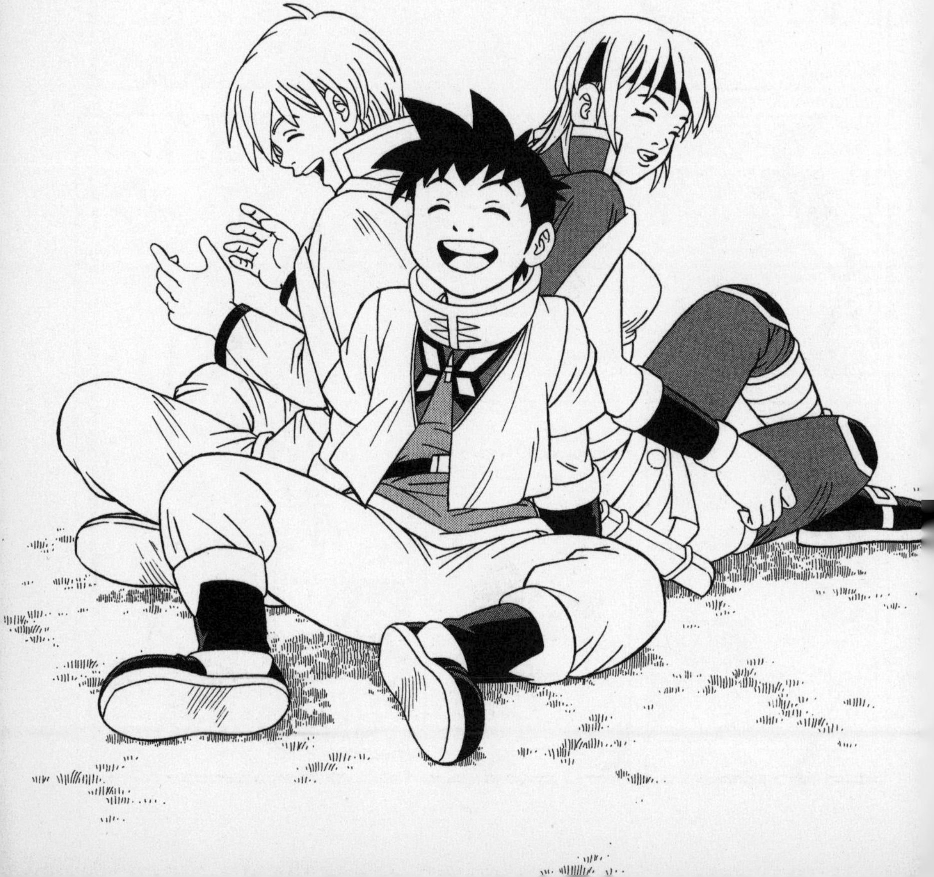

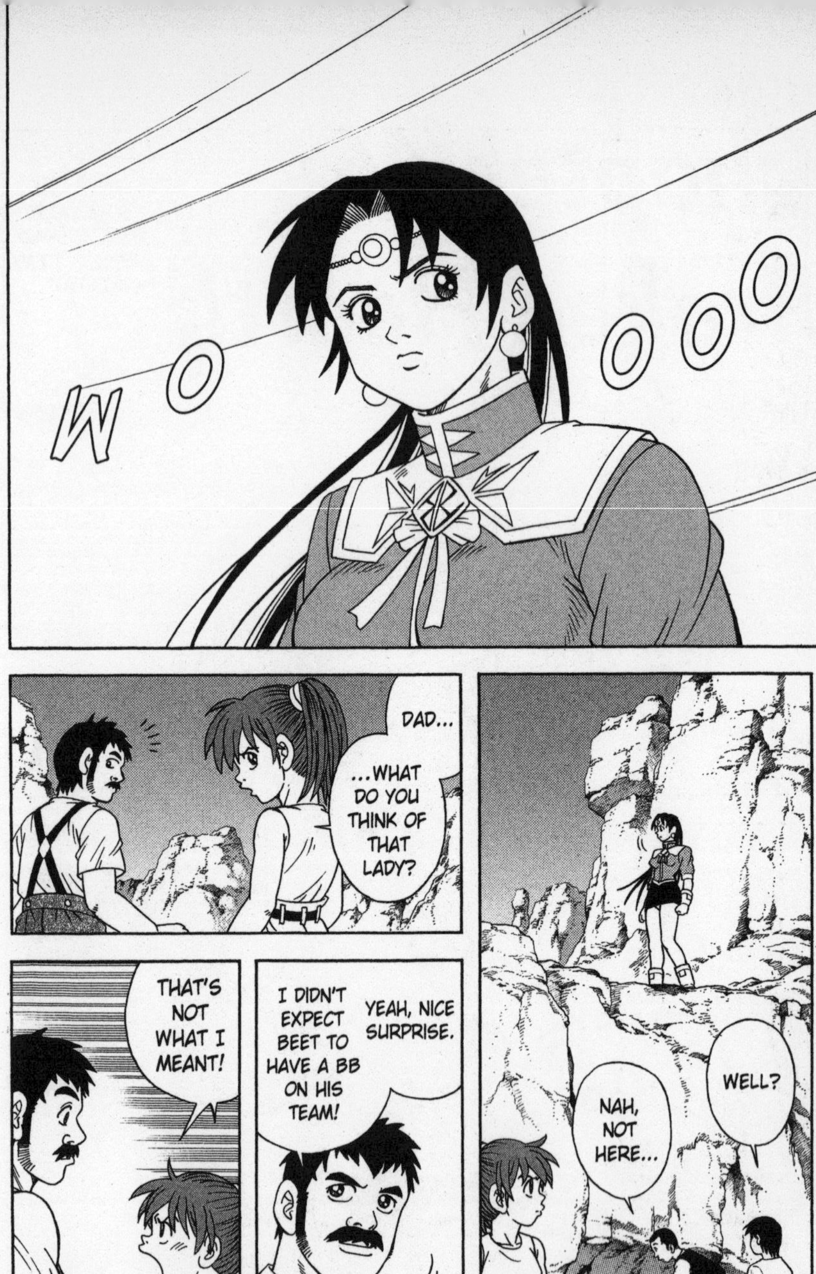
WOOOOO
WELL?
NAH, NOT HERE...
DAD...
...WHAT DO YOU THINK OF THAT LADY?
YEAH, NICE SURPRISE.
I DIDN'T EXPECT BEET TO HAVE A BB ON HIS TEAM!
THAT'S NOT WHAT I MEANT!

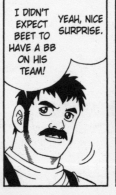

READ THIS WAY

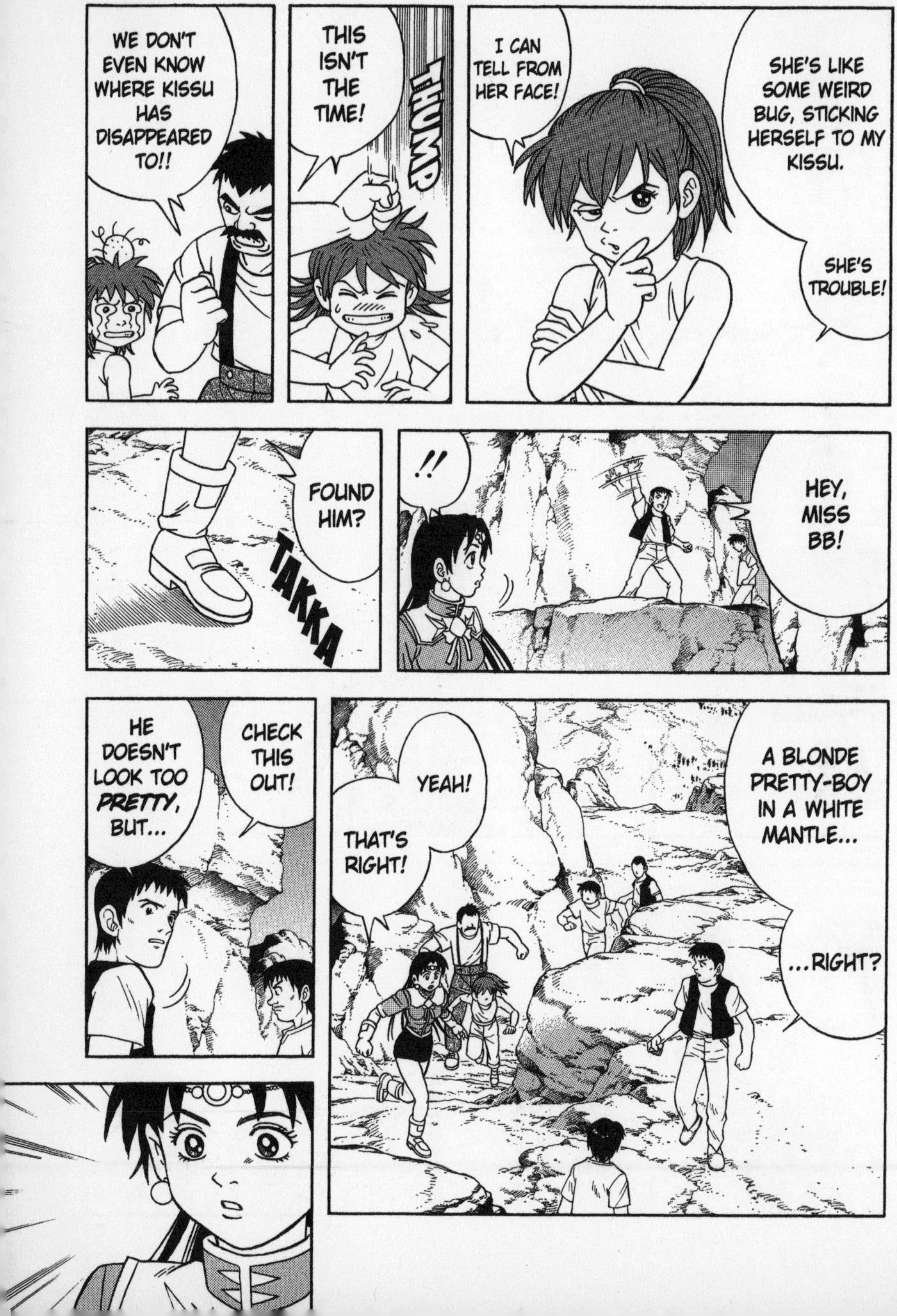
SHE'S LIKE SOME WEIRD BUG, STICKING HERSELF TO MY KISSU.
SHE'S TROUBLE!
I CAN TELL FROM HER FACE!
THIS ISN'T THE TIME!
THUMP
WE DON'T EVEN KNOW WHERE KISSU HAS DISAPPEARED TO!!
HEY, MISS BB!
!!
FOUND HIM?
TAKKA
A BLONDE PRETTY-BOY IN A WHITE MANTLE...
...RIGHT?
YEAH!
THAT'S RIGHT!
CHECK THIS OUT!
HE DOESN'T LOOK TOO *PRETTY*, BUT...

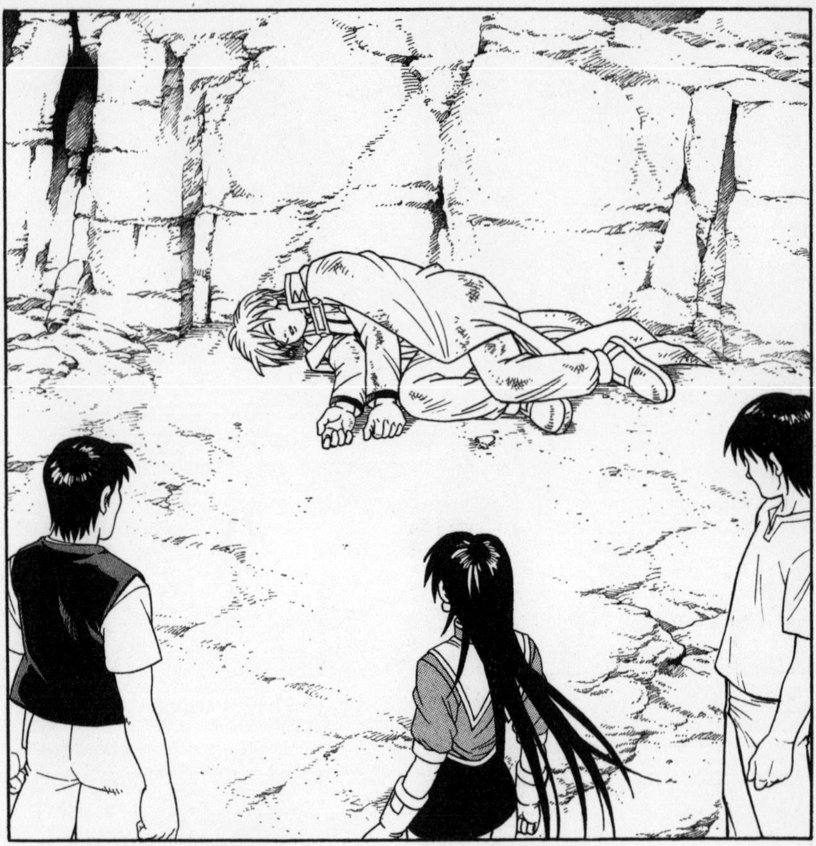

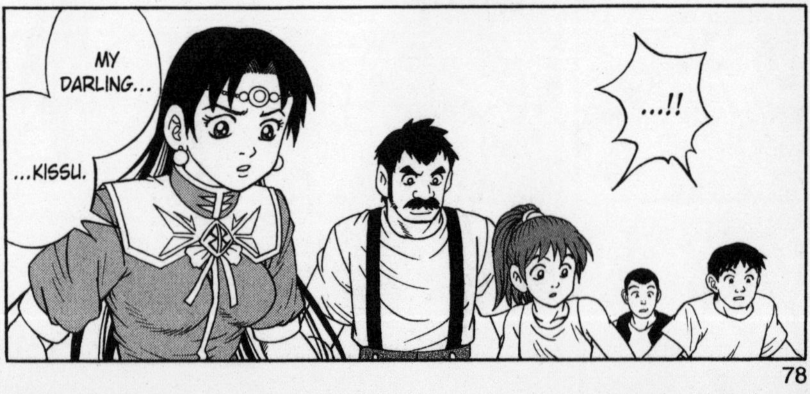
...!!
MY DARLING...
...KISSU.

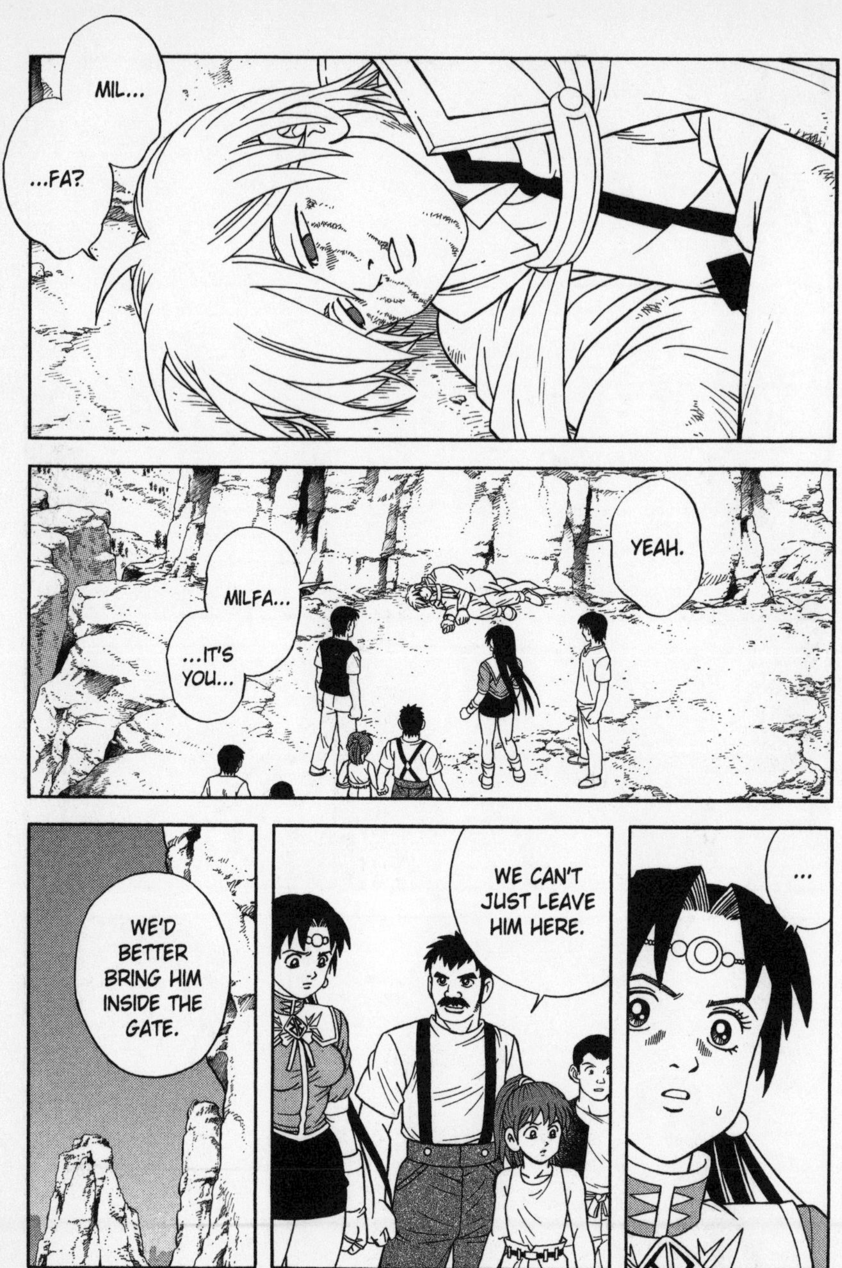
MIL...
...FA?
MILFA...
...IT'S YOU...
YEAH.
...
WE CAN'T JUST LEAVE HIM HERE.
WE'D BETTER BRING HIM INSIDE THE GATE.

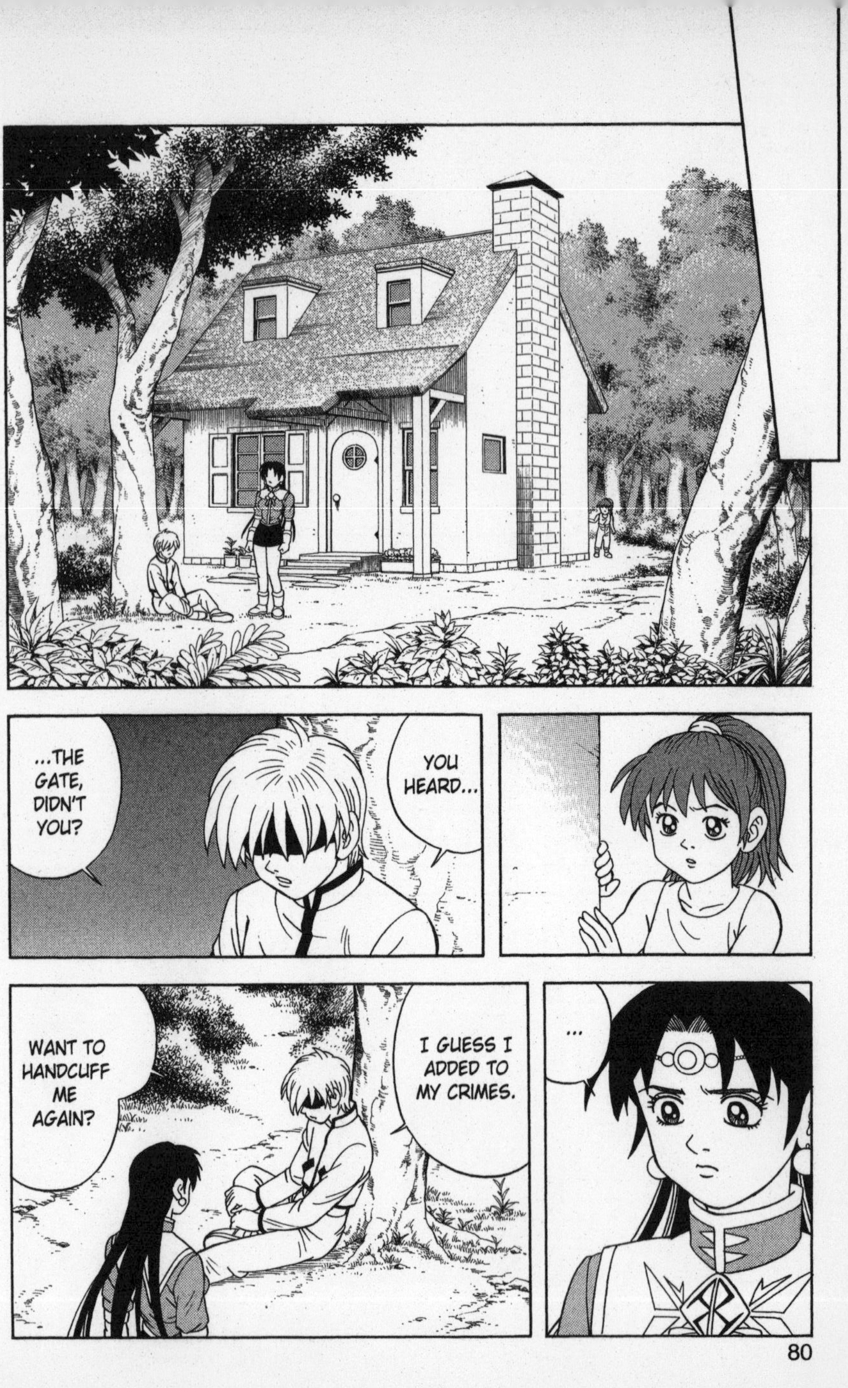
YOU HEARD...
...THE GATE, DIDN'T YOU?
...
I GUESS I ADDED TO MY CRIMES.
WANT TO HANDCUFF ME AGAIN?

READ THIS WAY

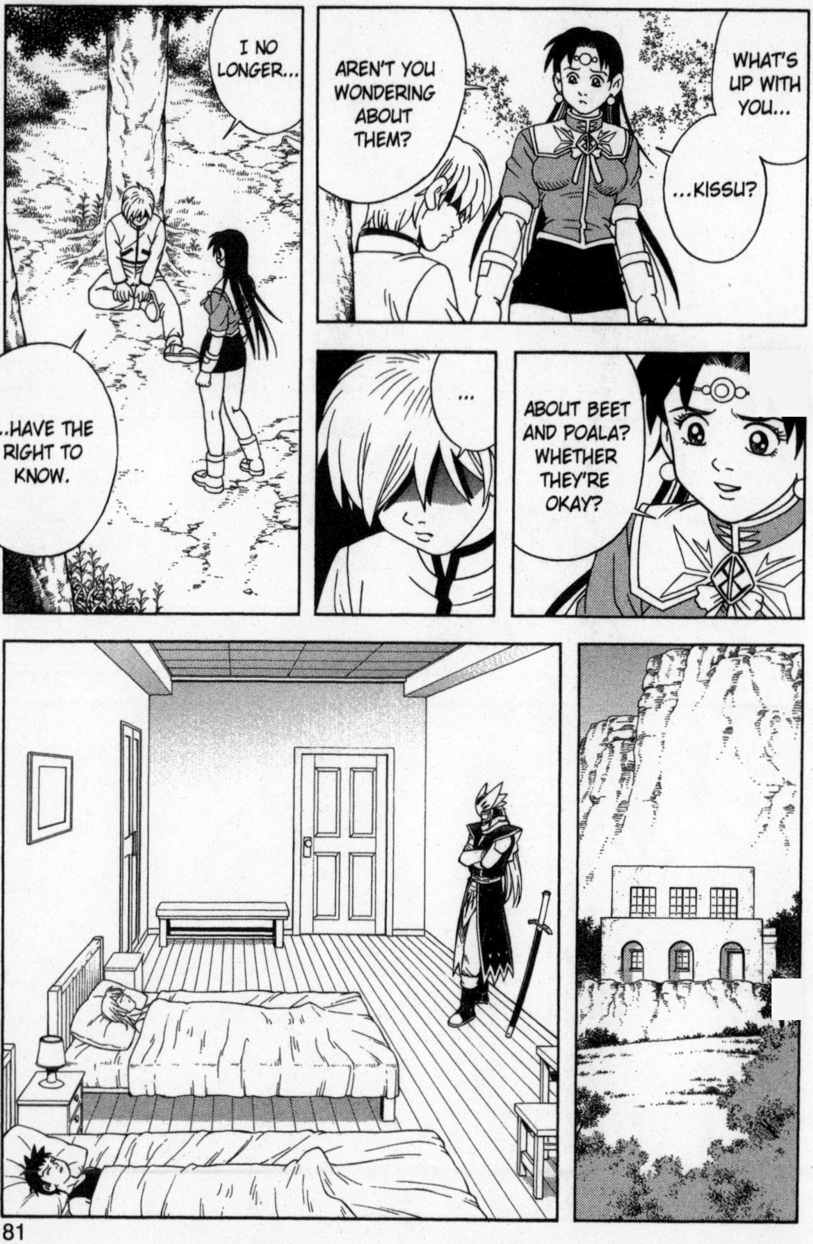
WHAT'S UP WITH YOU...
...KISSU?
AREN'T YOU WONDERING ABOUT THEM?
ABOUT BEET AND POALA? WHETHER THEY'RE OKAY?
...
I NO LONGER...
...HAVE THE RIGHT TO KNOW.

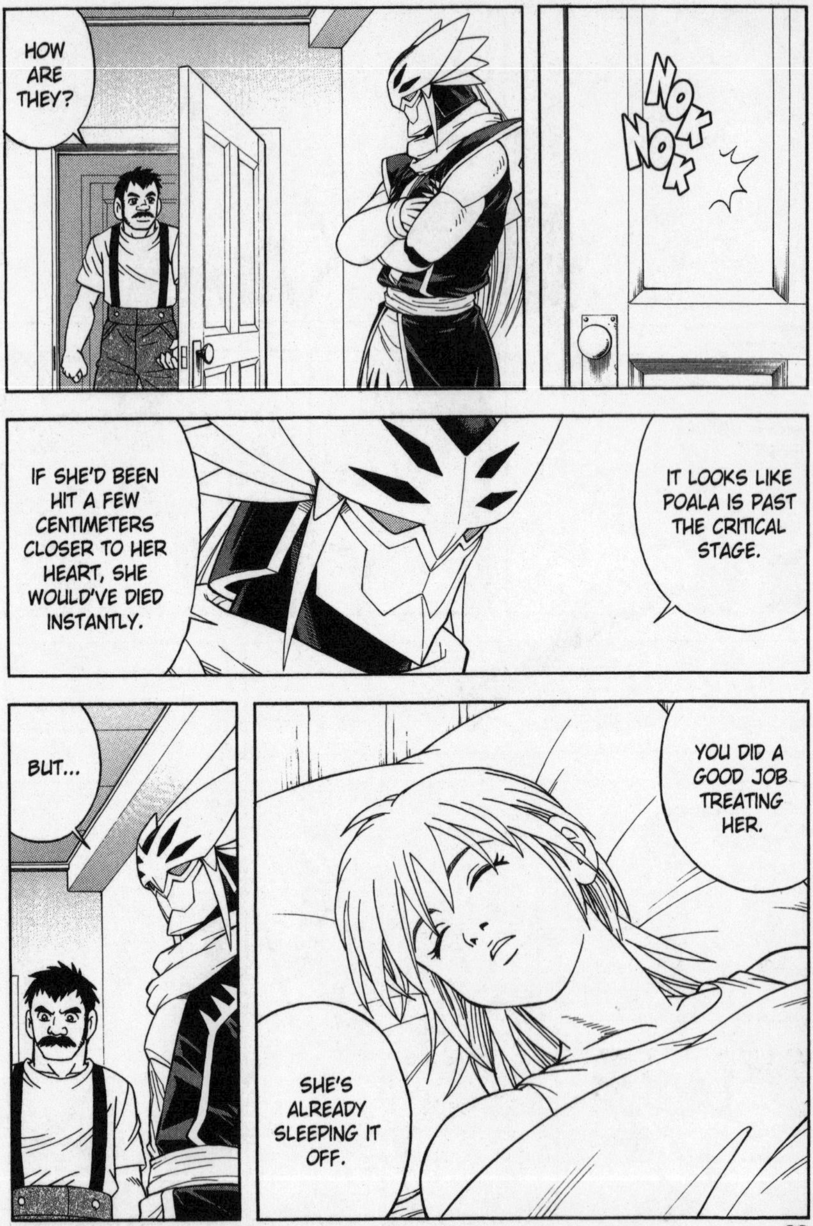
NOK NOK
HOW ARE THEY?
IT LOOKS LIKE POALA IS PAST THE CRITICAL STAGE.
IF SHE'D BEEN HIT A FEW CENTIMETERS CLOSER TO HER HEART, SHE WOULD'VE DIED INSTANTLY.
YOU DID A GOOD JOB TREATING HER.
SHE'S ALREADY SLEEPING IT OFF.
BUT...

READ THIS WAY

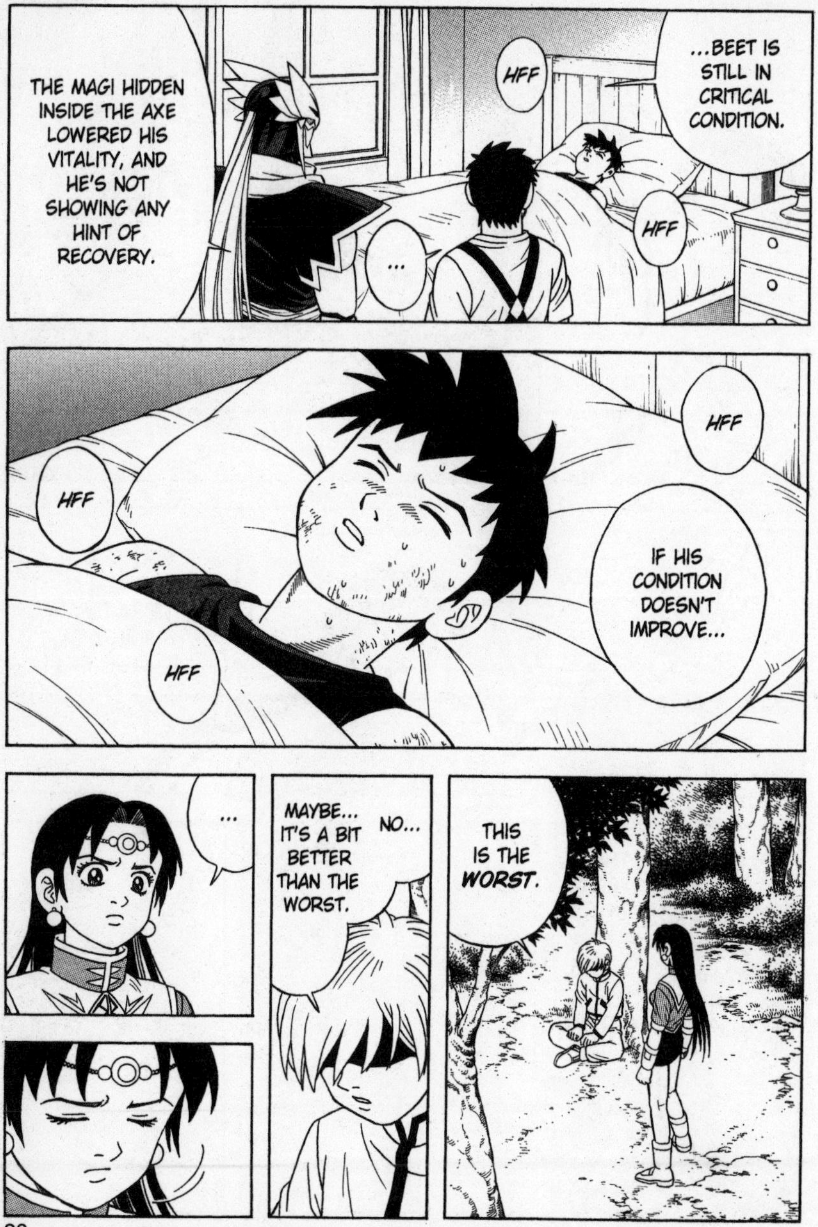
...BEET IS STILL IN CRITICAL CONDITION.
HFF
THE MAGI HIDDEN INSIDE THE AXE LOWERED HIS VITALITY, AND HE'S NOT SHOWING ANY HINT OF RECOVERY.
HFF
...
HFF
IF HIS CONDITION DOESN'T IMPROVE...
HFF
HFF
THIS IS THE *WORST*.
NO...
MAYBE... IT'S A BIT BETTER THAN THE WORST.
...

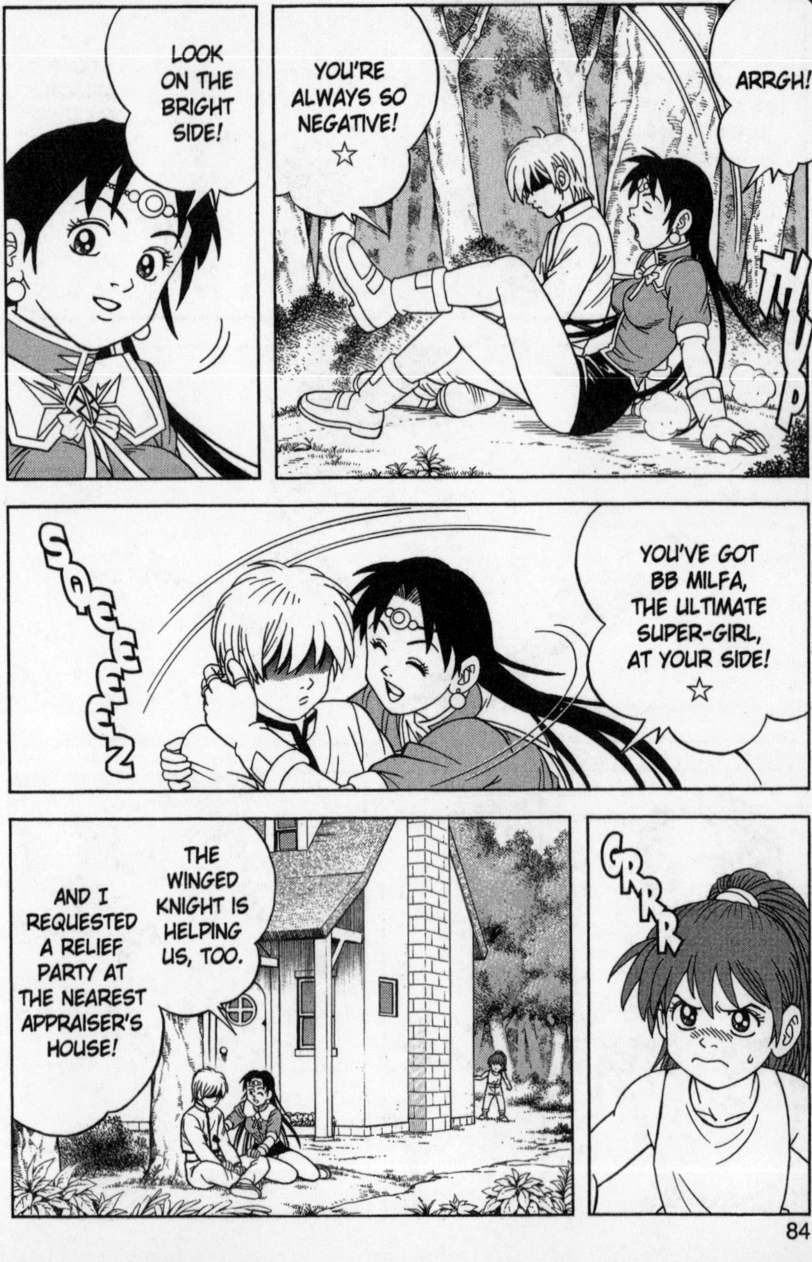
ARRGH!
THUD
YOU'RE ALWAYS SO NEGATIVE! ☆
LOOK ON THE BRIGHT SIDE!
YOU'VE GOT BB MILFA, THE ULTIMATE SUPER-GIRL, AT YOUR SIDE! ☆
SQEEEEZ
GRRRR
THE WINGED KNIGHT IS HELPING US, TOO.
AND I REQUESTED A RELIEF PARTY AT THE NEAREST APPRAISER'S HOUSE!

READ THIS WAY

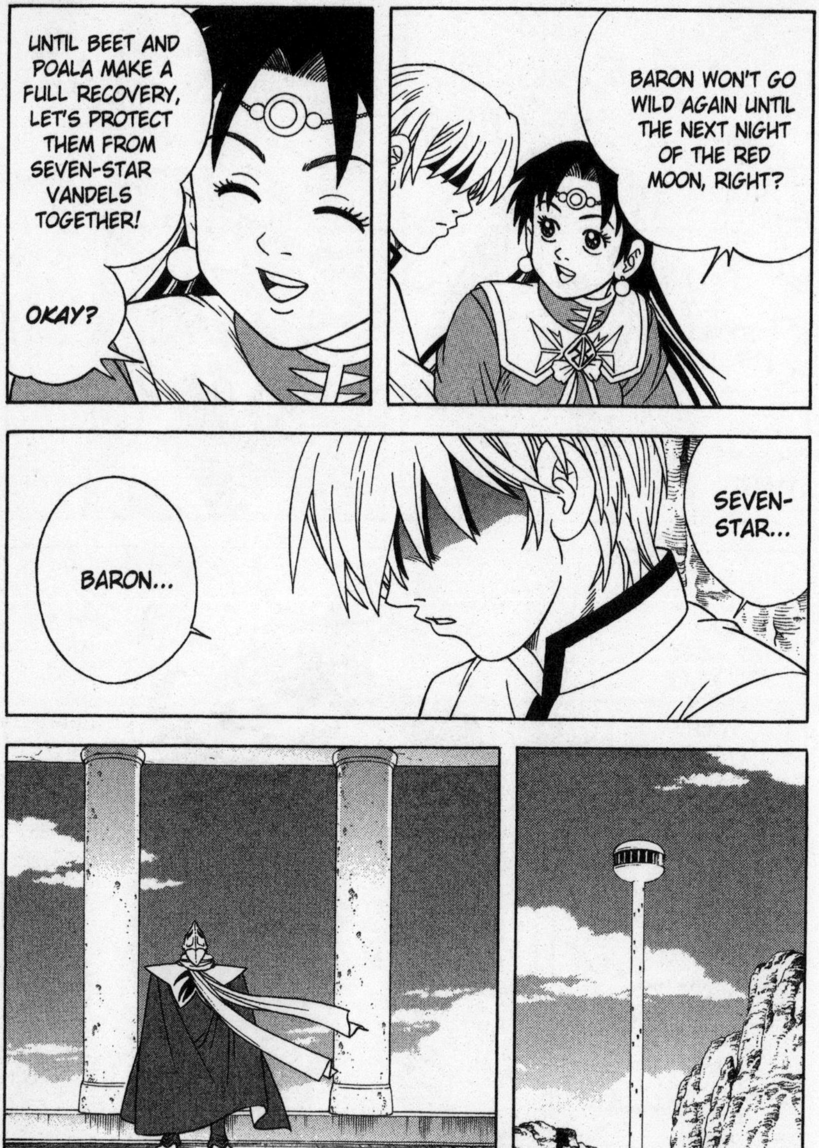
BARON WON'T GO WILD AGAIN UNTIL THE NEXT NIGHT OF THE RED MOON, RIGHT?
UNTIL BEET AND POALA MAKE A FULL RECOVERY, LET'S PROTECT THEM FROM SEVEN-STAR VANDELS TOGETHER!
OKAY?
SEVEN-STAR...
BARON...

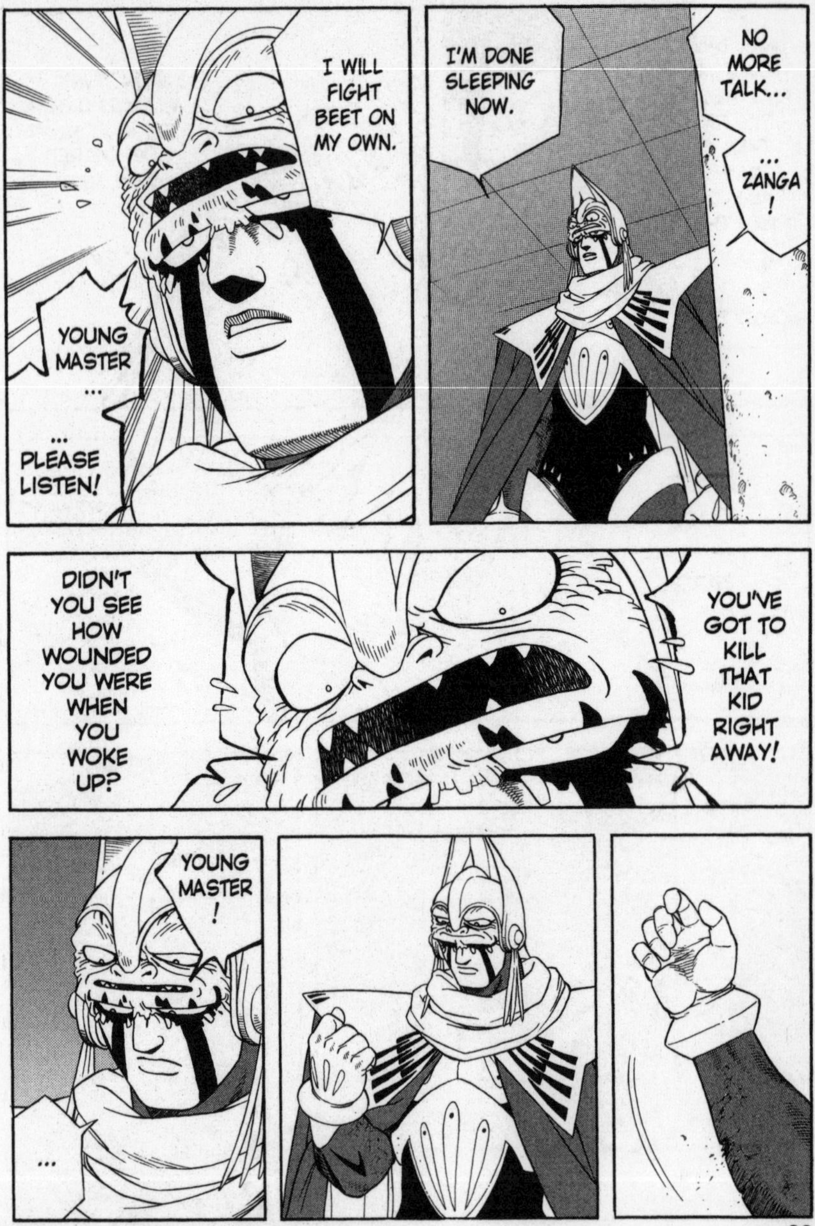
NO MORE TALK...
I'M DONE SLEEPING NOW.
...ZANGA!
I WILL FIGHT BEET ON MY OWN.
YOUNG MASTER...
...PLEASE LISTEN!
YOU'VE GOT TO KILL THAT KID RIGHT AWAY!
DIDN'T YOU SEE HOW WOUNDED YOU WERE WHEN YOU WOKE UP?
YOUNG MASTER!
...

READ THIS WAY

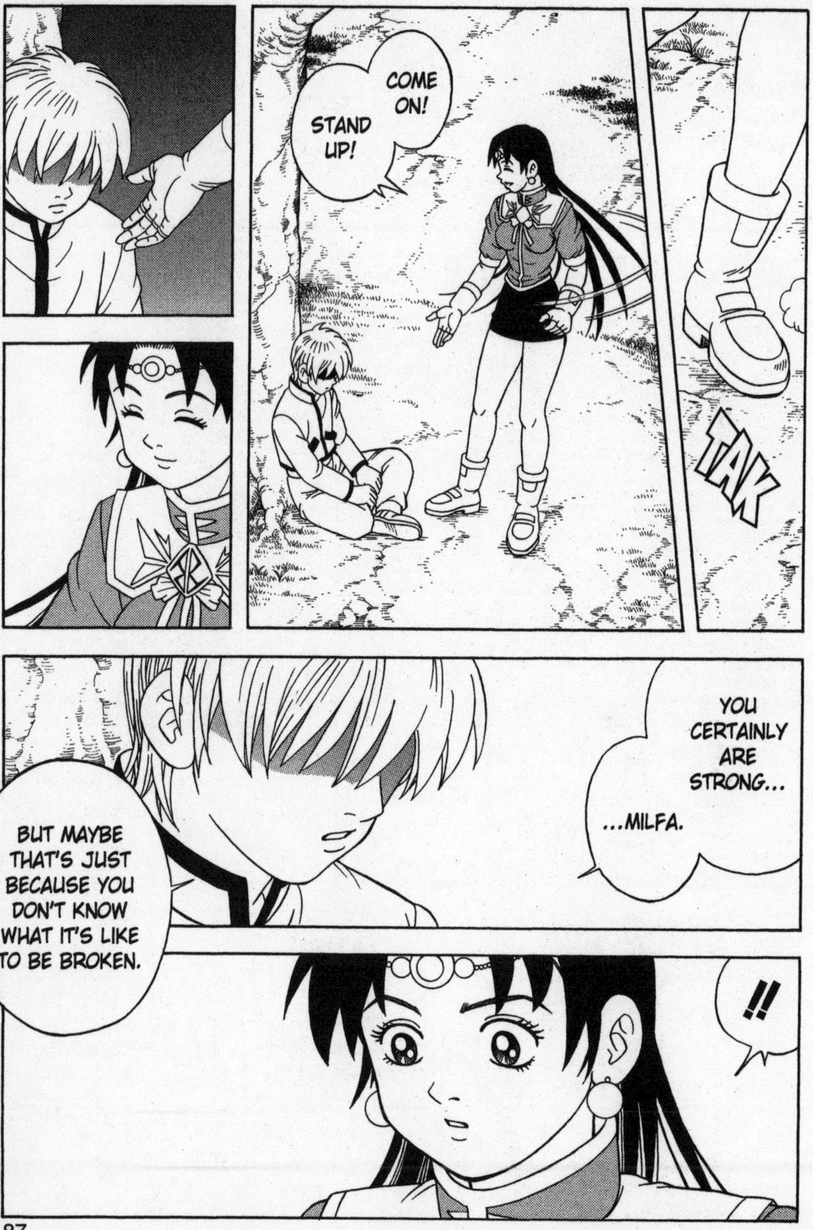
TAK
COME ON!
STAND UP!
YOU CERTAINLY ARE STRONG...
...MILFA.
BUT MAYBE THAT'S JUST BECAUSE YOU DON'T KNOW WHAT IT'S LIKE TO BE BROKEN.
!!

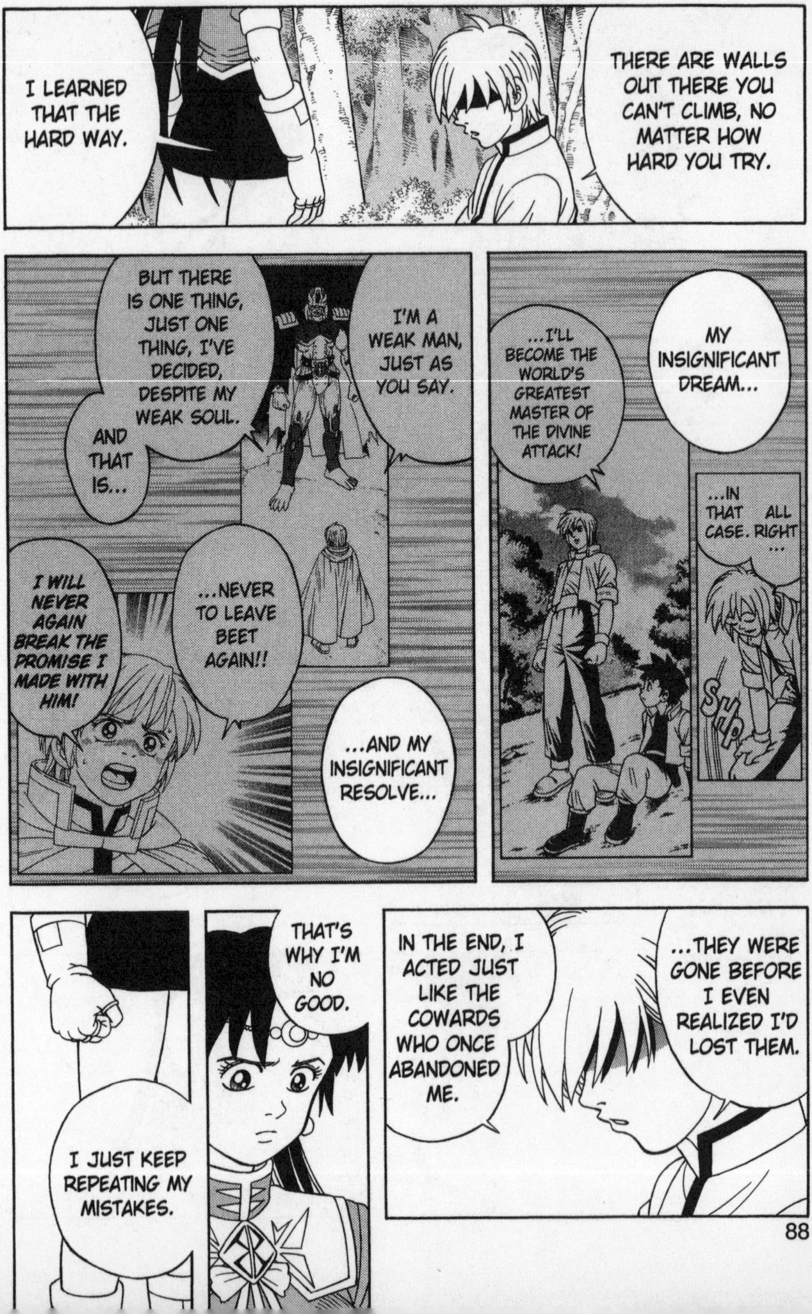
THERE ARE WALLS OUT THERE YOU CAN'T CLIMB, NO MATTER HOW HARD YOU TRY.
I LEARNED THAT THE HARD WAY.
MY INSIGNIFICANT DREAM...
...I'LL BECOME THE WORLD'S GREATEST MASTER OF THE DIVINE ATTACK!
ALL RIGHT...
...IN THAT CASE.
SHP
I'M A WEAK MAN, JUST AS YOU SAY.
BUT THERE IS ONE THING, JUST ONE THING, I'VE DECIDED, DESPITE MY WEAK SOUL.
AND THAT IS...
...NEVER TO LEAVE BEET AGAIN!!
I WILL NEVER AGAIN BREAK THE PROMISE I MADE WITH HIM!
...AND MY INSIGNIFICANT RESOLVE...
...THEY WERE GONE BEFORE I EVEN REALIZED I'D LOST THEM.
IN THE END, I ACTED JUST LIKE THE COWARDS WHO ONCE ABANDONED ME.
THAT'S WHY I'M NO GOOD.
I JUST KEEP REPEATING MY MISTAKES.

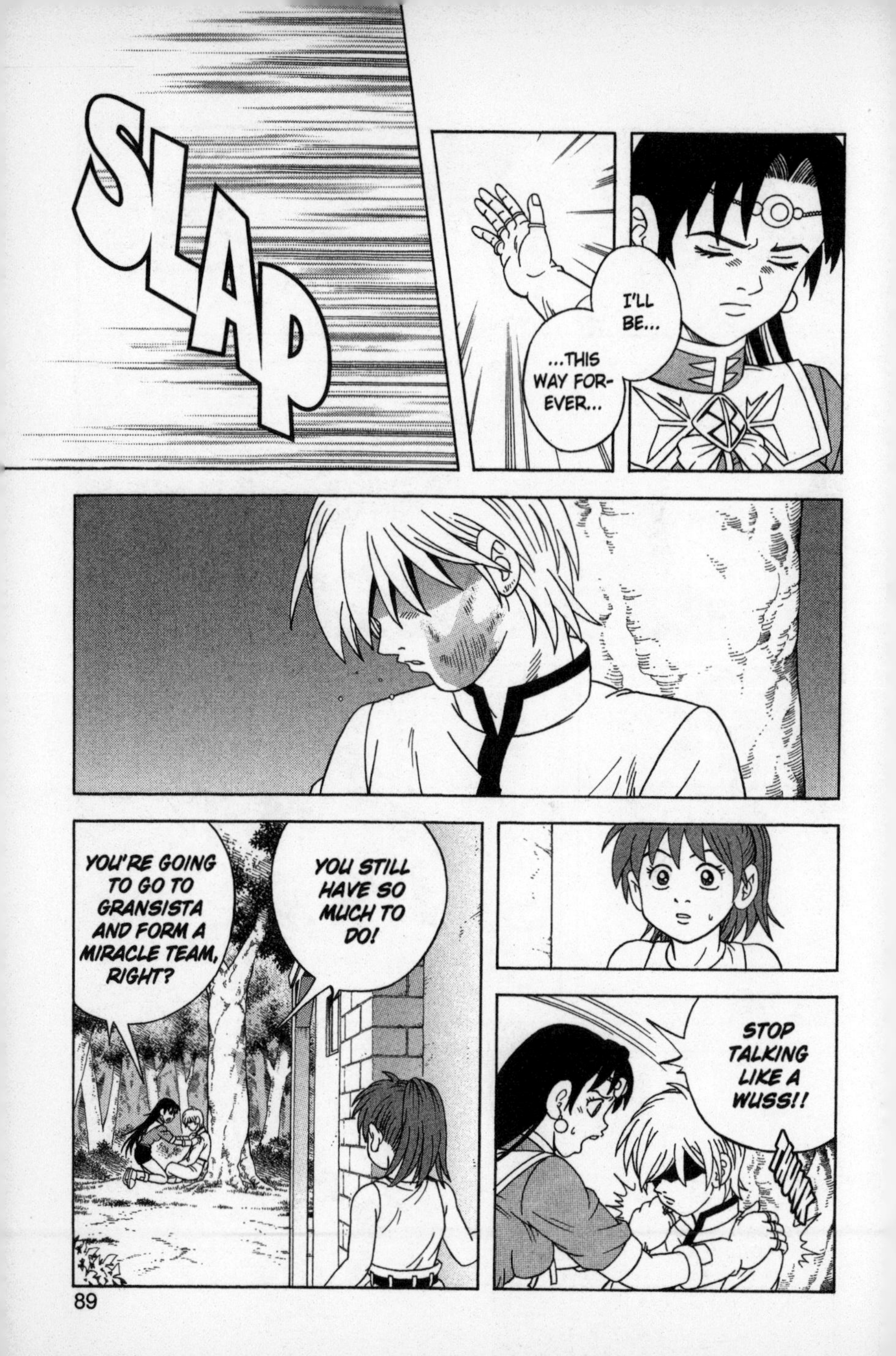
I'LL BE...
...THIS WAY FOR-EVER...
SLAP
STOP TALKING LIKE A WUSS!!
YOU STILL HAVE SO MUCH TO DO!
YOU'RE GOING TO GO TO GRANSISTA AND FORM A MIRACLE TEAM, RIGHT?

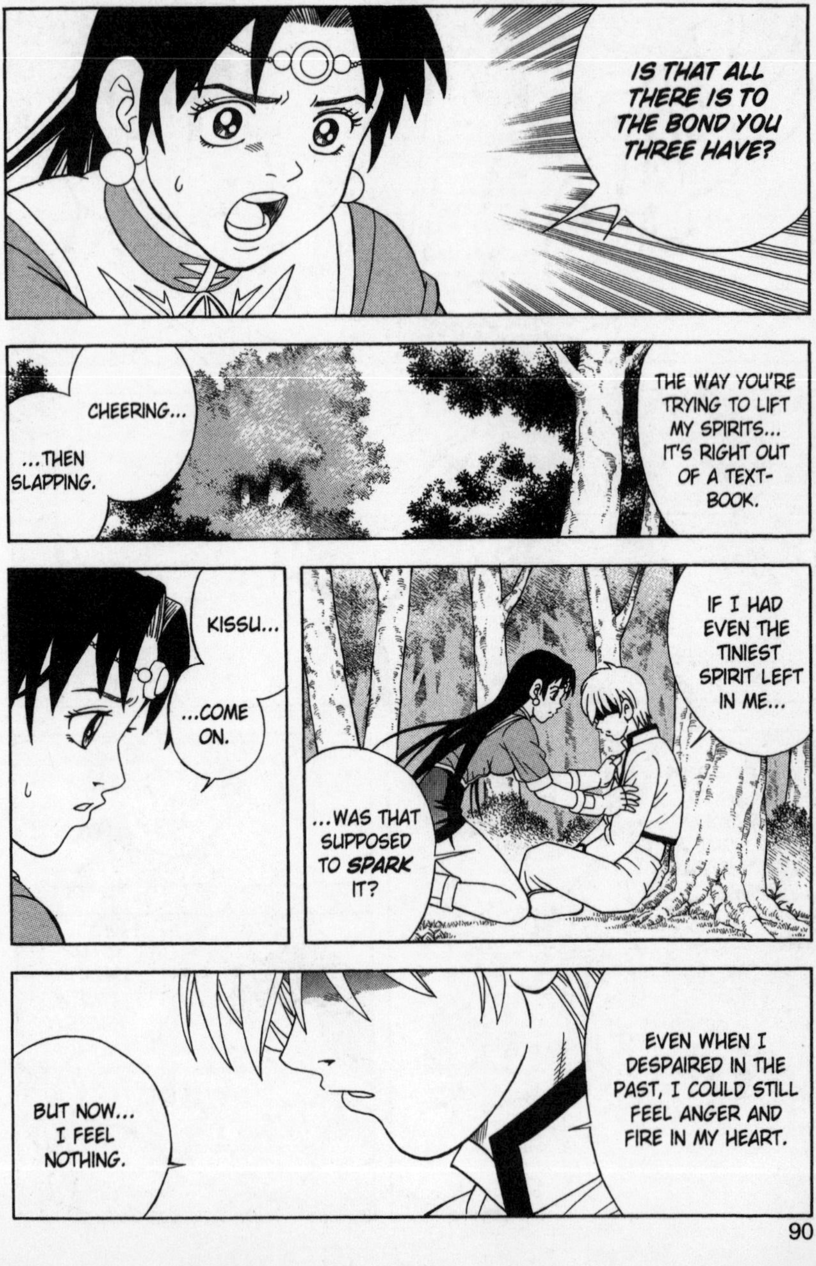
IS THAT ALL THERE IS TO THE BOND YOU THREE HAVE?
THE WAY YOU'RE TRYING TO LIFT MY SPIRITS... IT'S RIGHT OUT OF A TEXT-BOOK.
CHEERING...
...THEN SLAPPING.
IF I HAD EVEN THE TINIEST SPIRIT LEFT IN ME...
...WAS THAT SUPPOSED TO *SPARK* IT?
KISSU...
...COME ON.
EVEN WHEN I DESPAIRED IN THE PAST, I COULD STILL FEEL ANGER AND FIRE IN MY HEART.
BUT NOW... I FEEL NOTHING.

READ THIS WAY

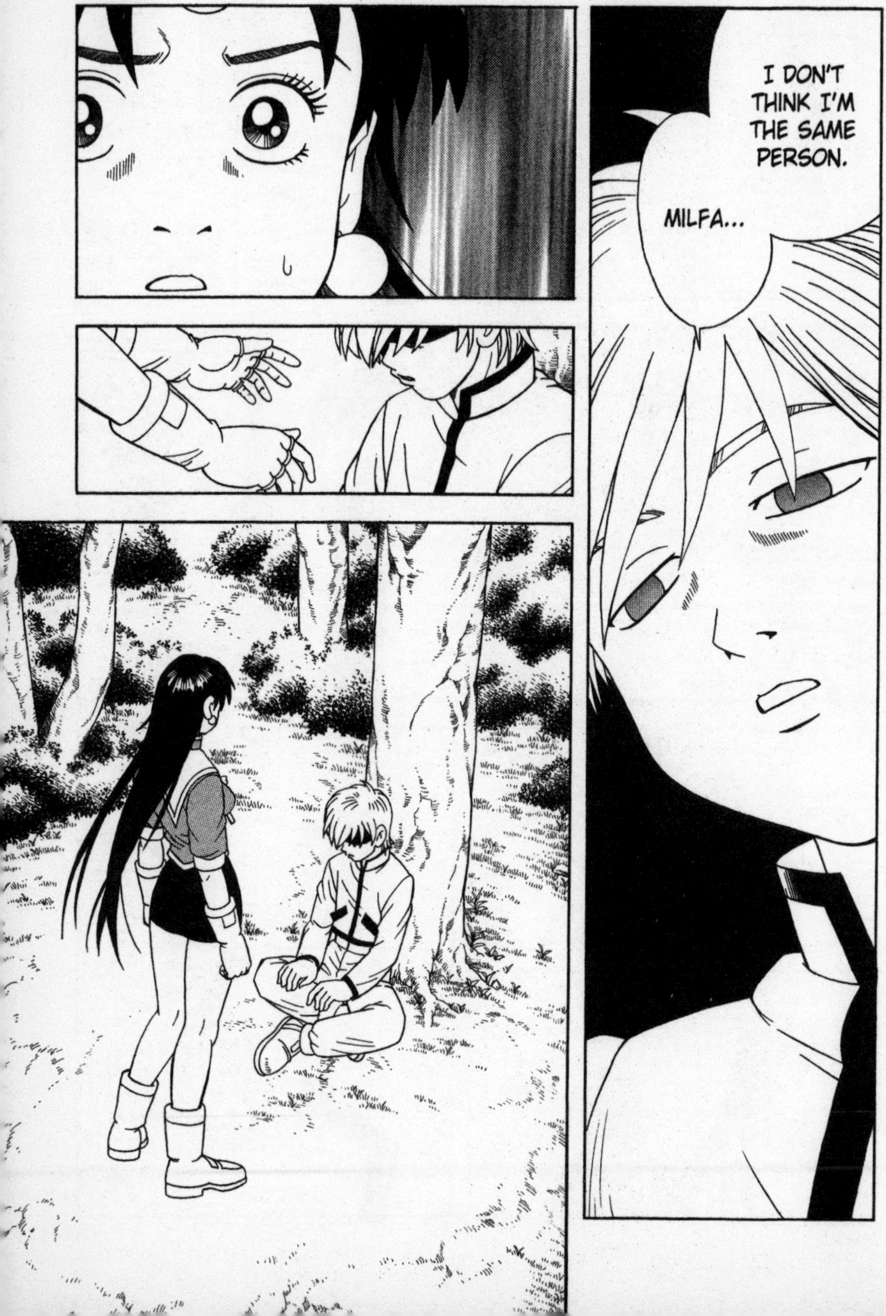
I DON'T THINK I'M THE SAME PERSON.
MILFA...

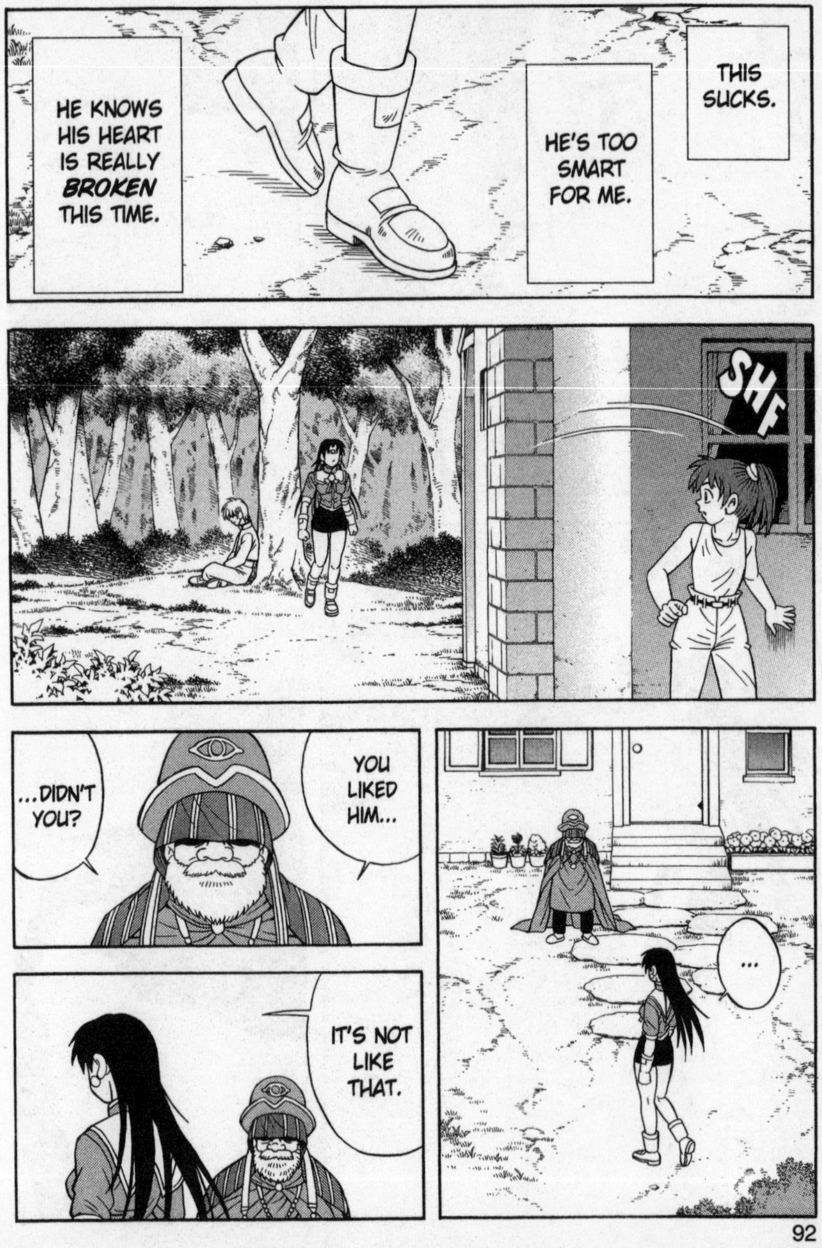
THIS SUCKS.
HE'S TOO SMART FOR ME.
HE KNOWS HIS HEART IS REALLY BROKEN THIS TIME.
SHF
...
YOU LIKED HIM...
...DIDN'T YOU?
IT'S NOT LIKE THAT.

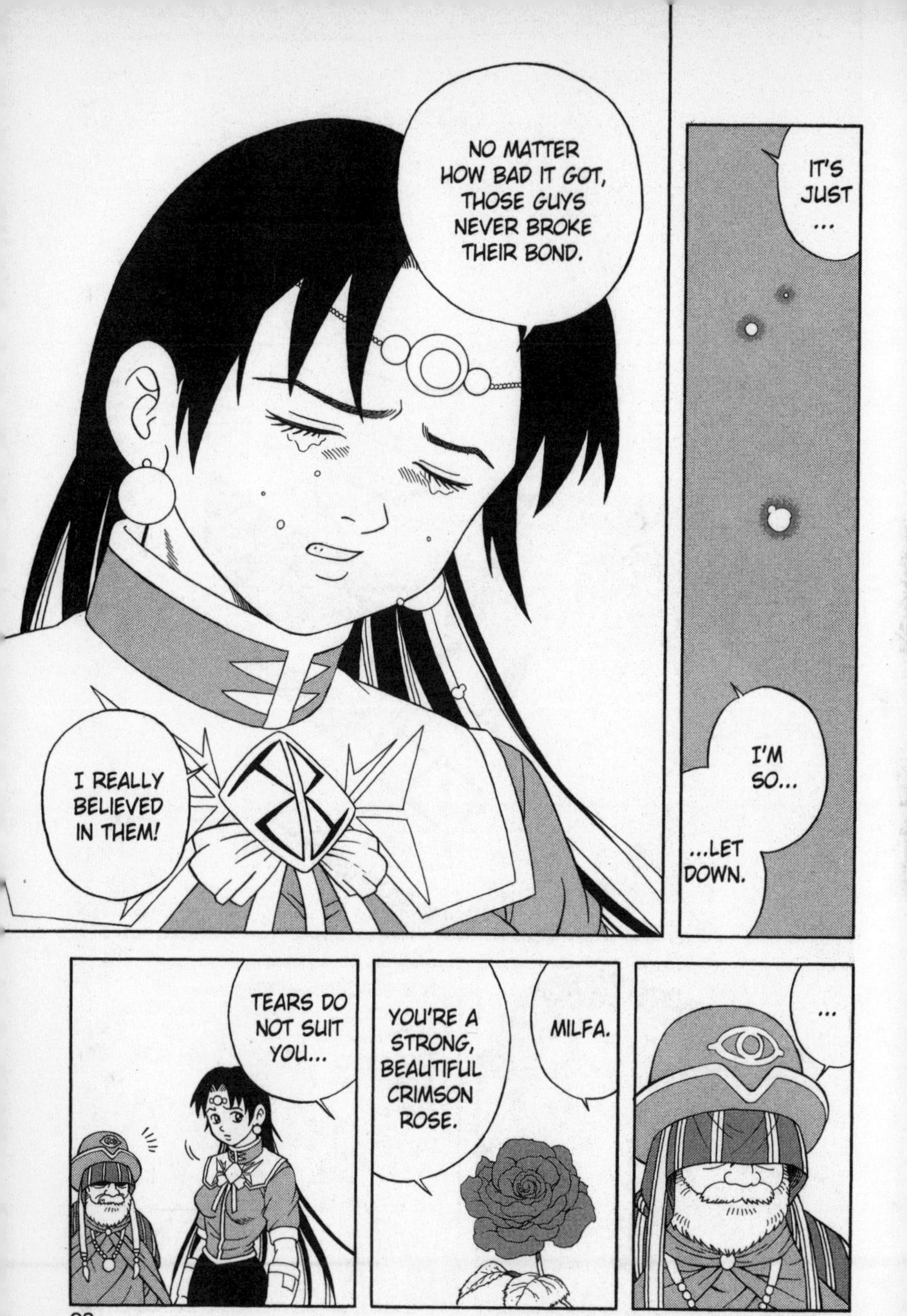
IT'S JUST ...
I'M SO...
...LET DOWN.
NO MATTER HOW BAD IT GOT, THOSE GUYS NEVER BROKE THEIR BOND.
I REALLY BELIEVED IN THEM!
...
MILFA.
YOU'RE A STRONG, BEAUTIFUL CRIMSON ROSE.
TEARS DO NOT SUIT YOU...

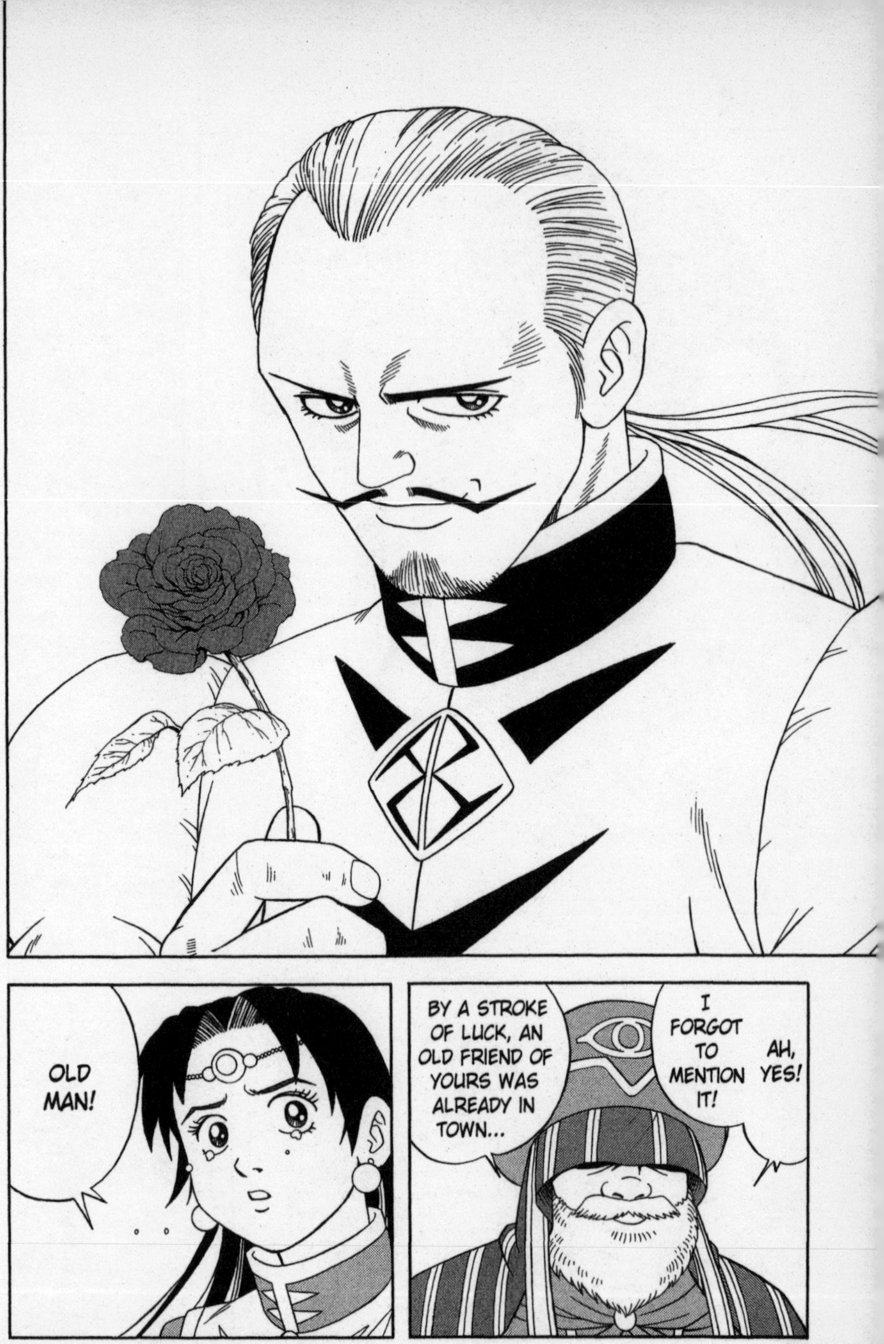
AH, YES!
I FORGOT TO MENTION IT!
BY A STROKE OF LUCK, AN OLD FRIEND OF YOURS WAS ALREADY IN TOWN...
OLD MAN!

READ THIS WAY

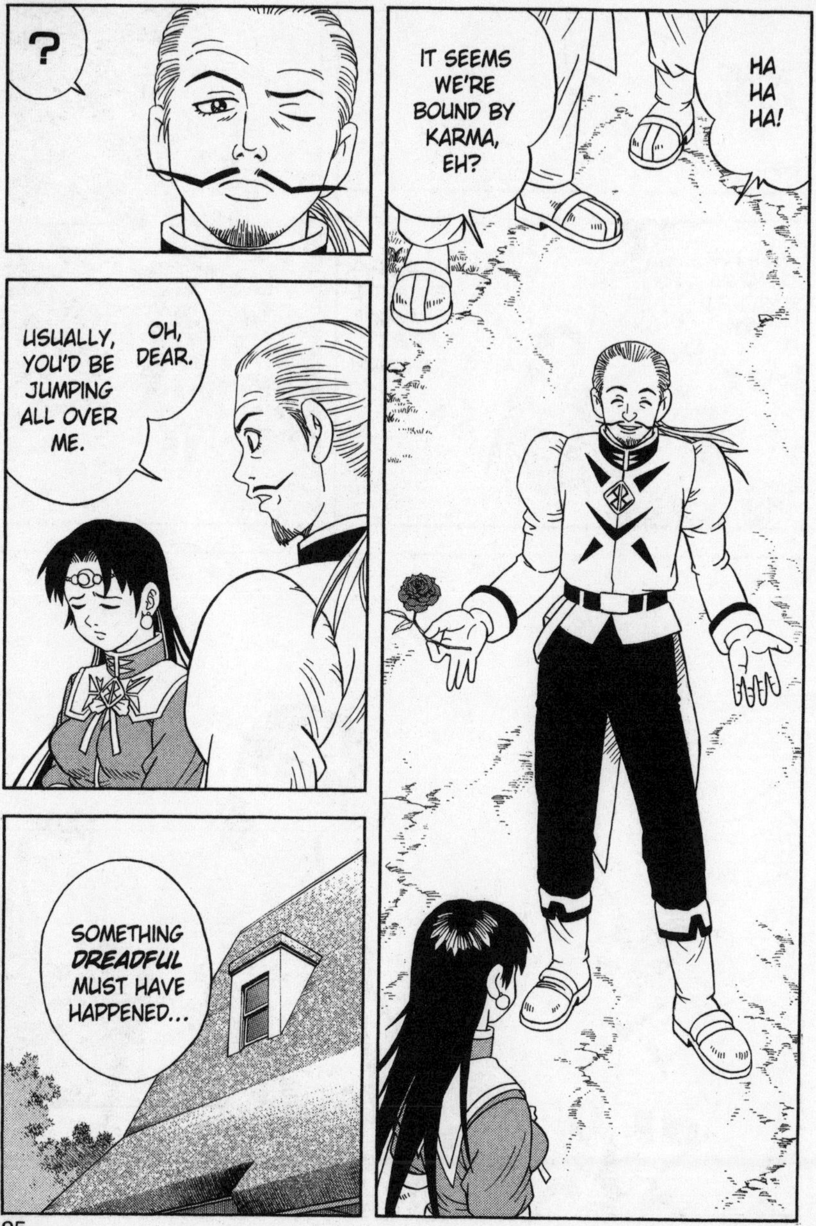
HA HA HA!
IT SEEMS WE'RE BOUND BY KARMA, EH?
?
OH, DEAR.
USUALLY, YOU'D BE JUMPING ALL OVER ME.
SOMETHING *DREADFUL* MUST HAVE HAPPENED...

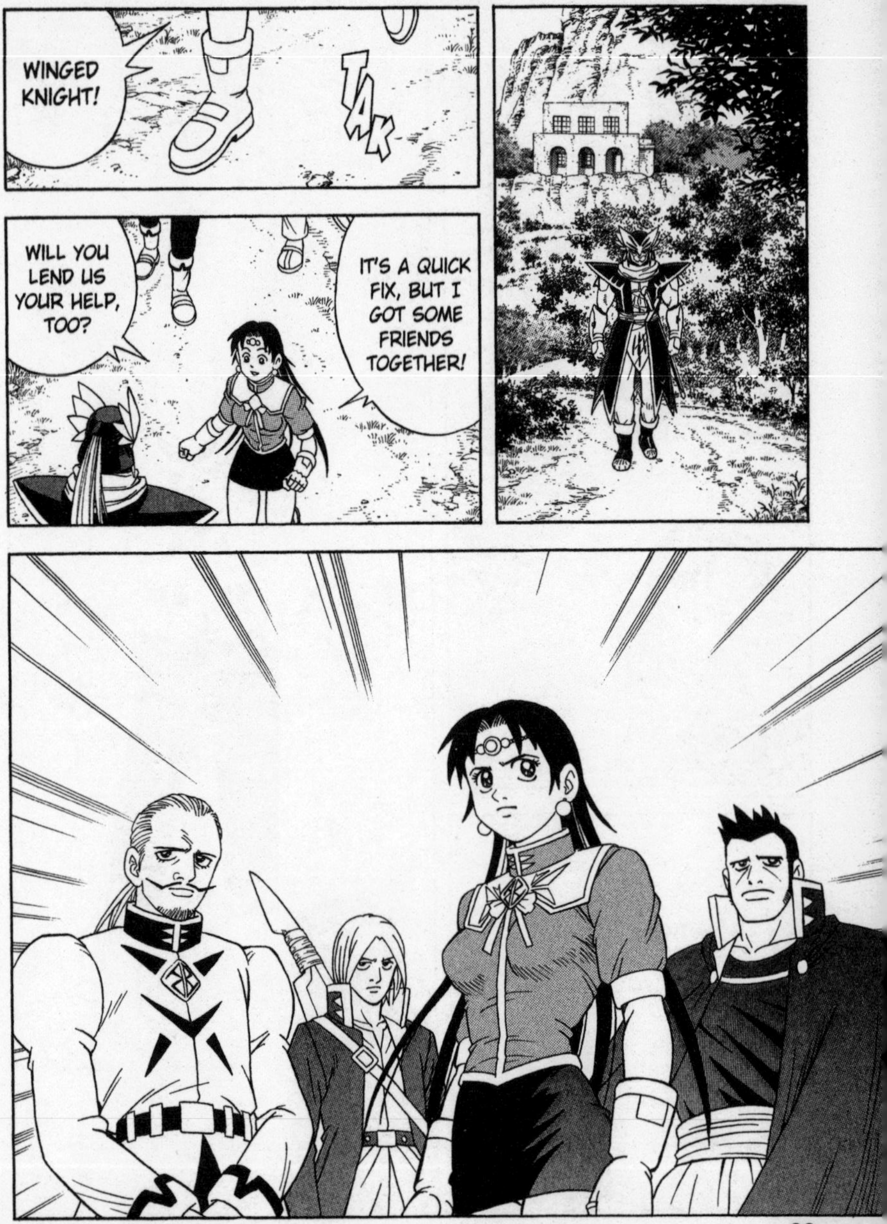
WINGED KNIGHT!
TAK
IT'S A QUICK FIX, BUT I GOT SOME FRIENDS TOGETHER!
WILL YOU LEND US YOUR HELP, TOO?

READ THIS WAY

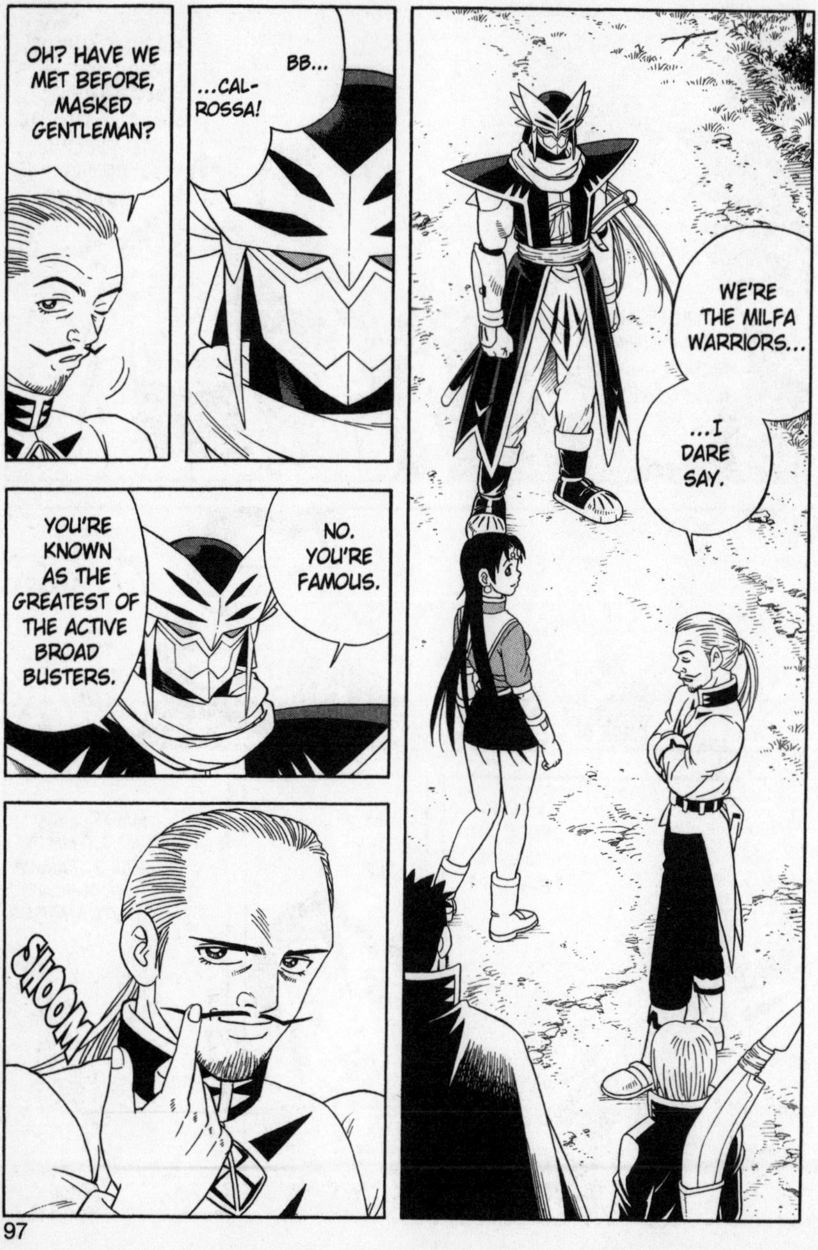

WE'RE THE MILFA WARRIORS...
...I DARE SAY.
BB...
...CAL-ROSSA!
OH? HAVE WE MET BEFORE, MASKED GENTLEMAN?
NO. YOU'RE FAMOUS.
YOU'RE KNOWN AS THE GREATEST OF THE ACTIVE BROAD BUSTERS.
SHOOM

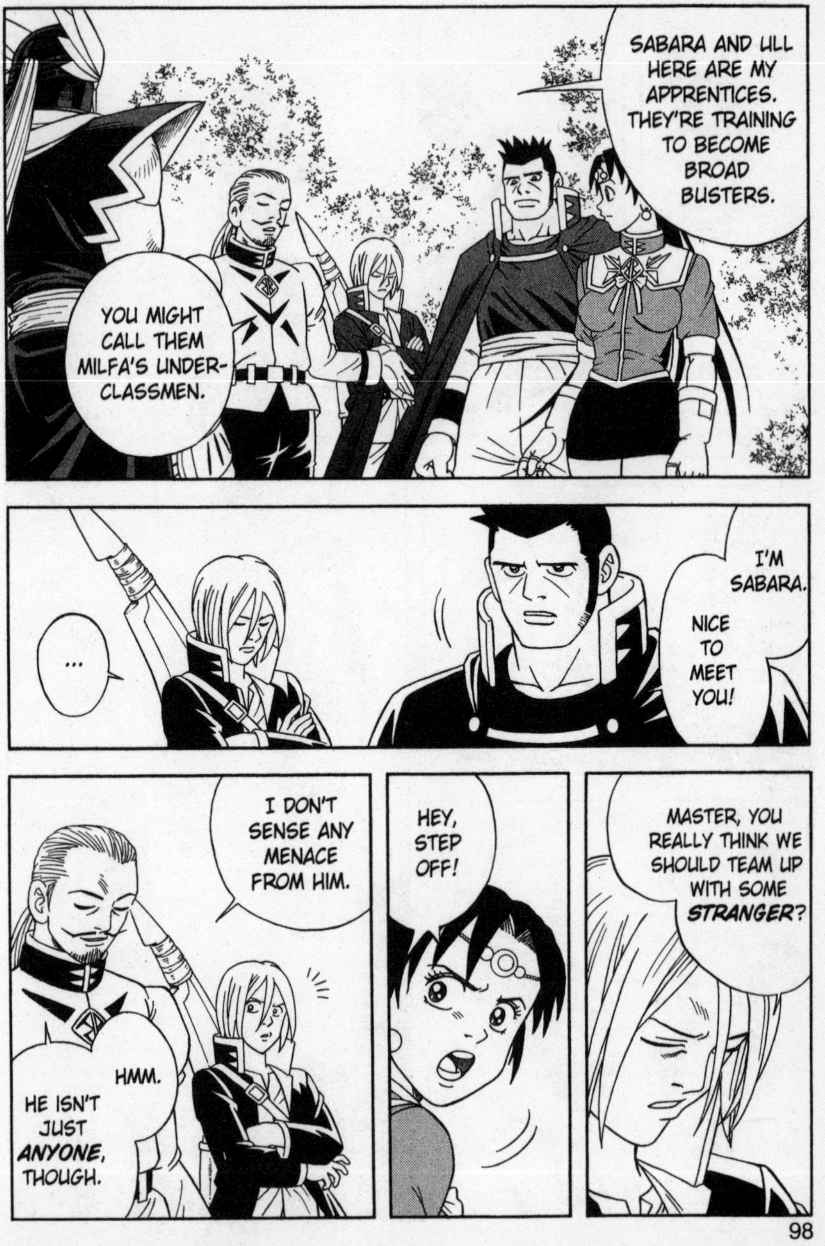
SABARA AND ULL HERE ARE MY APPRENTICES. THEY'RE TRAINING TO BECOME BROAD BUSTERS.
YOU MIGHT CALL THEM MILFA'S UNDER-CLASSMEN.
I'M SABARA.
NICE TO MEET YOU!
...
MASTER, YOU REALLY THINK WE SHOULD TEAM UP WITH SOME *STRANGER*?
HEY, STEP OFF!
I DON'T SENSE ANY MENACE FROM HIM.
HMM.
HE ISN'T JUST *ANYONE*, THOUGH.

READ THIS WAY

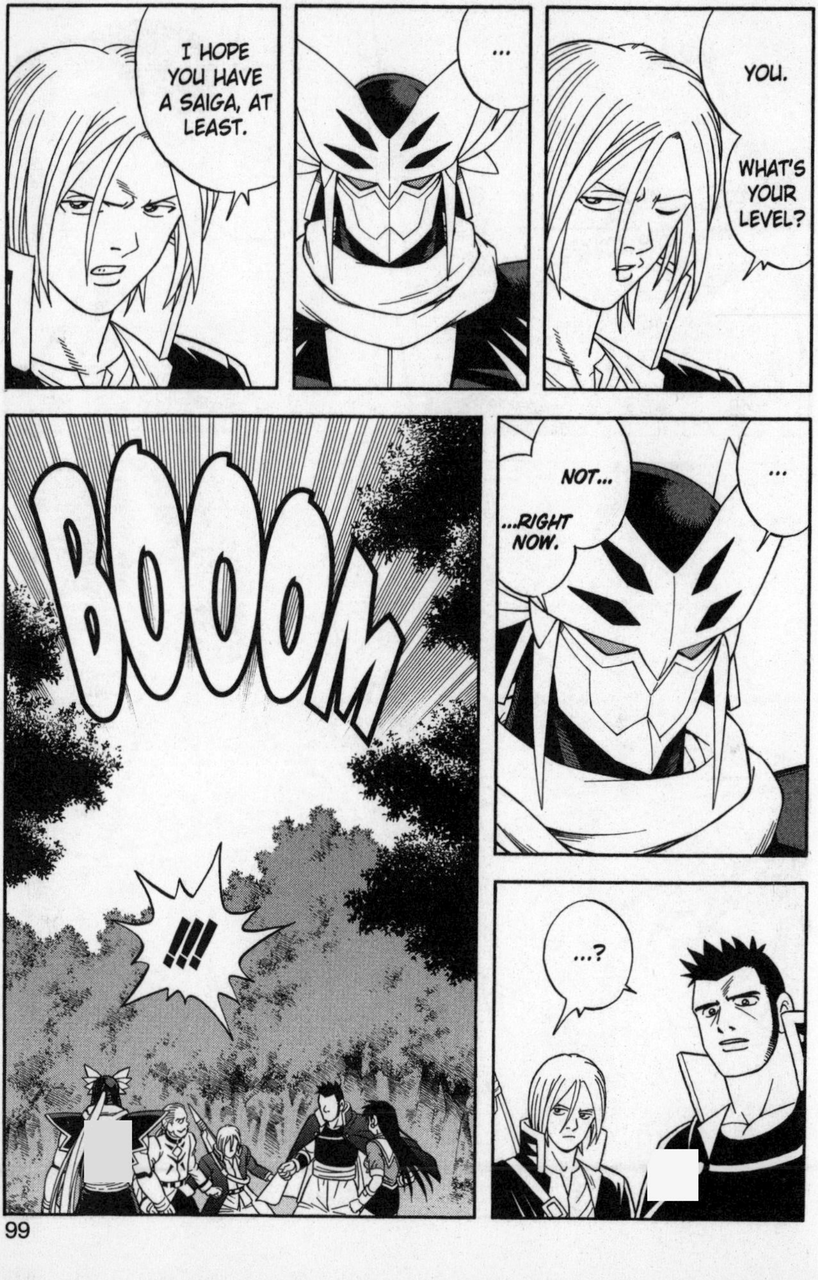
YOU.
WHAT'S YOUR LEVEL?
...
I HOPE YOU HAVE A SAIGA, AT LEAST.
...
NOT...
...RIGHT NOW.
...?
BOOOM
!!!

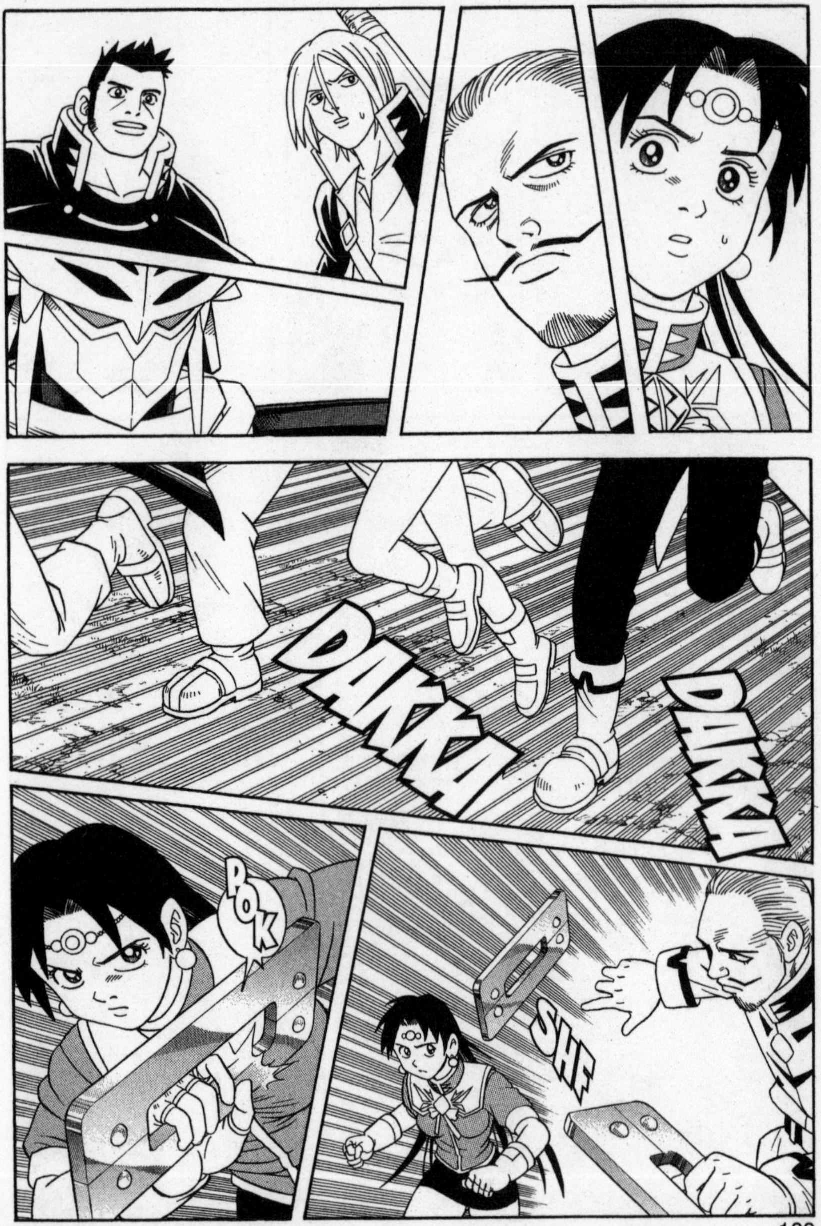
DAKKA
DAKKA
SHF
POK

READ THIS WAY

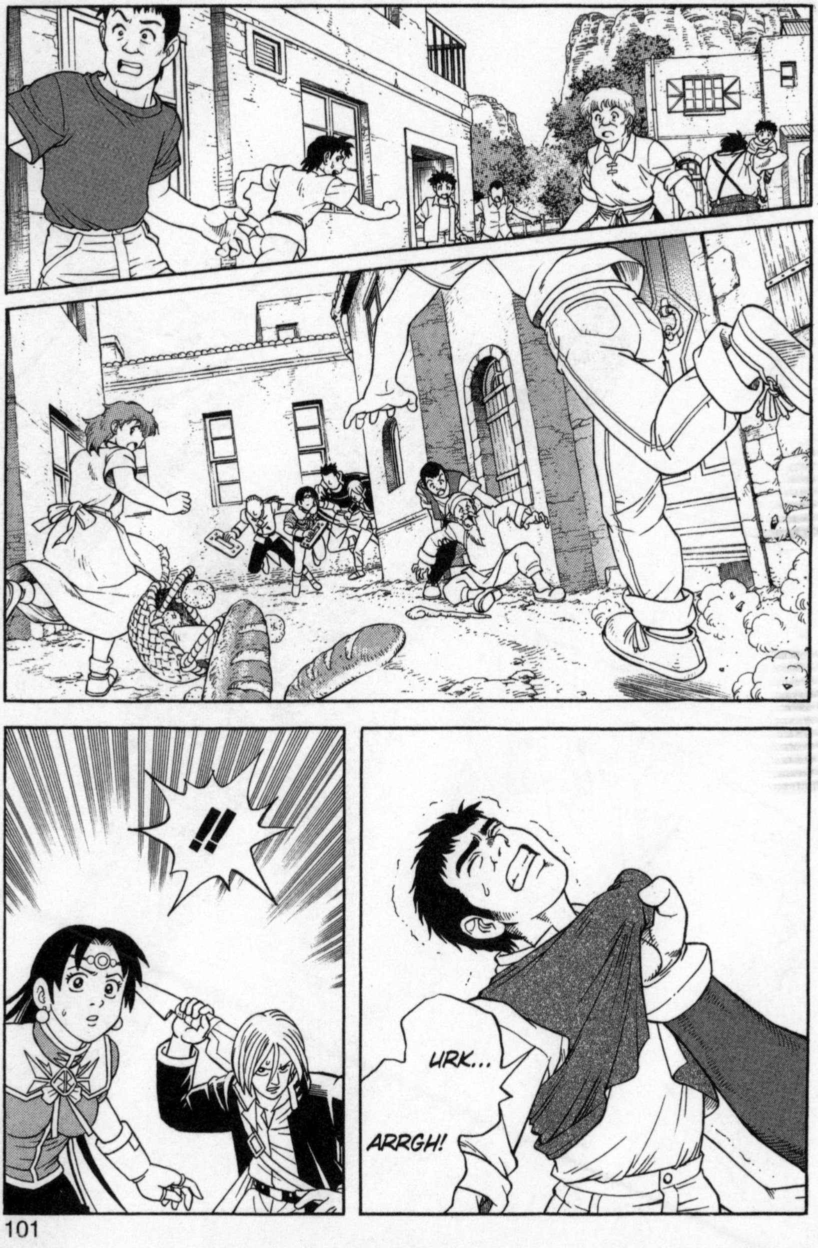
URK...
ARRGH!
!!

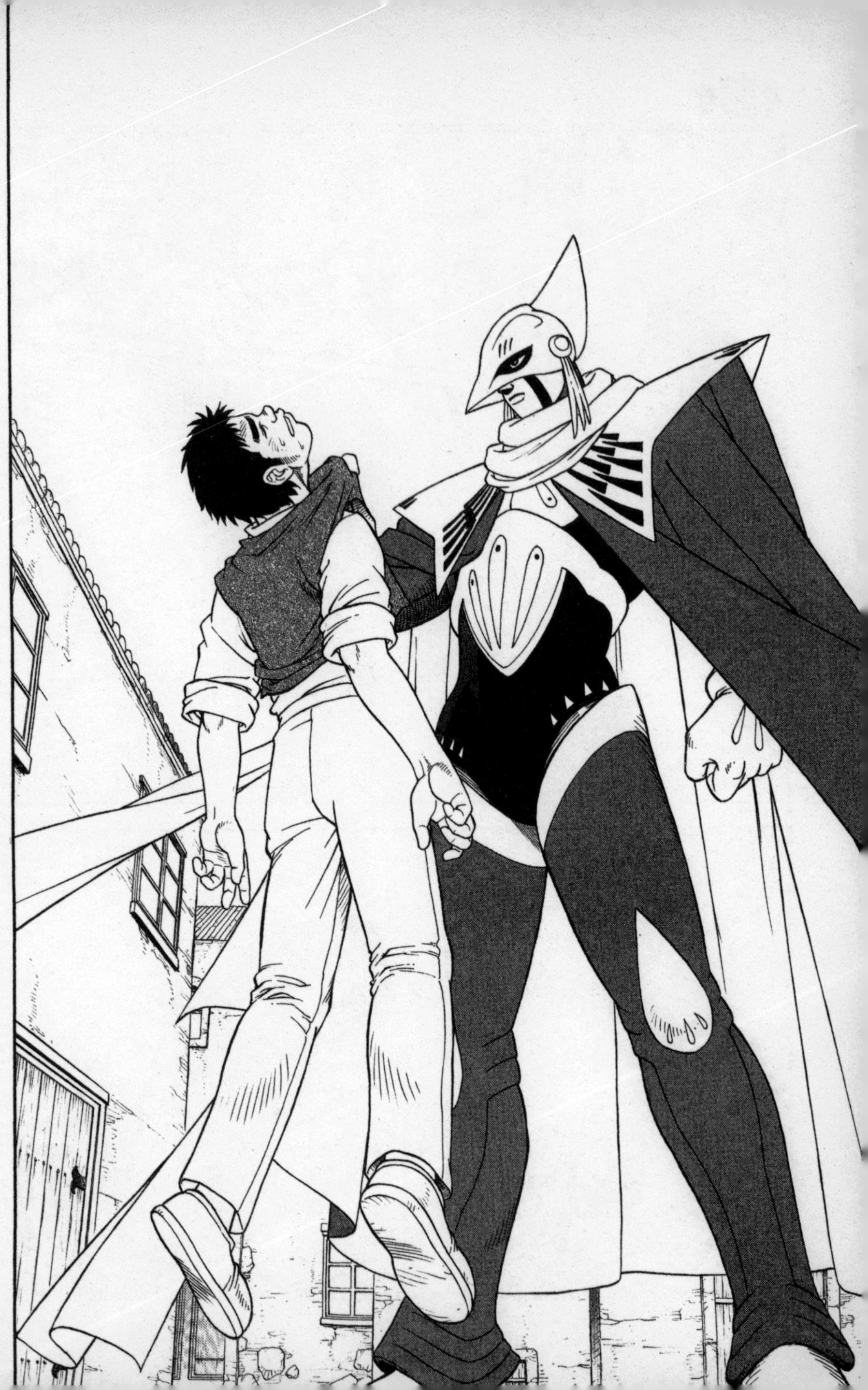

READ THIS WAY

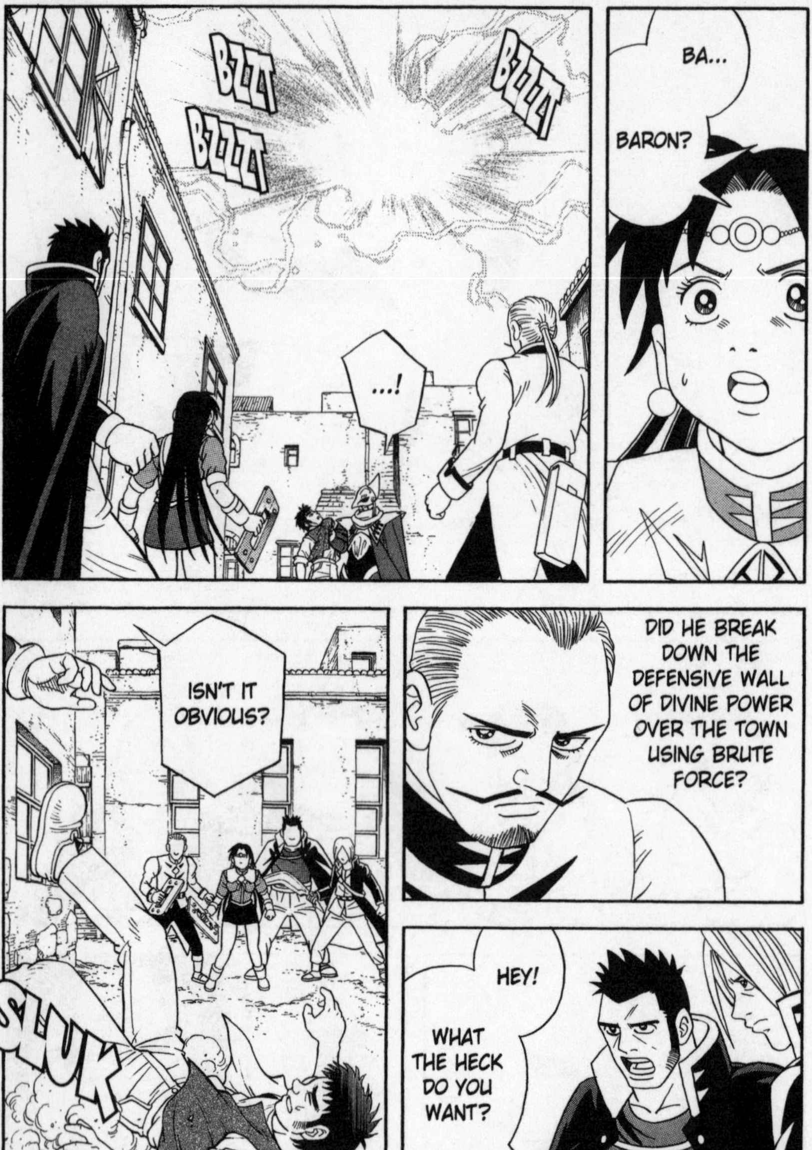
BA...
BARON?
BZZZT
BZZZT
BZZZT
...!
DID HE BREAK DOWN THE DEFENSIVE WALL OF DIVINE POWER OVER THE TOWN USING BRUTE FORCE?
HEY!
WHAT THE HECK DO YOU WANT?
ISN'T IT OBVIOUS?
SLUK

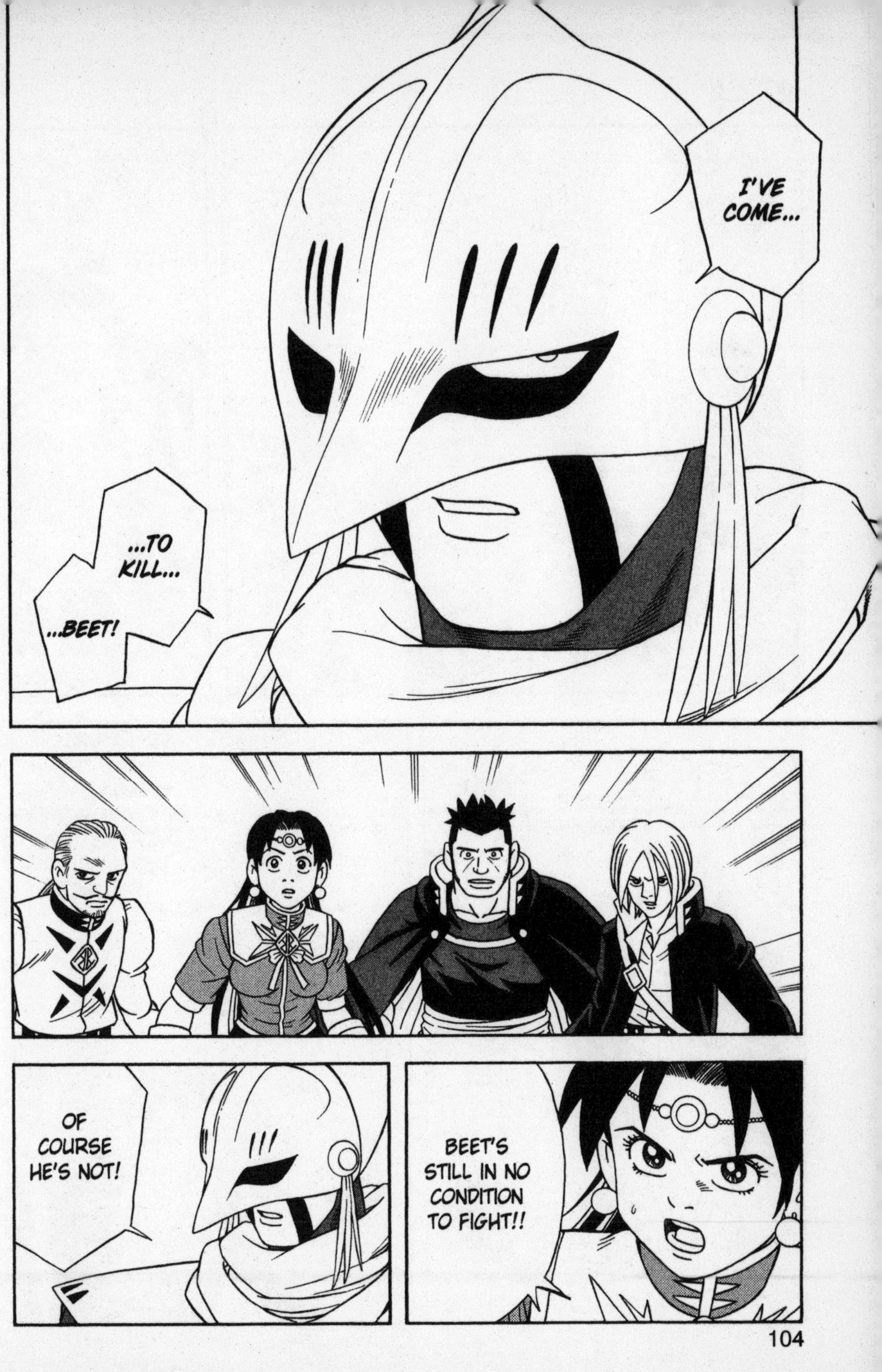
I'VE COME...
...TO KILL...
...BEET!
BEET'S STILL IN NO CONDITION TO FIGHT!!
OF COURSE HE'S NOT!

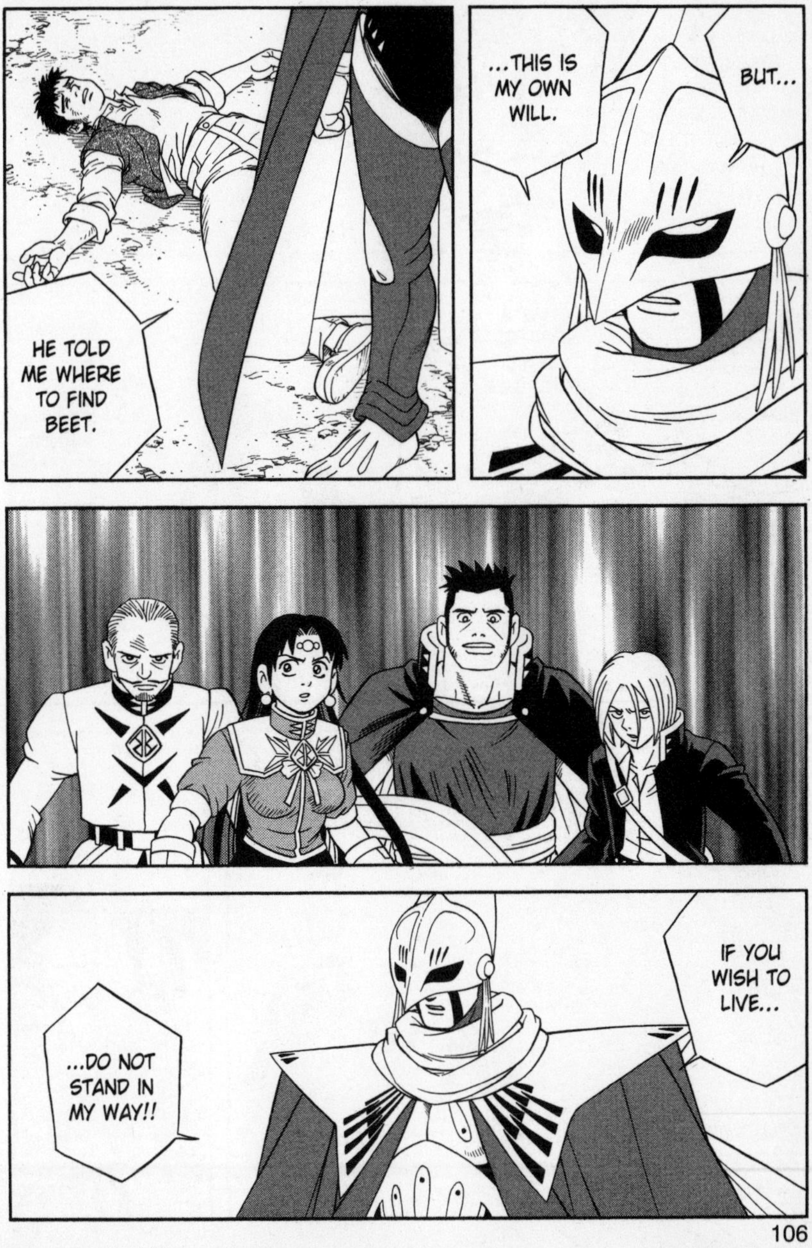

...THIS IS MY OWN WILL.
BUT...
HE TOLD ME WHERE TO FIND BEET.
IF YOU WISH TO LIVE...
...DO NOT STAND IN MY WAY!!

READ THIS WAY

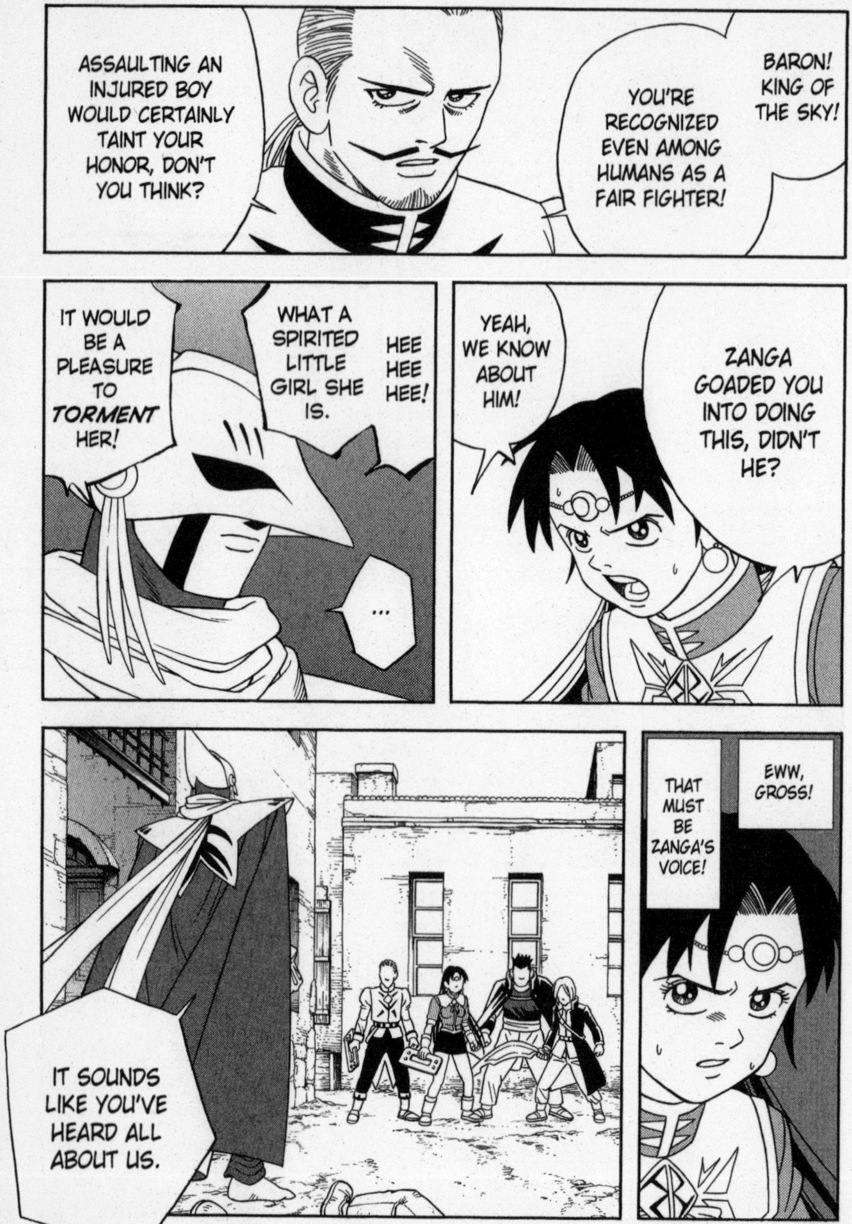
BARON! KING OF THE SKY!
YOU'RE RECOGNIZED EVEN AMONG HUMANS AS A FAIR FIGHTER!
ASSAULTING AN INJURED BOY WOULD CERTAINLY TAINT YOUR HONOR, DON'T YOU THINK?
ZANGA GOADED YOU INTO DOING THIS, DIDN'T HE?
YEAH, WE KNOW ABOUT HIM!
HEE HEE HEE!
WHAT A SPIRITED LITTLE GIRL SHE IS.
IT WOULD BE A PLEASURE TO *TORMENT* HER!
...
EWW, GROSS!
THAT MUST BE ZANGA'S VOICE!
IT SOUNDS LIKE YOU'VE HEARD ALL ABOUT US.

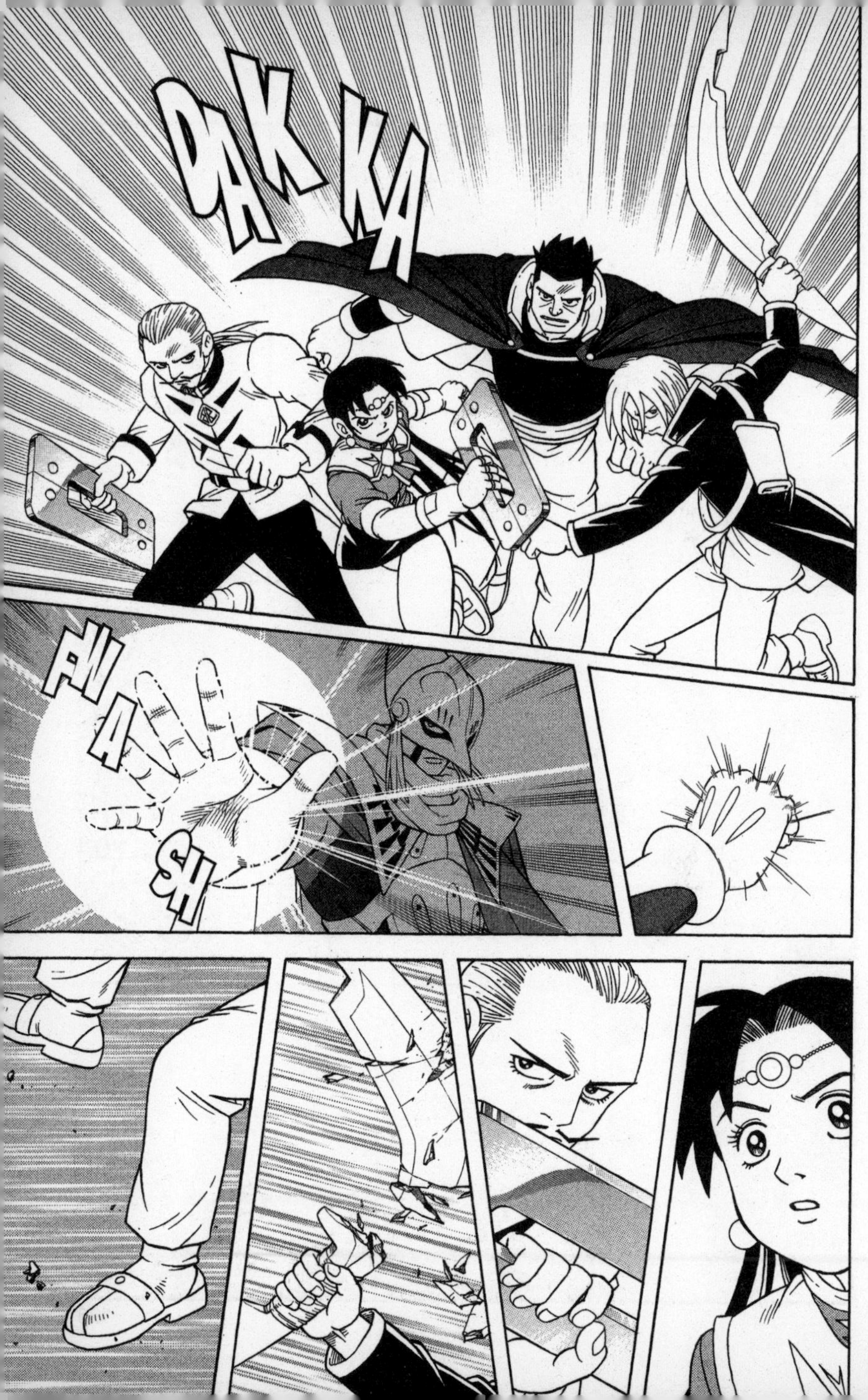
DAKKA
FWASH

UGH!

GEEZ!

HE SHATTERED THE GOLDEN CUFFS WITHOUT SO MUCH AS TOUCHING THEM...

CRAMM

BA-M

!!

READ THIS WAY

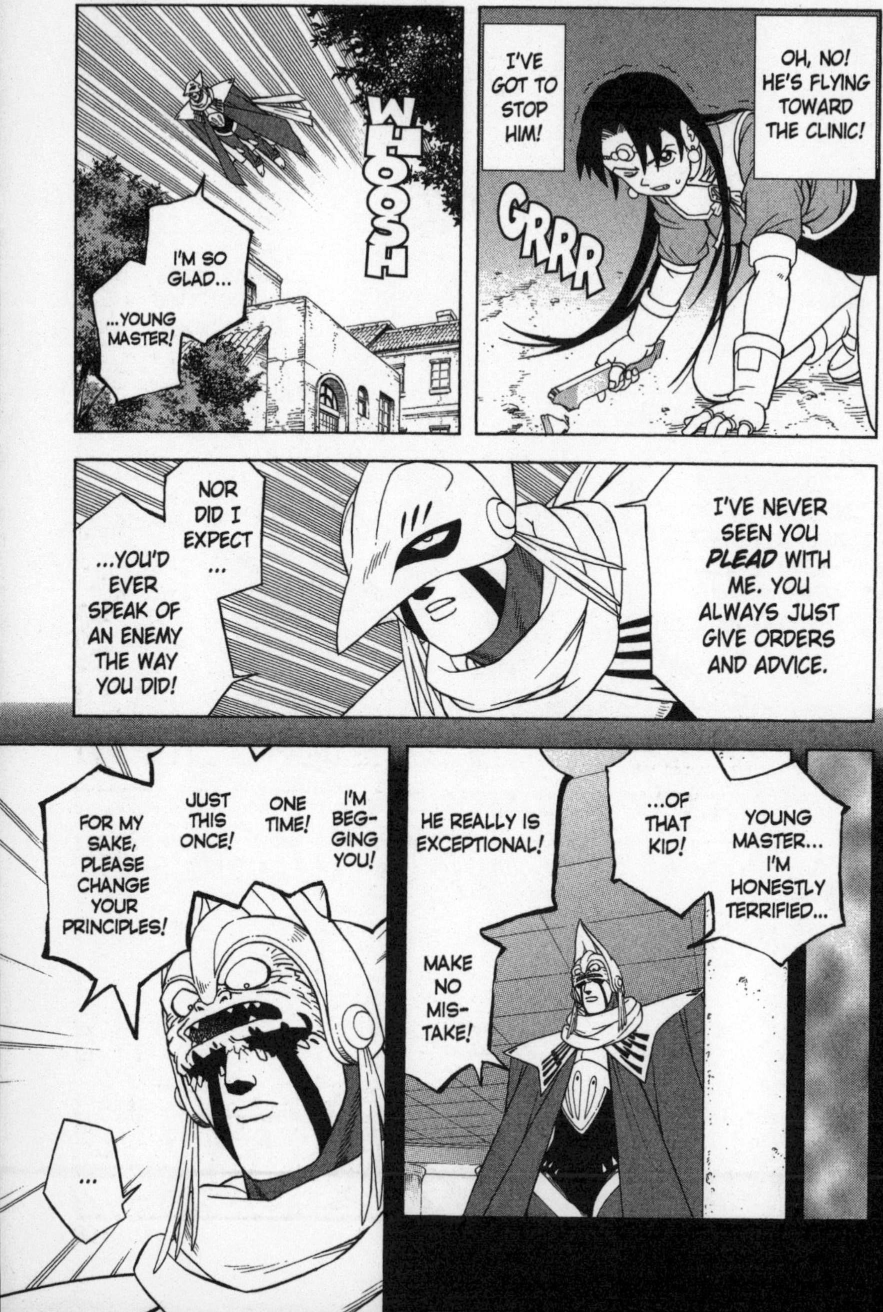
OH, NO! HE'S FLYING TOWARD THE CLINIC!
I'VE GOT TO STOP HIM!
GRRRR
WHOOSH
I'M SO GLAD...
...YOUNG MASTER!
I'VE NEVER SEEN YOU PLEAD WITH ME. YOU ALWAYS JUST GIVE ORDERS AND ADVICE.
NOR DID I EXPECT ...
...YOU'D EVER SPEAK OF AN ENEMY THE WAY YOU DID!
YOUNG MASTER... I'M HONESTLY TERRIFIED...
...OF THAT KID!
HE REALLY IS EXCEPTIONAL!
MAKE NO MIS-TAKE!
I'M BEG-GING YOU!
ONE TIME!
JUST THIS ONCE!
FOR MY SAKE, PLEASE CHANGE YOUR PRINCIPLES!
...

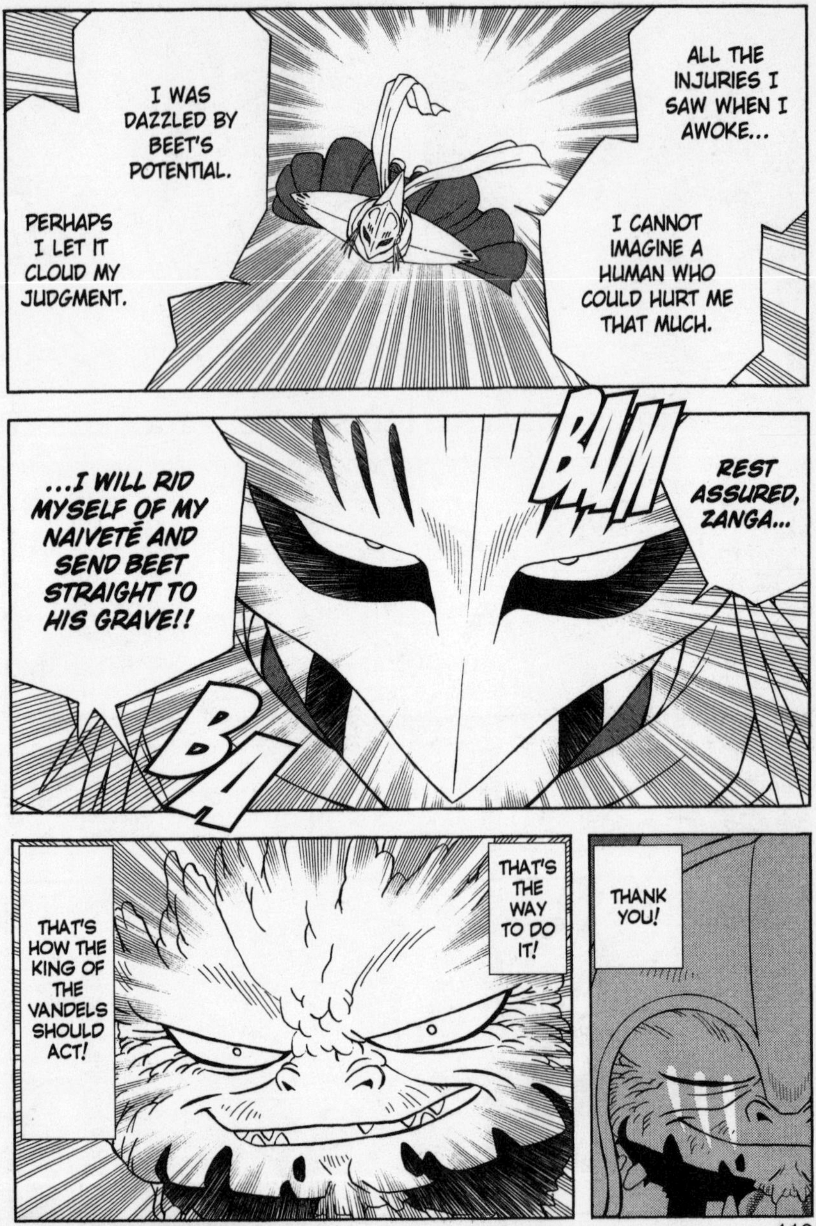
ALL THE INJURIES I SAW WHEN I AWOKE...
I CANNOT IMAGINE A HUMAN WHO COULD HURT ME THAT MUCH.
I WAS DAZZLED BY BEET'S POTENTIAL.
PERHAPS I LET IT CLOUD MY JUDGMENT.
BAM
REST ASSURED, ZANGA...
...I WILL RID MYSELF OF MY NAIVETÉ AND SEND BEET STRAIGHT TO HIS GRAVE!!
BA
THANK YOU!
THAT'S THE WAY TO DO IT!
THAT'S HOW THE KING OF THE VANDELS SHOULD ACT!

READ THIS WAY

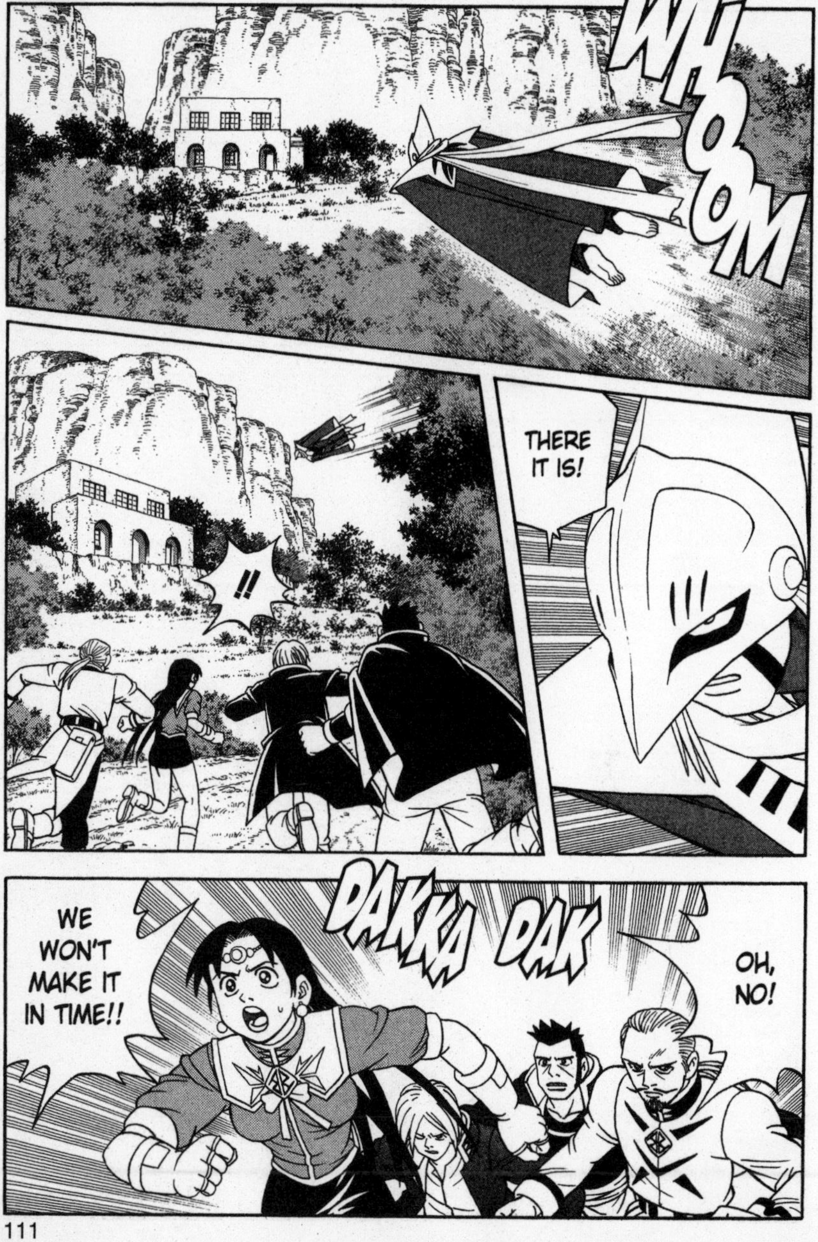
WHOOM
THERE IT IS!
!!
DAKKA DAK
OH, NO!
WE WON'T MAKE IT IN TIME!!

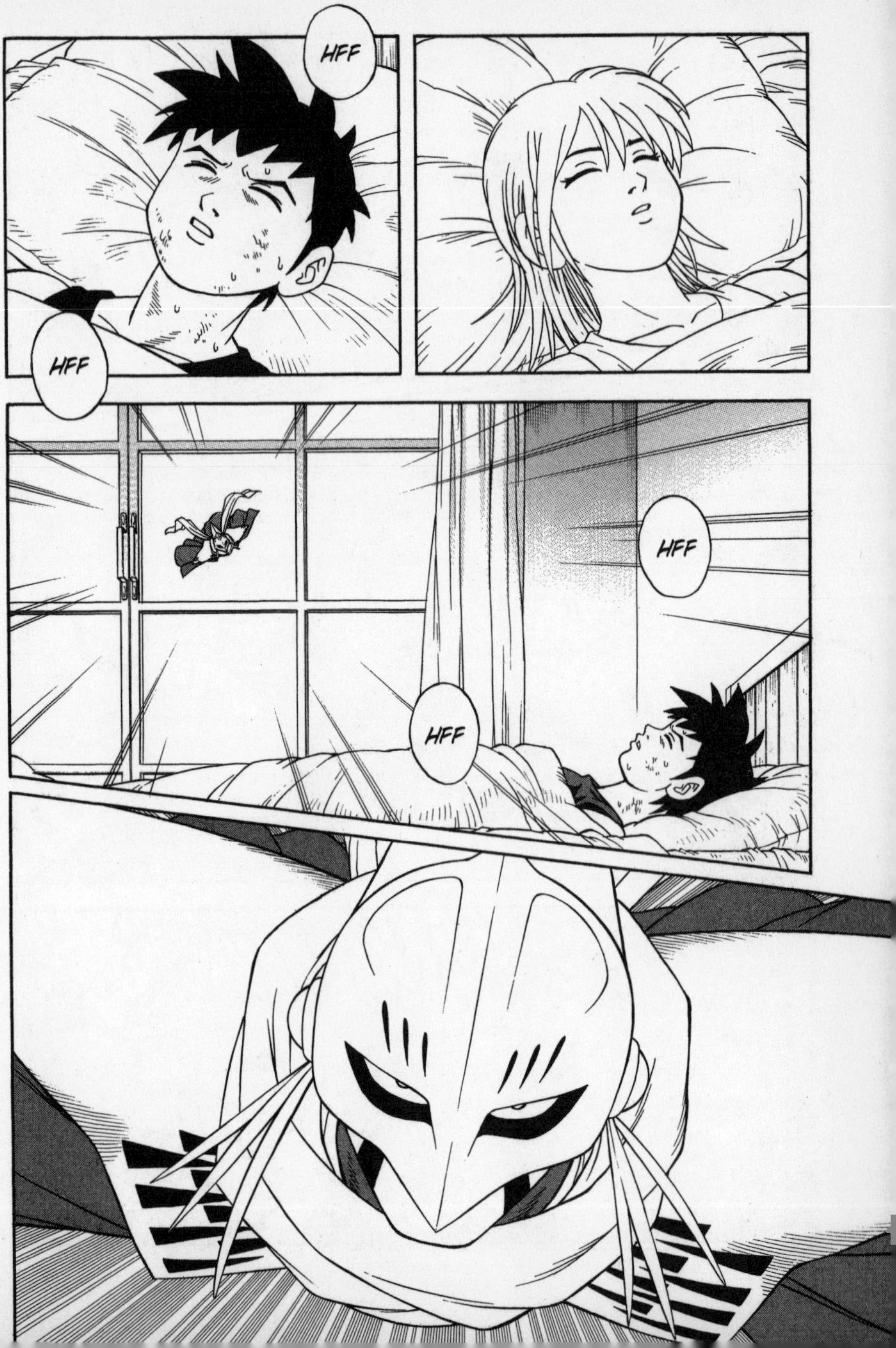
HFF
HFF
HFF
HFF

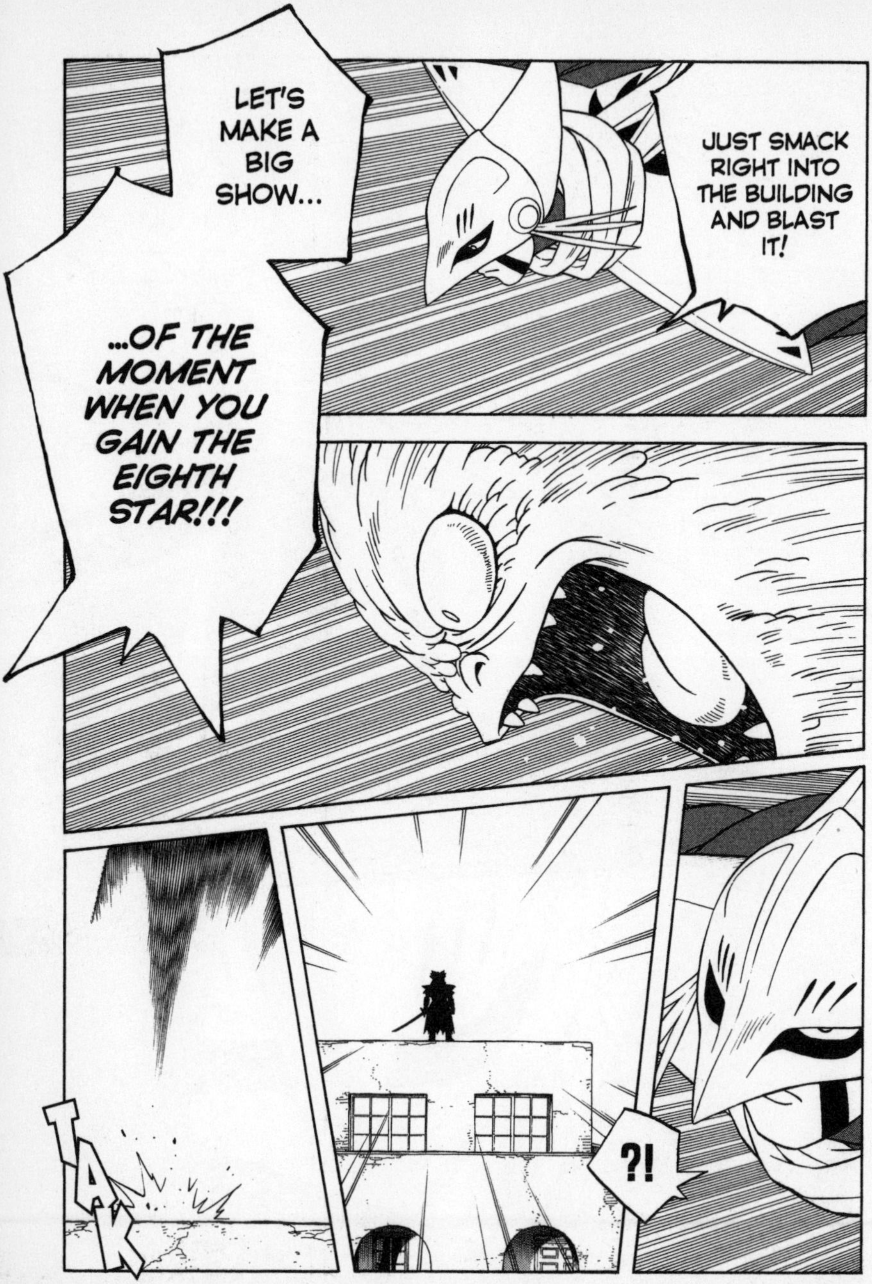
JUST SMACK RIGHT INTO THE BUILDING AND BLAST IT!
LET'S MAKE A BIG SHOW...
...OF THE MOMENT WHEN YOU GAIN THE EIGHTH STAR!!!
?!
TAK

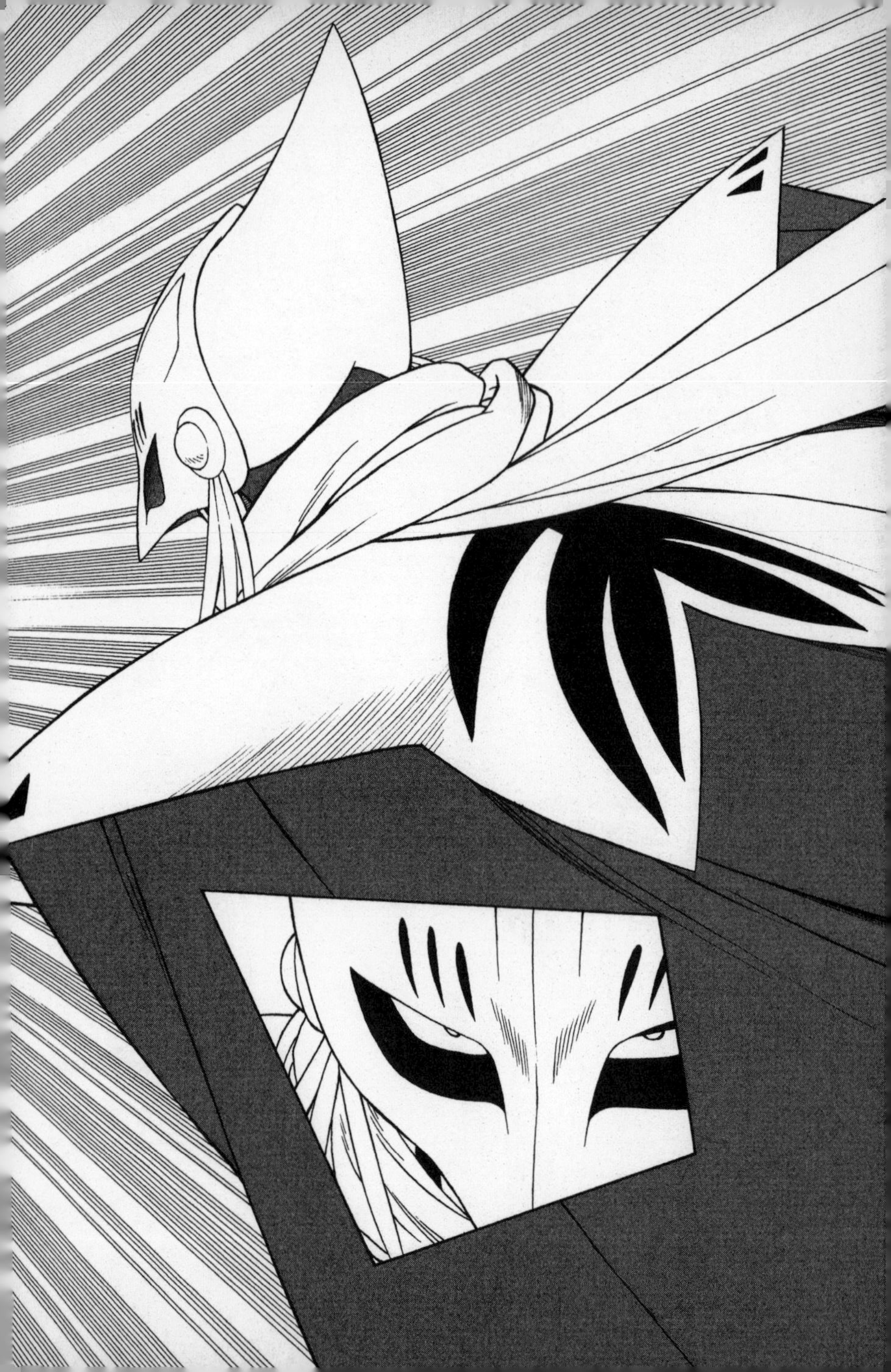

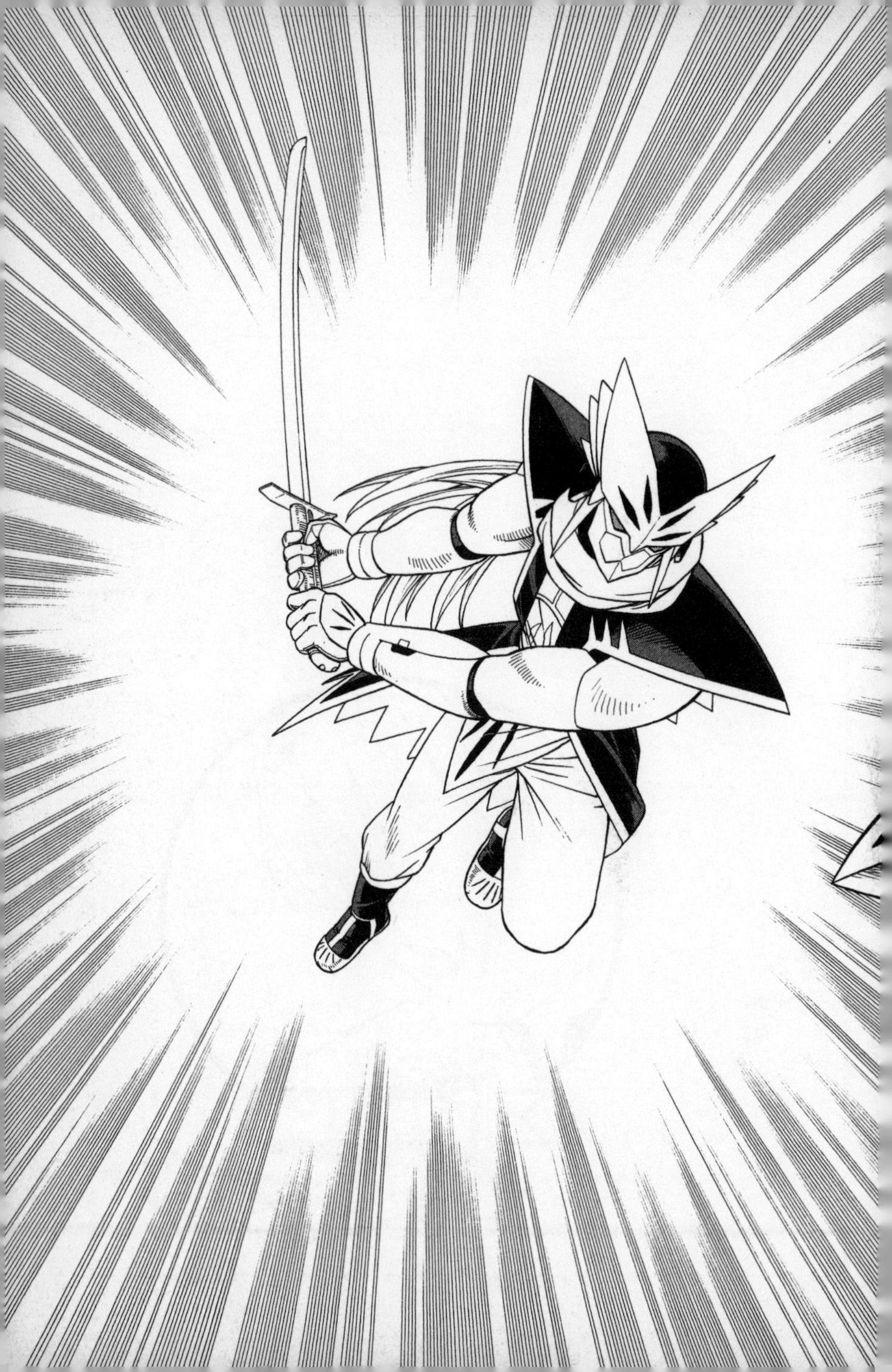

BEET
THE VANDEL BUSTER

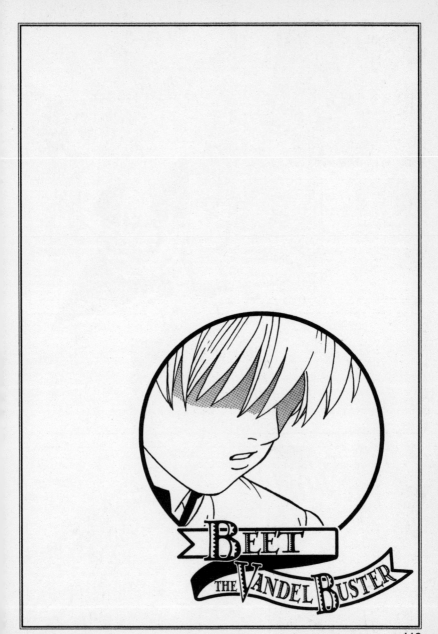

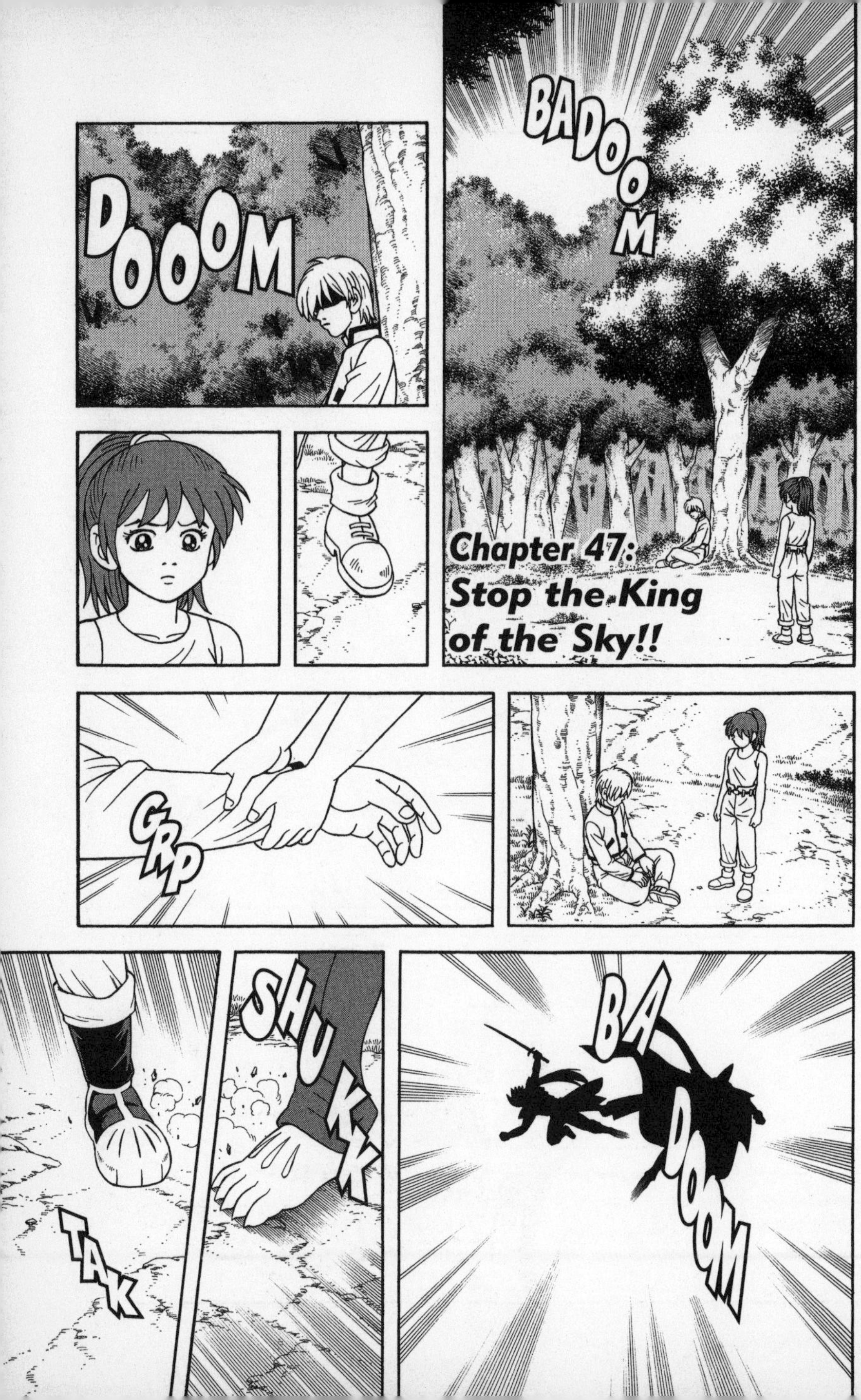
BADOOOM
Chapter 47: Stop the King of the Sky!!
DOOOM
GRP
BA DOOOM
SHUKK
TAK

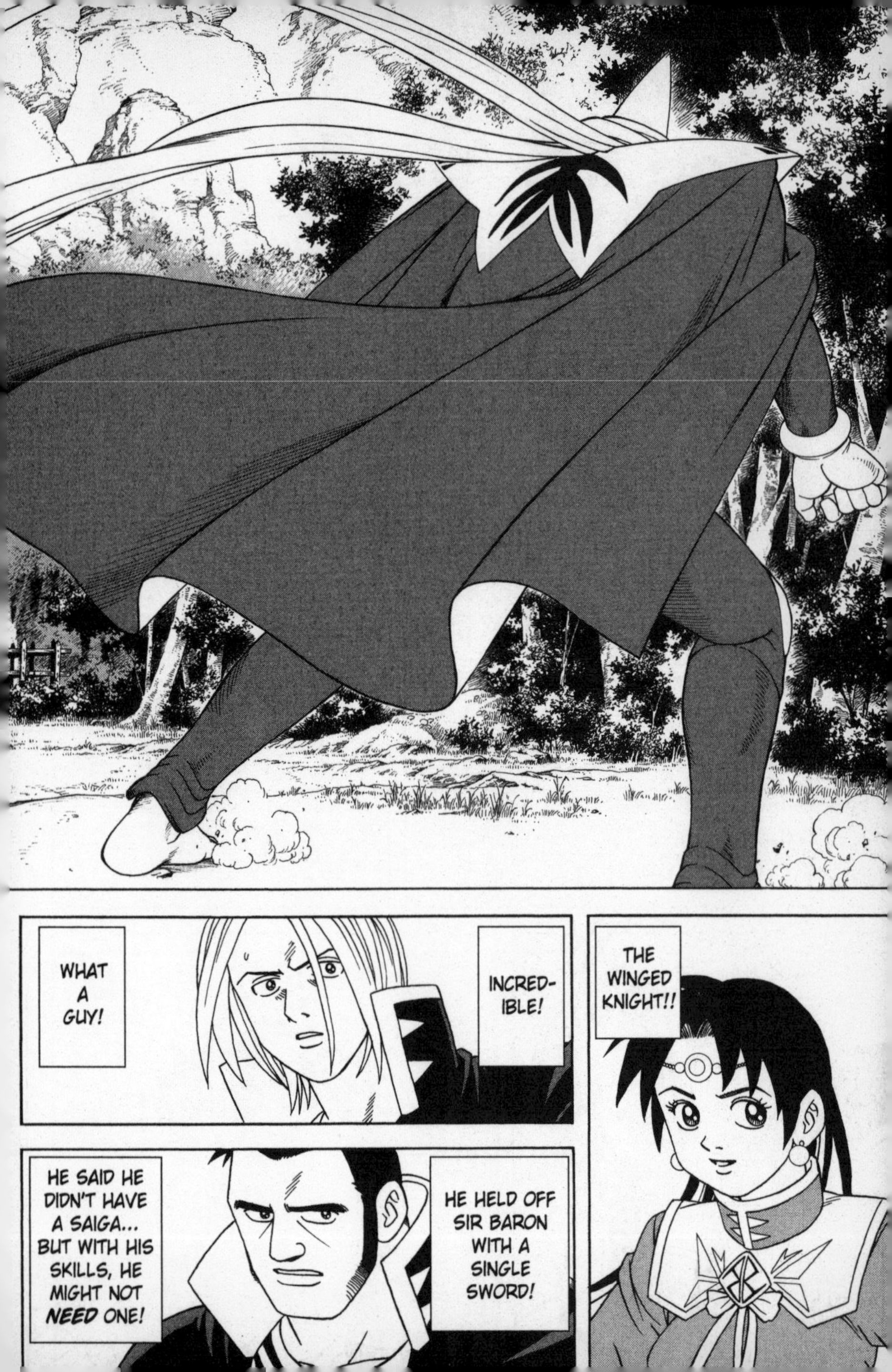
THE WINGED KNIGHT!!
INCRED-IBLE!
WHAT A GUY!
HE HELD OFF SIR BARON WITH A SINGLE SWORD!
HE SAID HE DIDN'T HAVE A SAIGA... BUT WITH HIS SKILLS, HE MIGHT NOT **NEED** ONE!

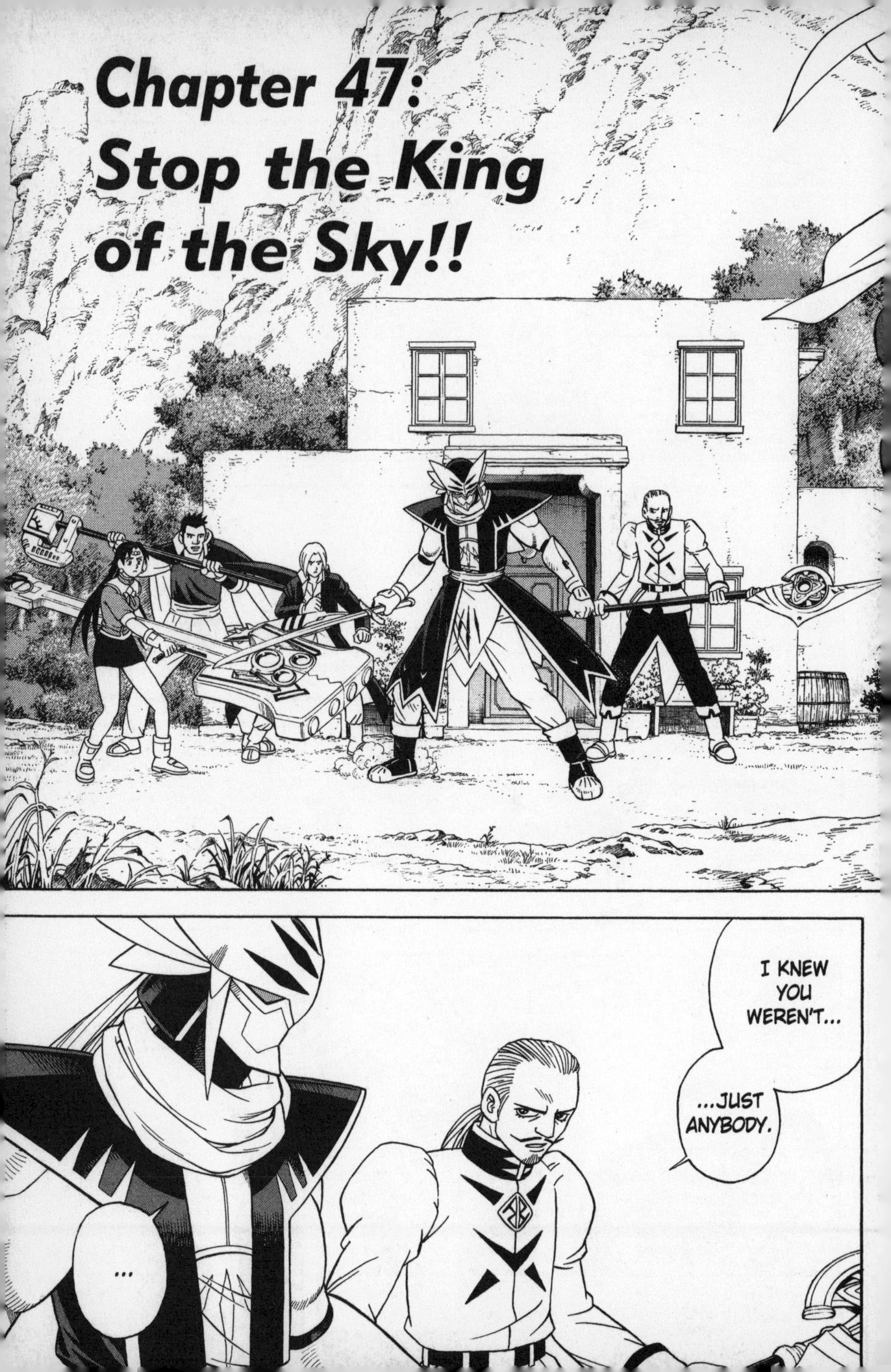
Chapter 47:
Stop the King of the Sky!!
I KNEW YOU WEREN'T...
...JUST ANYBODY.
...

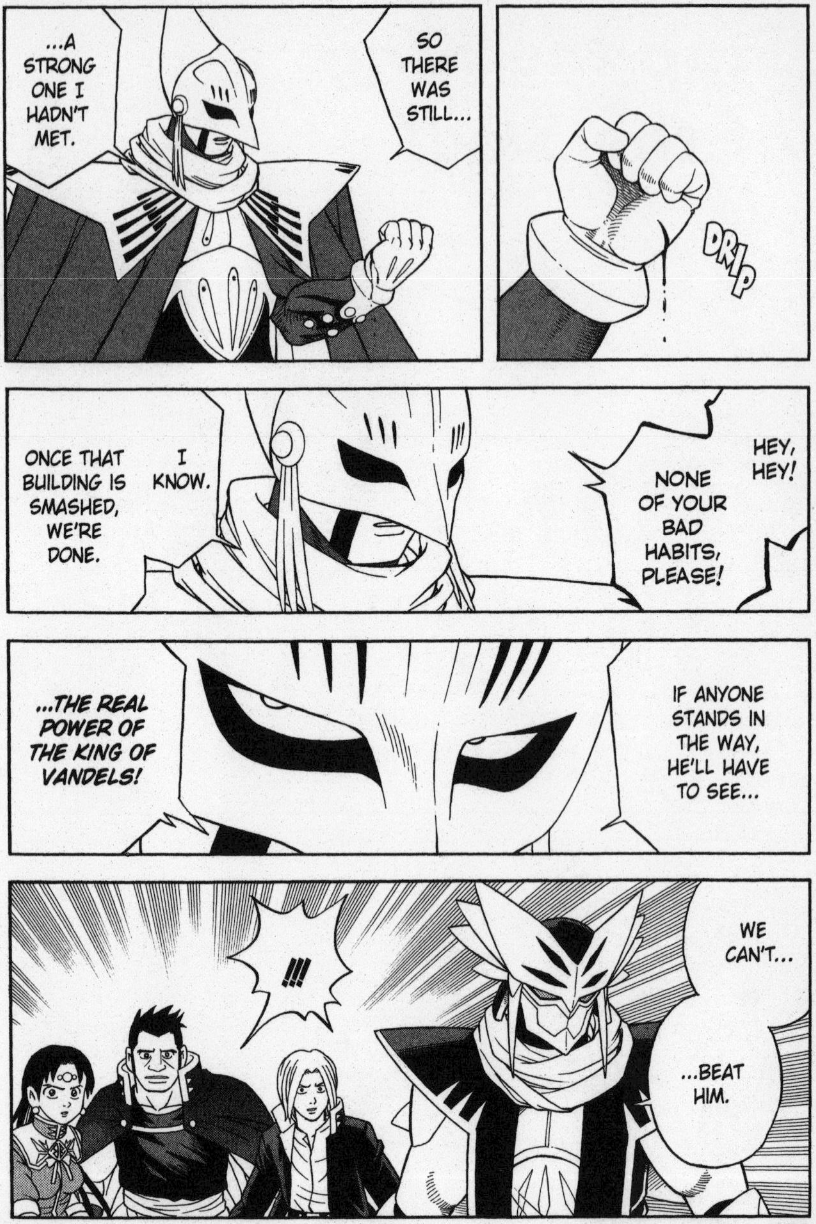
DRIP
SO THERE WAS STILL...
...A STRONG ONE I HADN'T MET.
HEY, HEY!
NONE OF YOUR BAD HABITS, PLEASE!
I KNOW.
ONCE THAT BUILDING IS SMASHED, WE'RE DONE.
IF ANYONE STANDS IN THE WAY, HE'LL HAVE TO SEE...
...THE REAL POWER OF THE KING OF VANDELS!
WE CAN'T...
...BEAT HIM.
!!!

READ THIS WAY

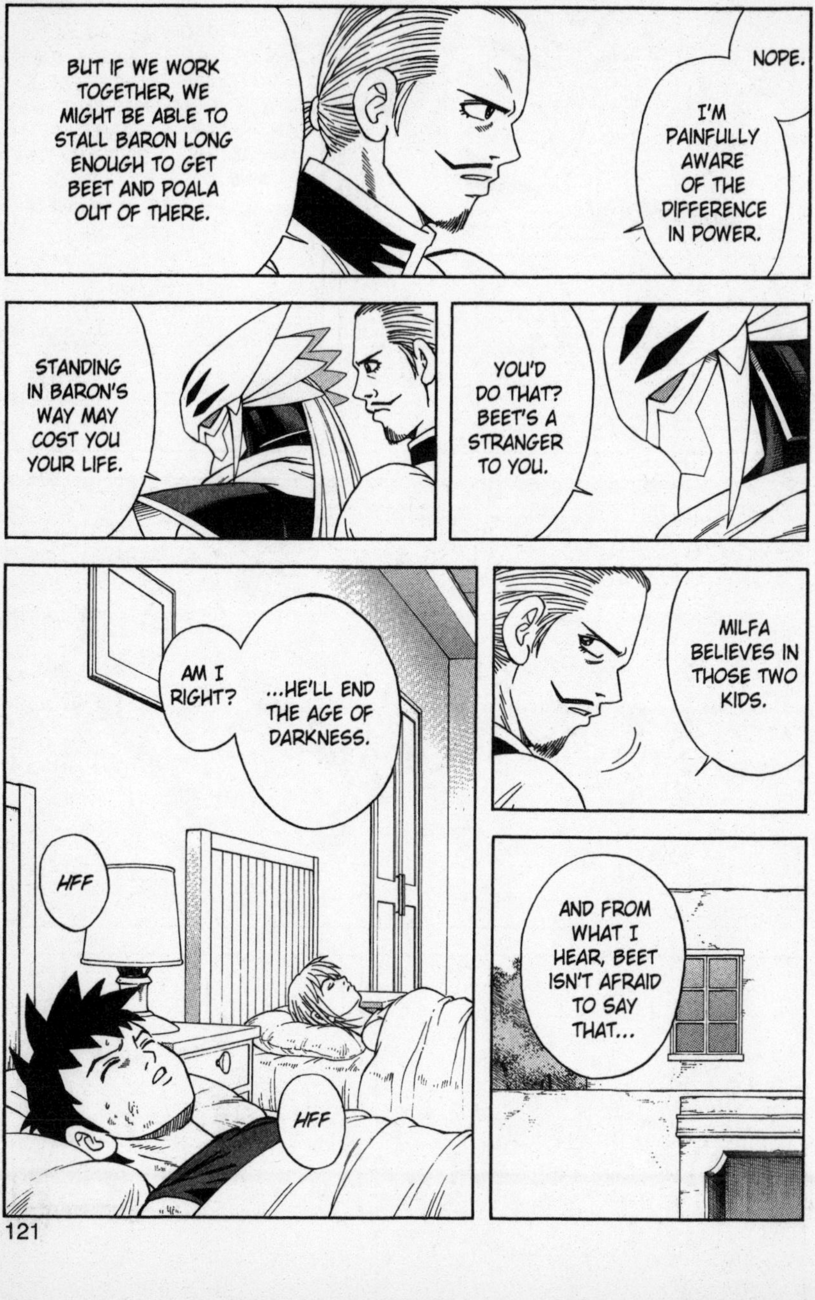
NOPE.
I'M PAINFULLY AWARE OF THE DIFFERENCE IN POWER.
BUT IF WE WORK TOGETHER, WE MIGHT BE ABLE TO STALL BARON LONG ENOUGH TO GET BEET AND POALA OUT OF THERE.
YOU'D DO THAT? BEET'S A STRANGER TO YOU.
STANDING IN BARON'S WAY MAY COST YOU YOUR LIFE.
MILFA BELIEVES IN THOSE TWO KIDS.
AND FROM WHAT I HEAR, BEET ISN'T AFRAID TO SAY THAT...
...HE'LL END THE AGE OF DARKNESS.
AM I RIGHT?
HFF
HFF

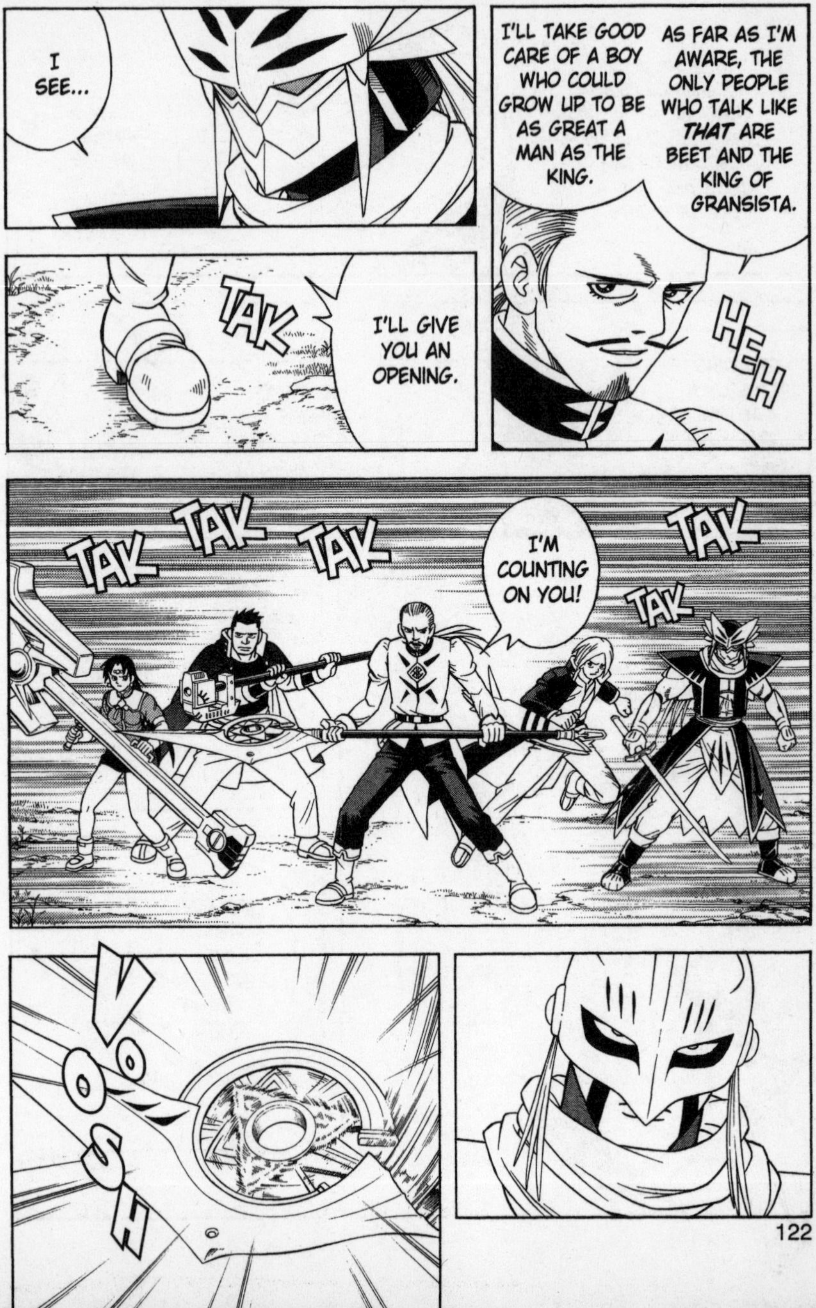
AS FAR AS I'M AWARE, THE ONLY PEOPLE WHO TALK LIKE *THAT* ARE BEET AND THE KING OF GRANSISTA.
I'LL TAKE GOOD CARE OF A BOY WHO COULD GROW UP TO BE AS GREAT A MAN AS THE KING.
HEH
I SEE...
TAK
I'LL GIVE YOU AN OPENING.
TAK
TAK
I'M COUNTING ON YOU!
TAK
TAK
TAK
VOOSH

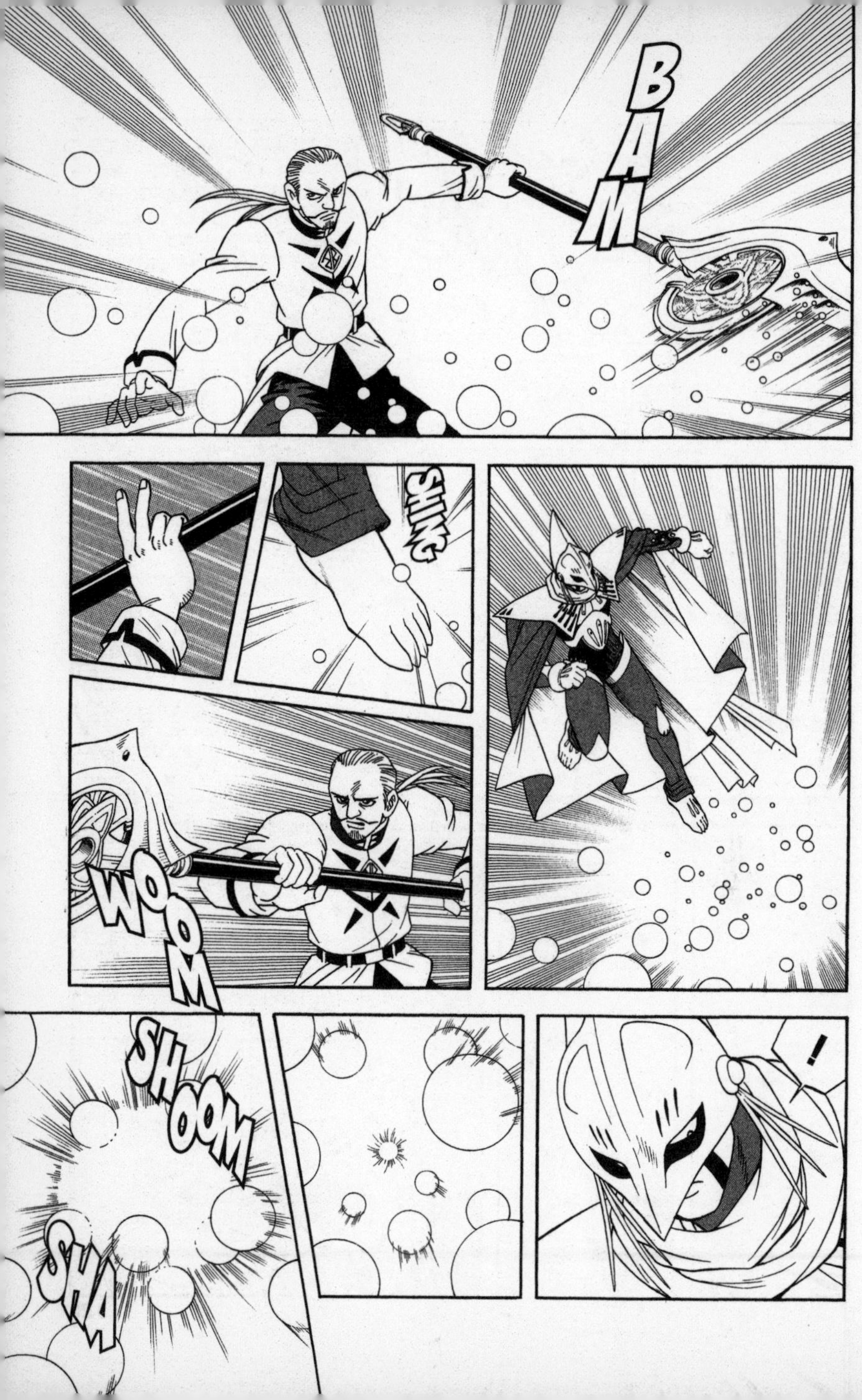
BAM
SHING
WOOOM
!
SHOOM
SHA

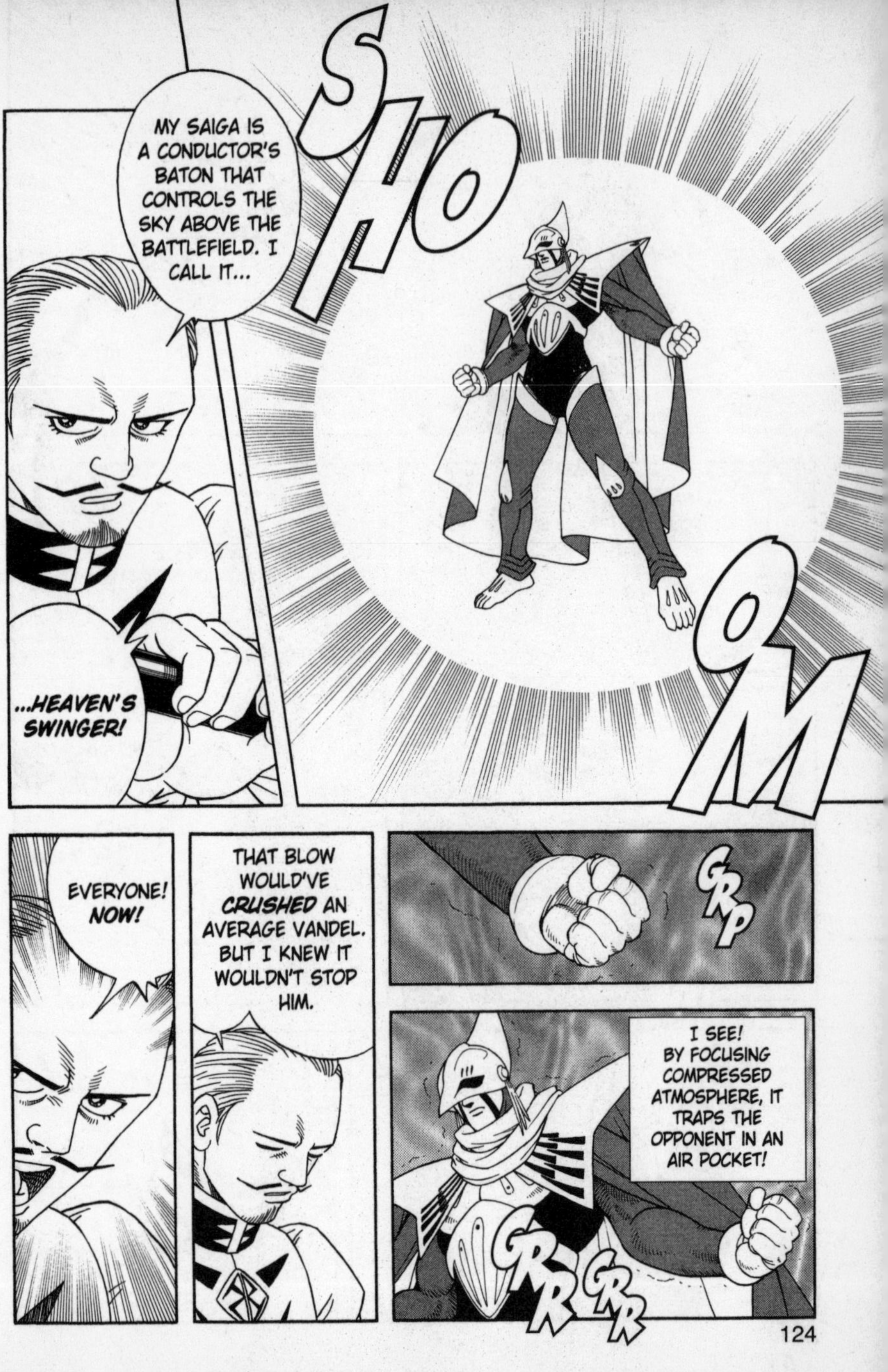
SHOOM
MY SAIGA IS A CONDUCTOR'S BATON THAT CONTROLS THE SKY ABOVE THE BATTLEFIELD. I CALL IT...
...HEAVEN'S SWINGER!
GRP
I SEE! BY FOCUSING COMPRESSED ATMOSPHERE, IT TRAPS THE OPPONENT IN AN AIR POCKET!
GRR GRR
THAT BLOW WOULD'VE CRUSHED AN AVERAGE VANDEL. BUT I KNEW IT WOULDN'T STOP HIM.
EVERYONE! NOW!

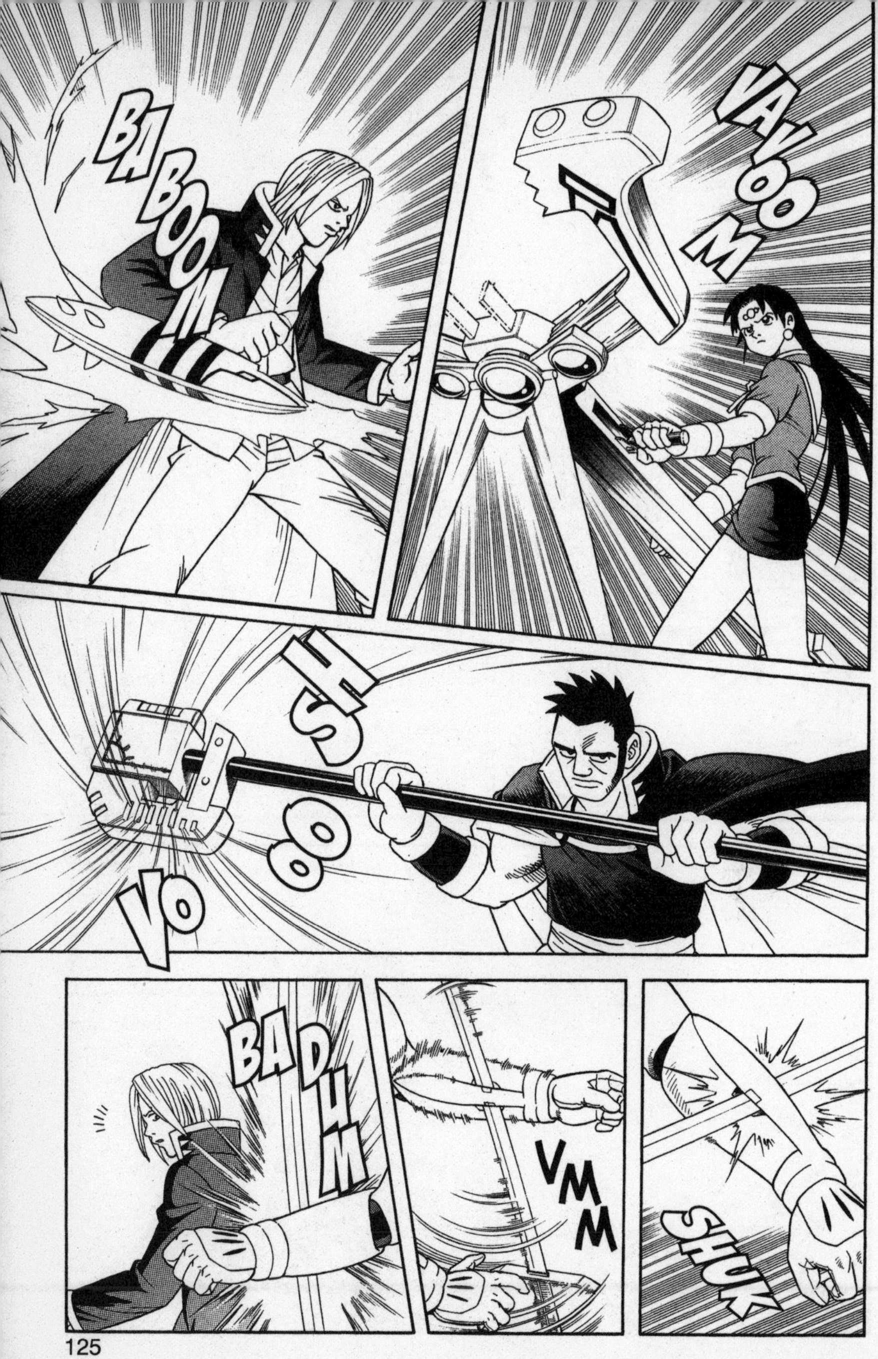
VAVOOM
BABOOM
VOOOSH
SHUK
VMM
BADUM

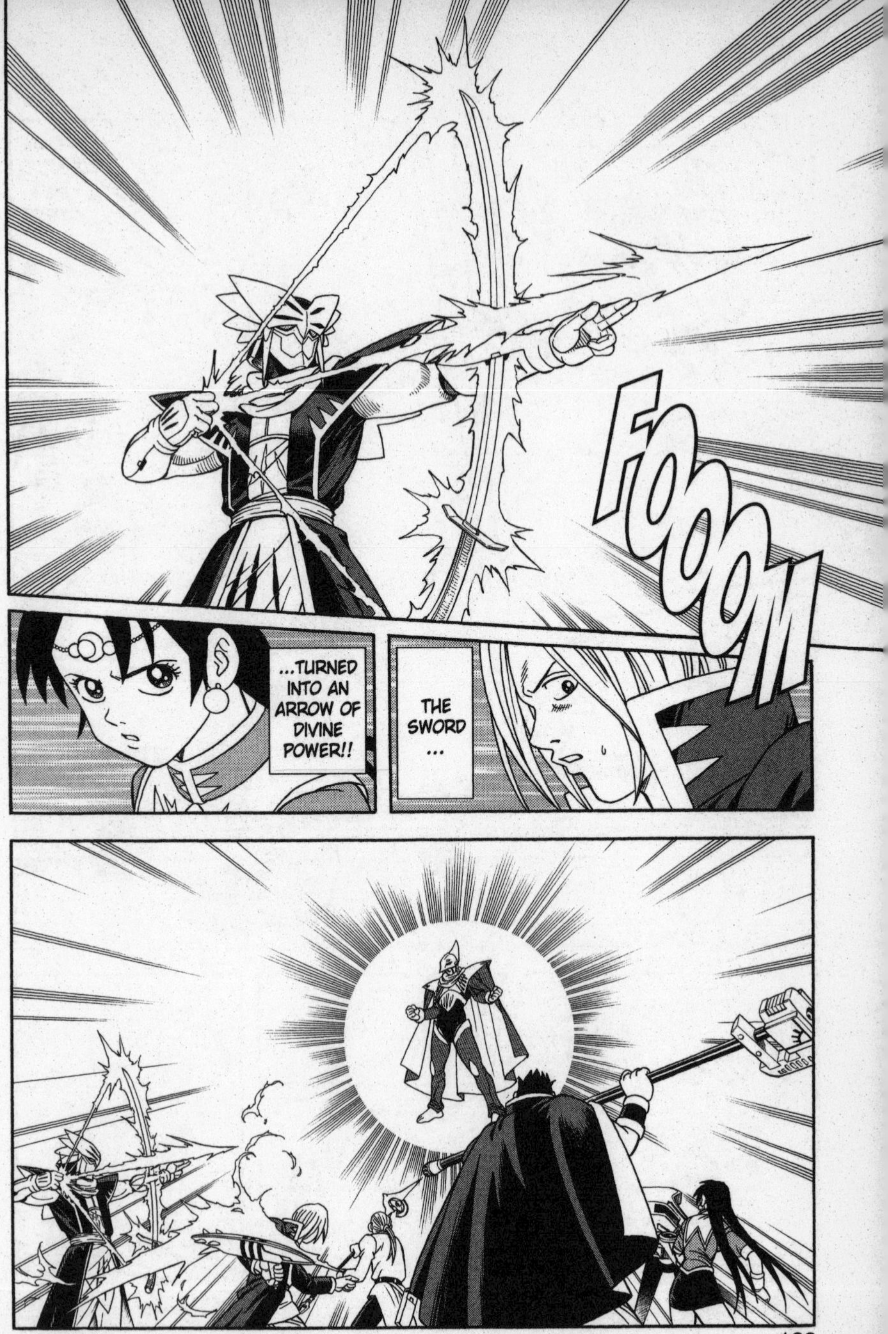
FOOOM
THE SWORD ...
...TURNED INTO AN ARROW OF DIVINE POWER!!

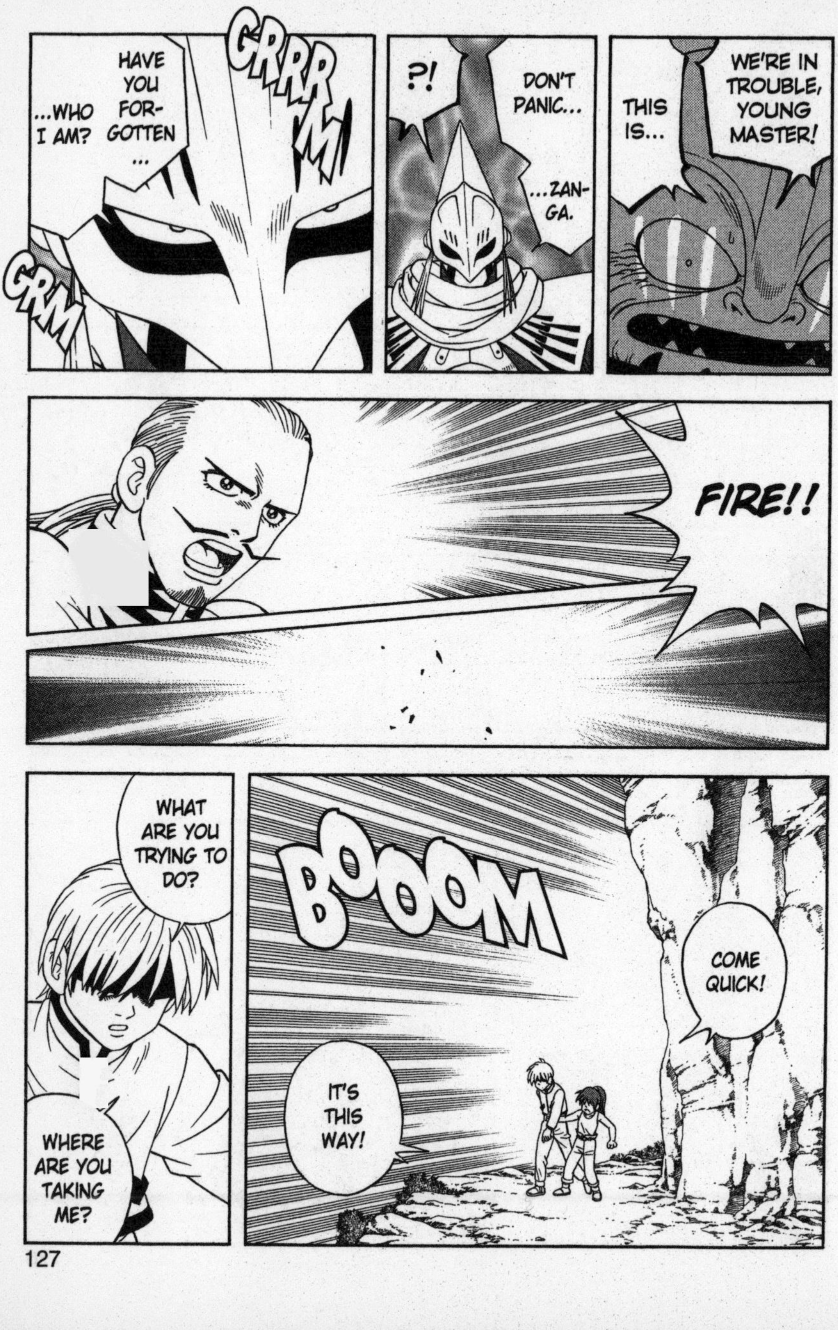

WE'RE IN TROUBLE, YOUNG MASTER!
THIS IS...
DON'T PANIC...
...ZAN-GA.
?!
GRRRM
HAVE YOU FOR-GOTTEN...
...WHO I AM?
GRM
FIRE!!
BOOOM
COME QUICK!
IT'S THIS WAY!
WHAT ARE YOU TRYING TO DO?
WHERE ARE YOU TAKING ME?

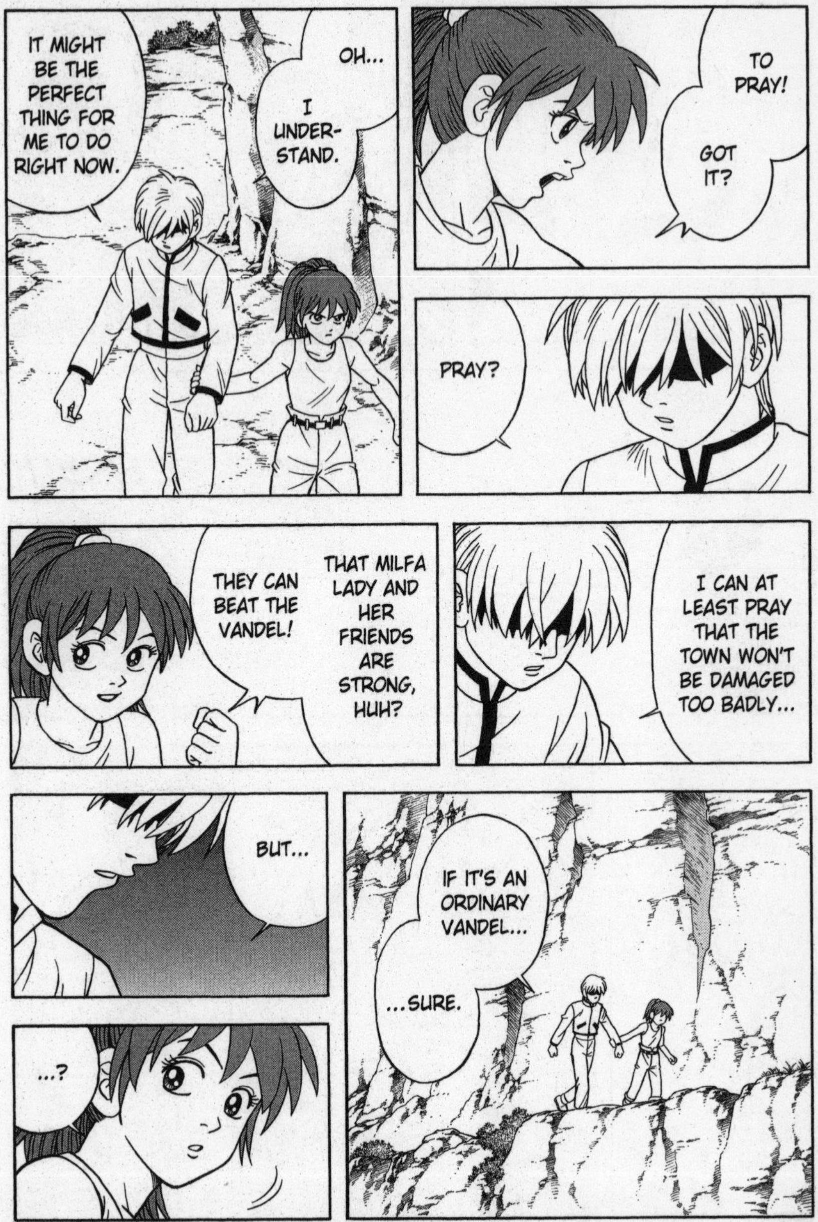
TO PRAY!
GOT IT?
PRAY?
OH...
I UNDERSTAND.
IT MIGHT BE THE PERFECT THING FOR ME TO DO RIGHT NOW.
I CAN AT LEAST PRAY THAT THE TOWN WON'T BE DAMAGED TOO BADLY...
THAT MILFA LADY AND HER FRIENDS ARE STRONG, HUH?
THEY CAN BEAT THE VANDEL!
IF IT'S AN ORDINARY VANDEL...
...SURE.
BUT...
...?

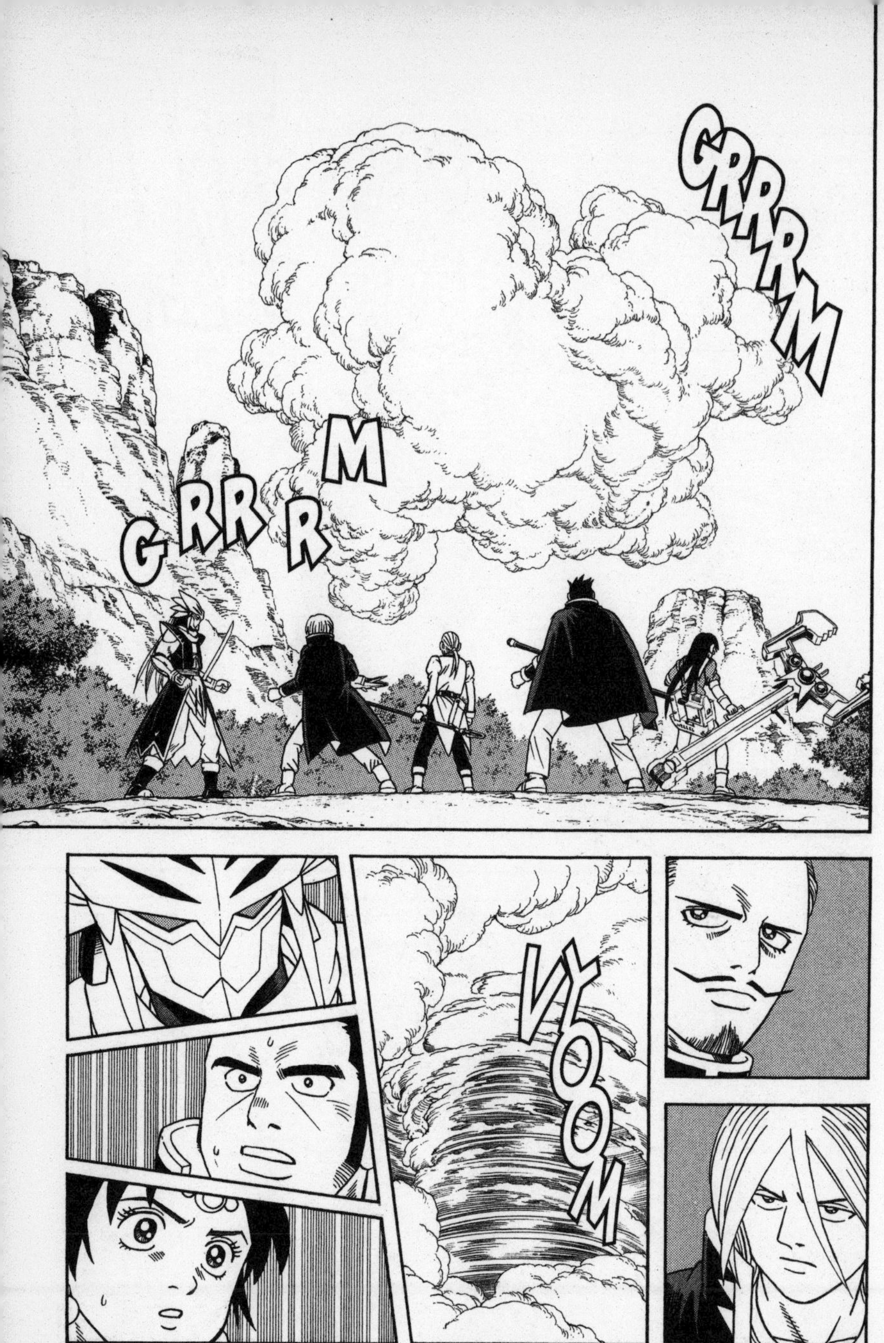
GRRRM
GRRRM
VYOOM

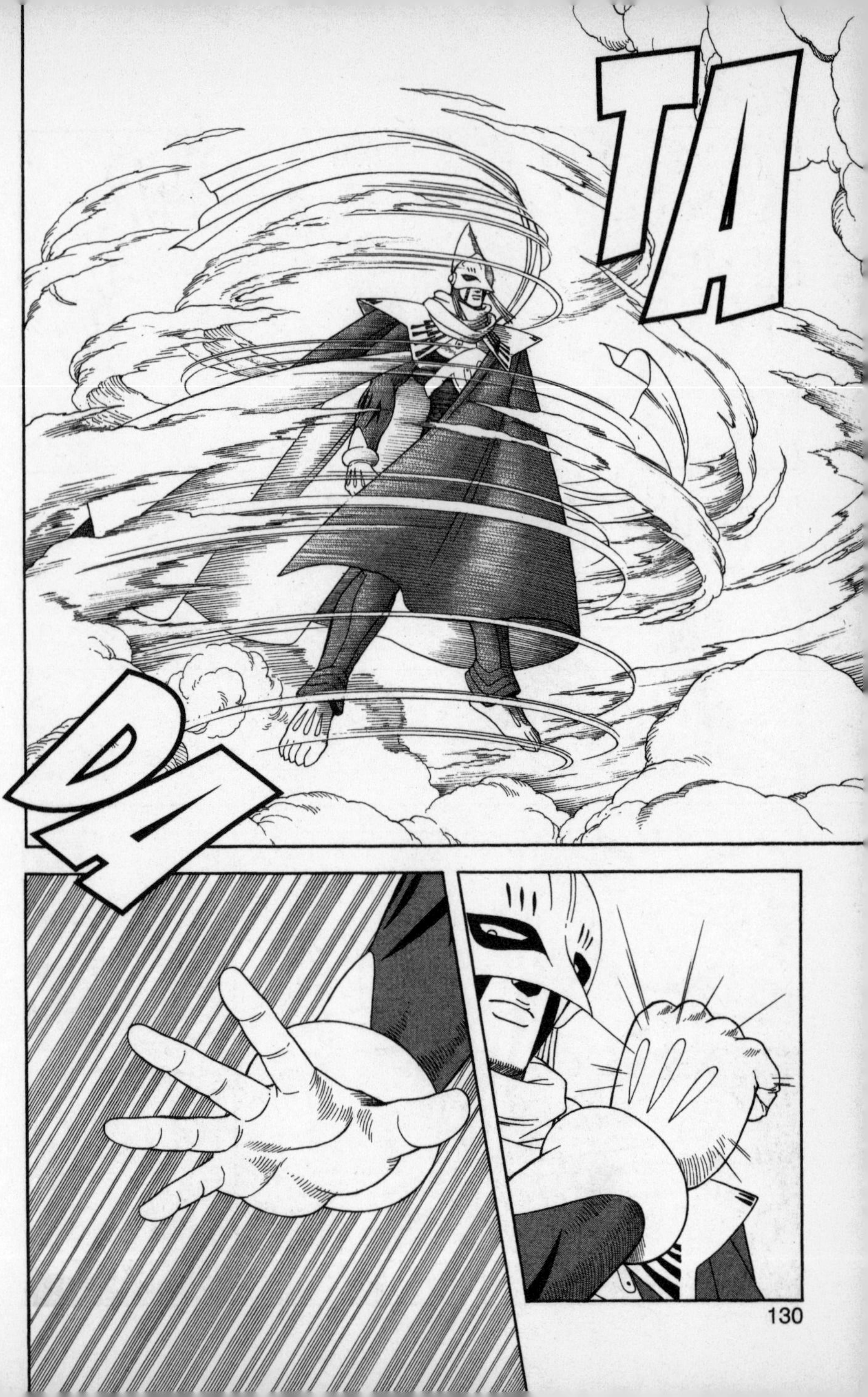
TA
DA

READ THIS WAY

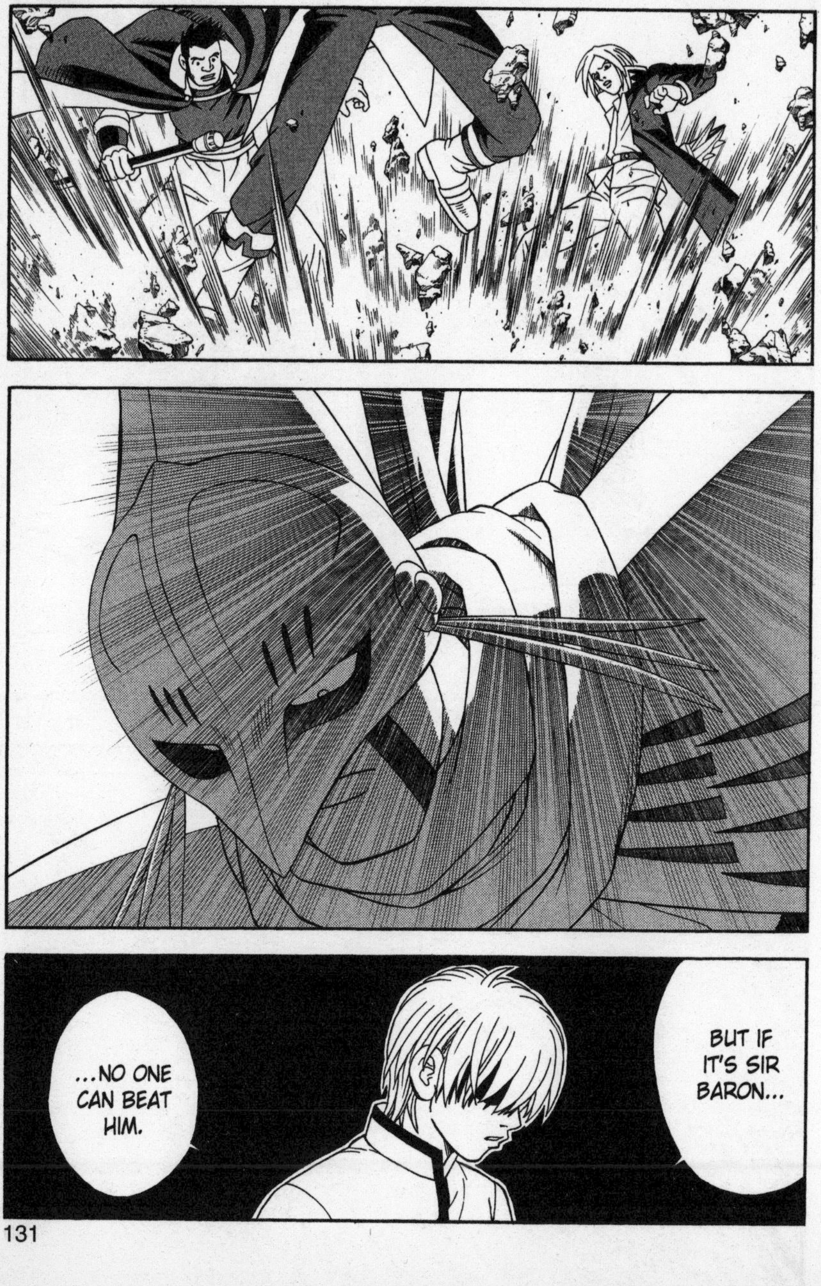
BUT IF IT'S SIR BARON...
...NO ONE CAN BEAT HIM.

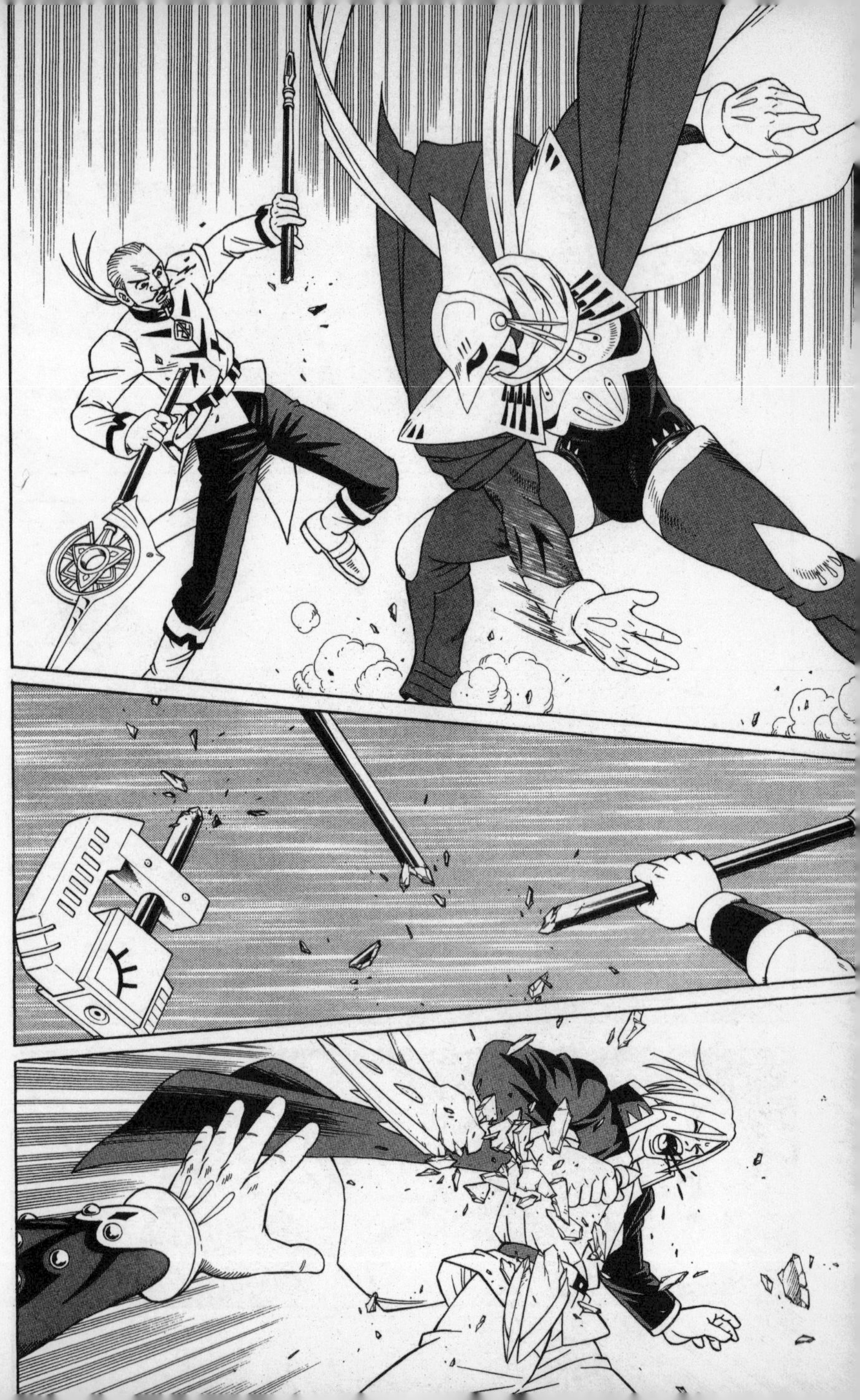

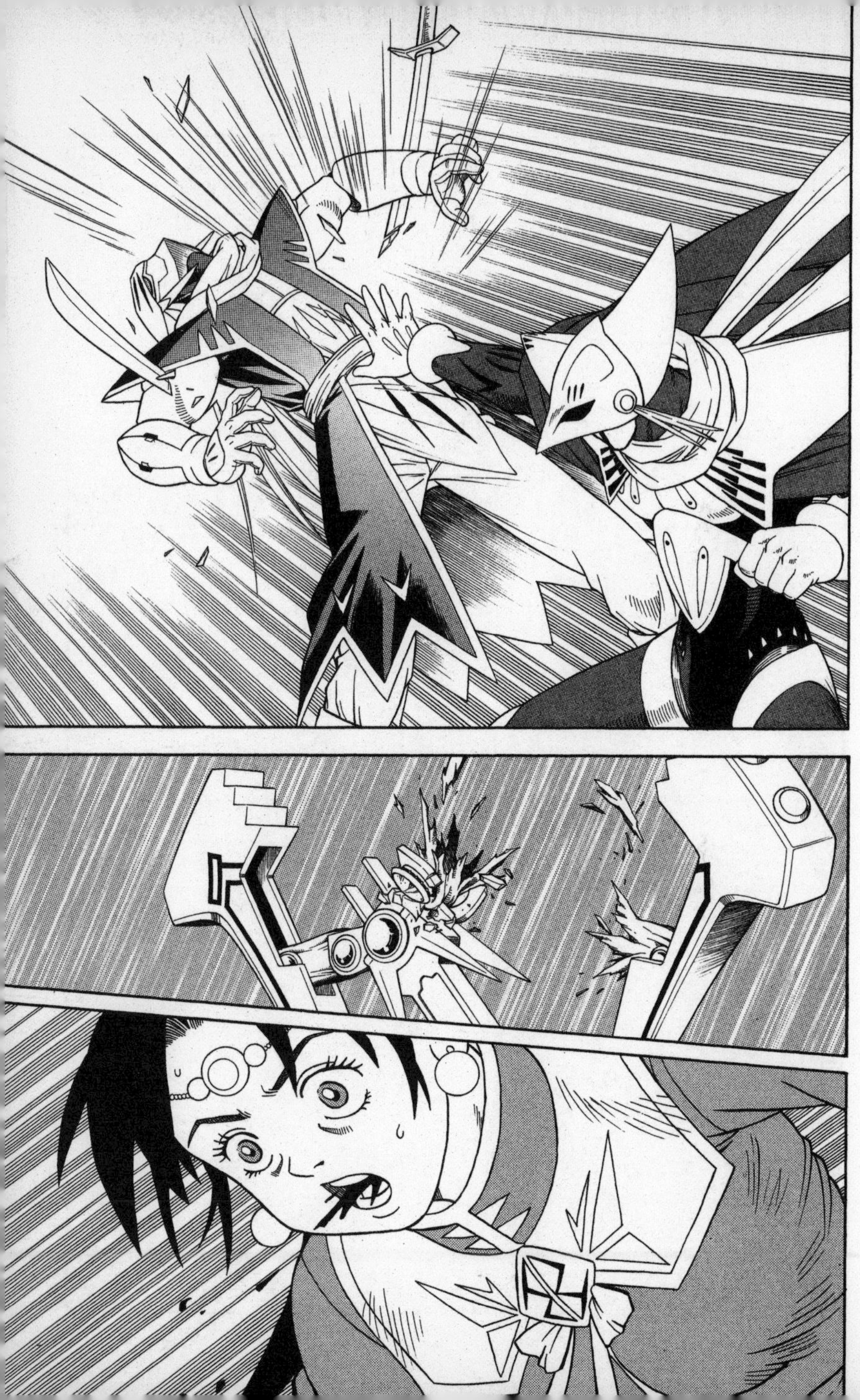

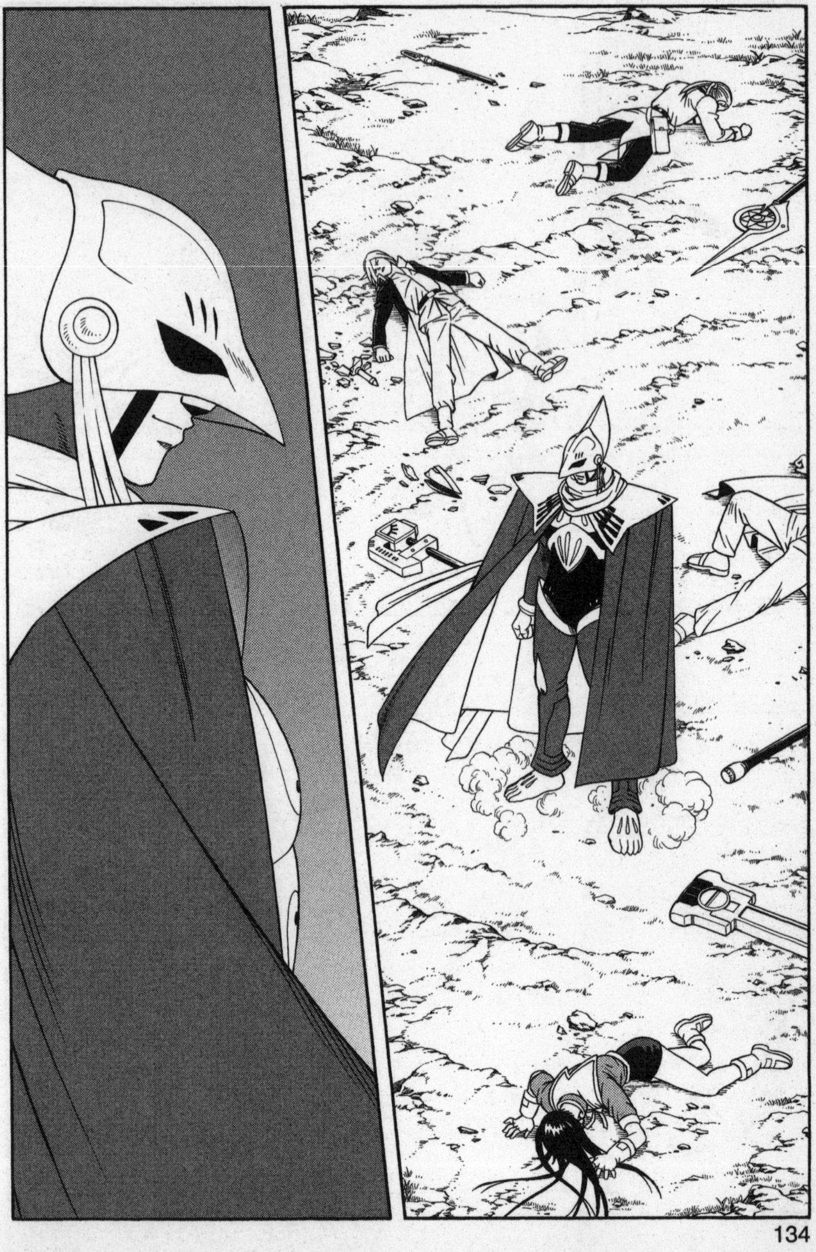

READ THIS WAY

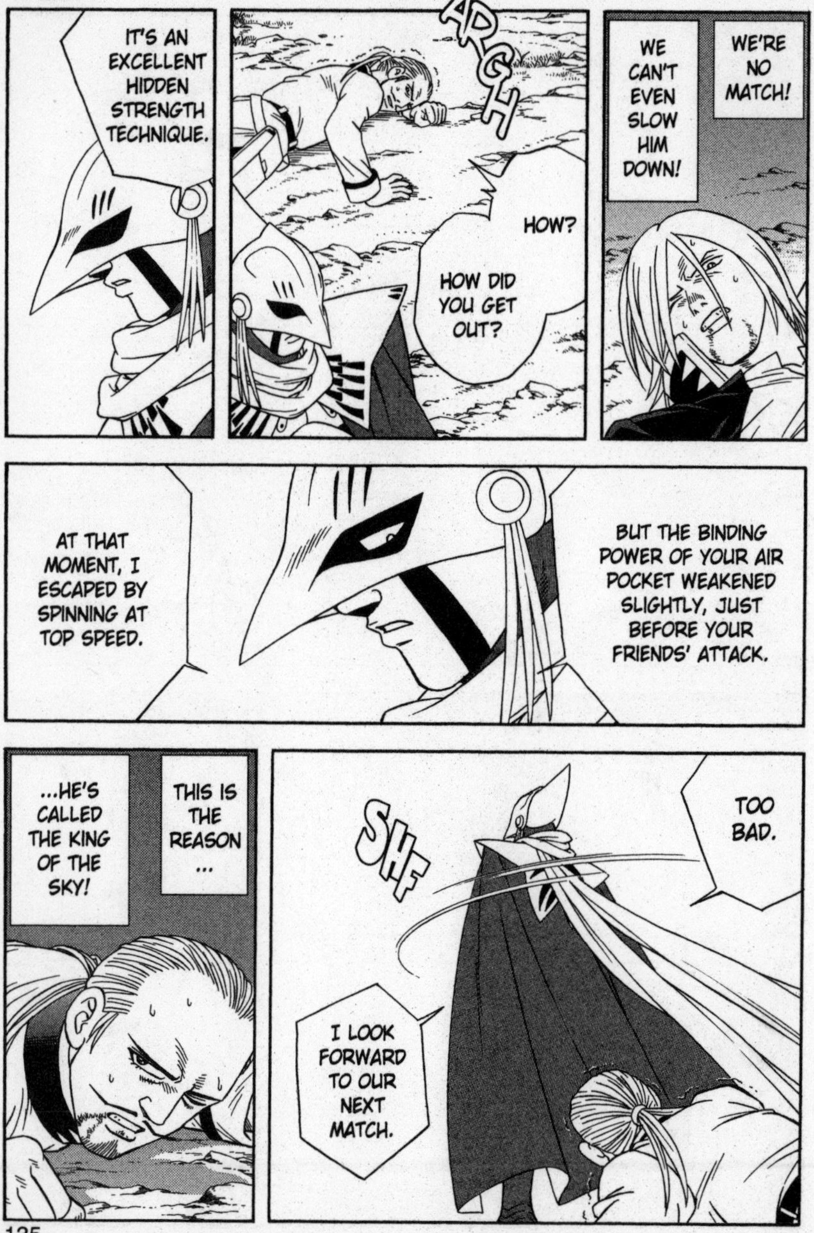
WE'RE NO MATCH!
WE CAN'T EVEN SLOW HIM DOWN!
ARGH
HOW?
HOW DID YOU GET OUT?
IT'S AN EXCELLENT HIDDEN STRENGTH TECHNIQUE.
BUT THE BINDING POWER OF YOUR AIR POCKET WEAKENED SLIGHTLY, JUST BEFORE YOUR FRIENDS' ATTACK.
AT THAT MOMENT, I ESCAPED BY SPINNING AT TOP SPEED.
TOO BAD.
SHF
I LOOK FORWARD TO OUR NEXT MATCH.
THIS IS THE REASON ...
...HE'S CALLED THE KING OF THE SKY!

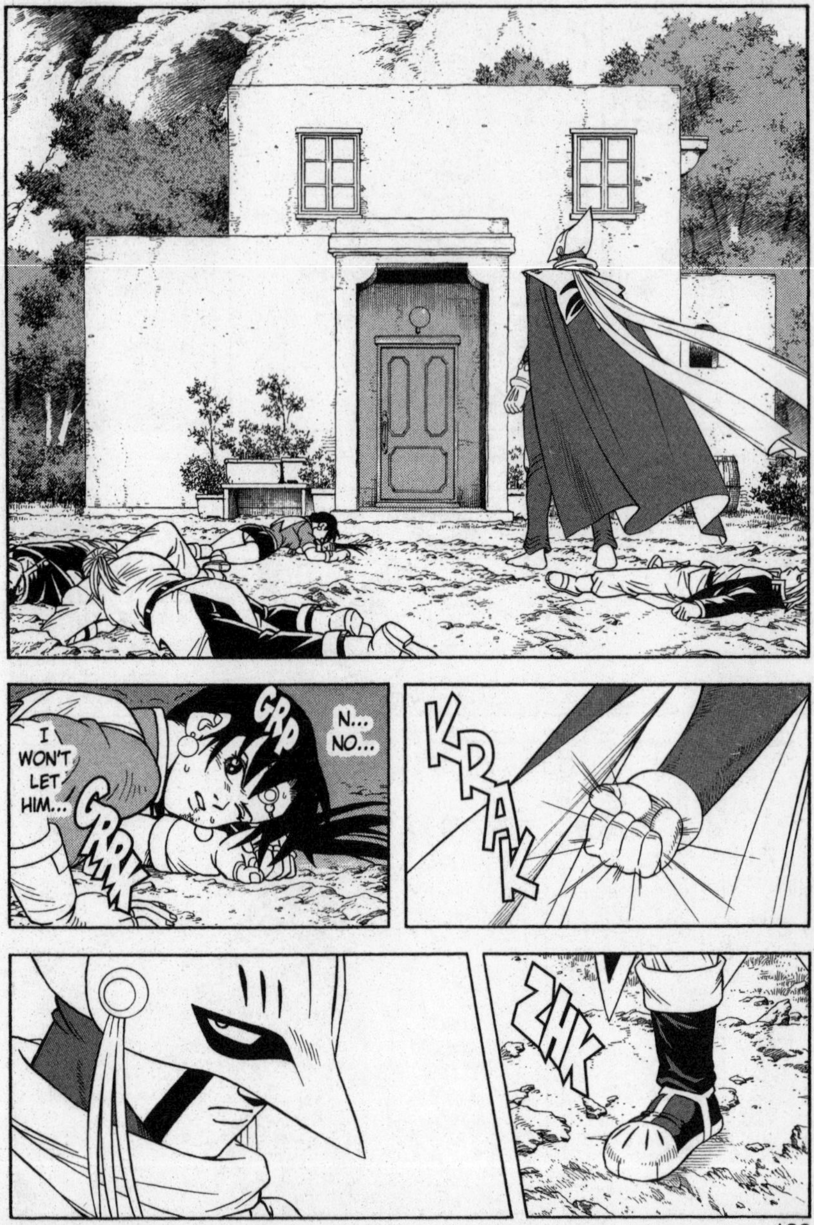
KRAK
N... NO...
GRP
I WON'T LET HIM...
GRRK
ZHK

READ THIS WAY

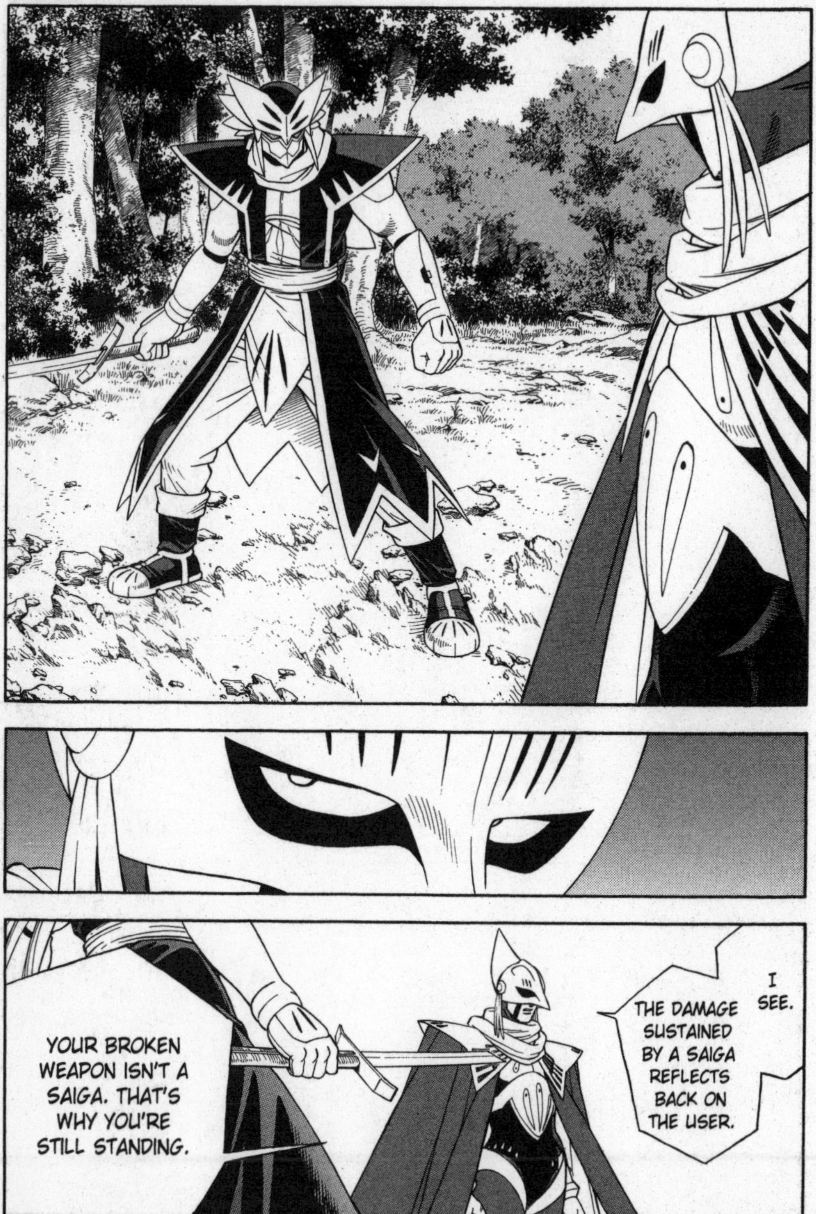
I SEE.
THE DAMAGE SUSTAINED BY A SAIGA REFLECTS BACK ON THE USER.
YOUR BROKEN WEAPON ISN'T A SAIGA. THAT'S WHY YOU'RE STILL STANDING.

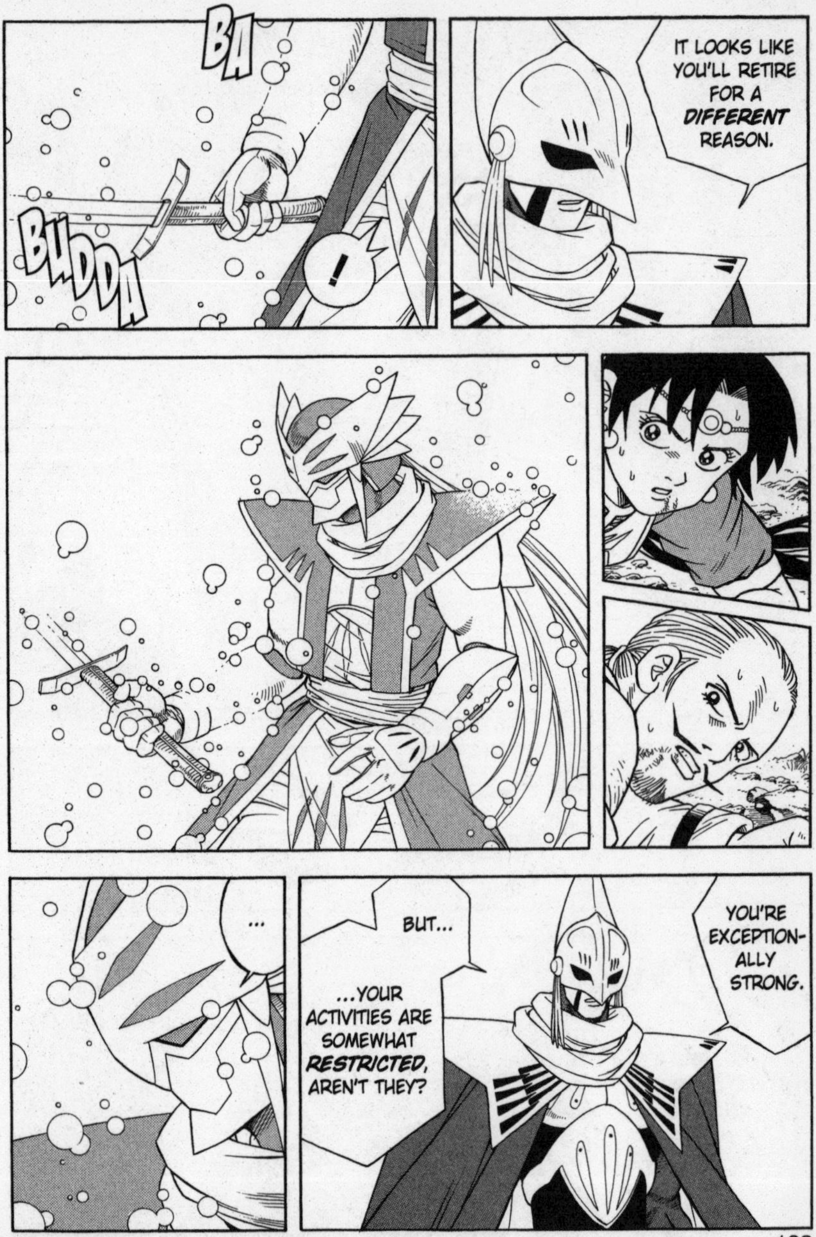
IT LOOKS LIKE YOU'LL RETIRE FOR A DIFFERENT REASON.
BA
BUDDA
!
YOU'RE EXCEPTION-ALLY STRONG.
BUT...
...YOUR ACTIVITIES ARE SOMEWHAT RESTRICTED, AREN'T THEY?
...

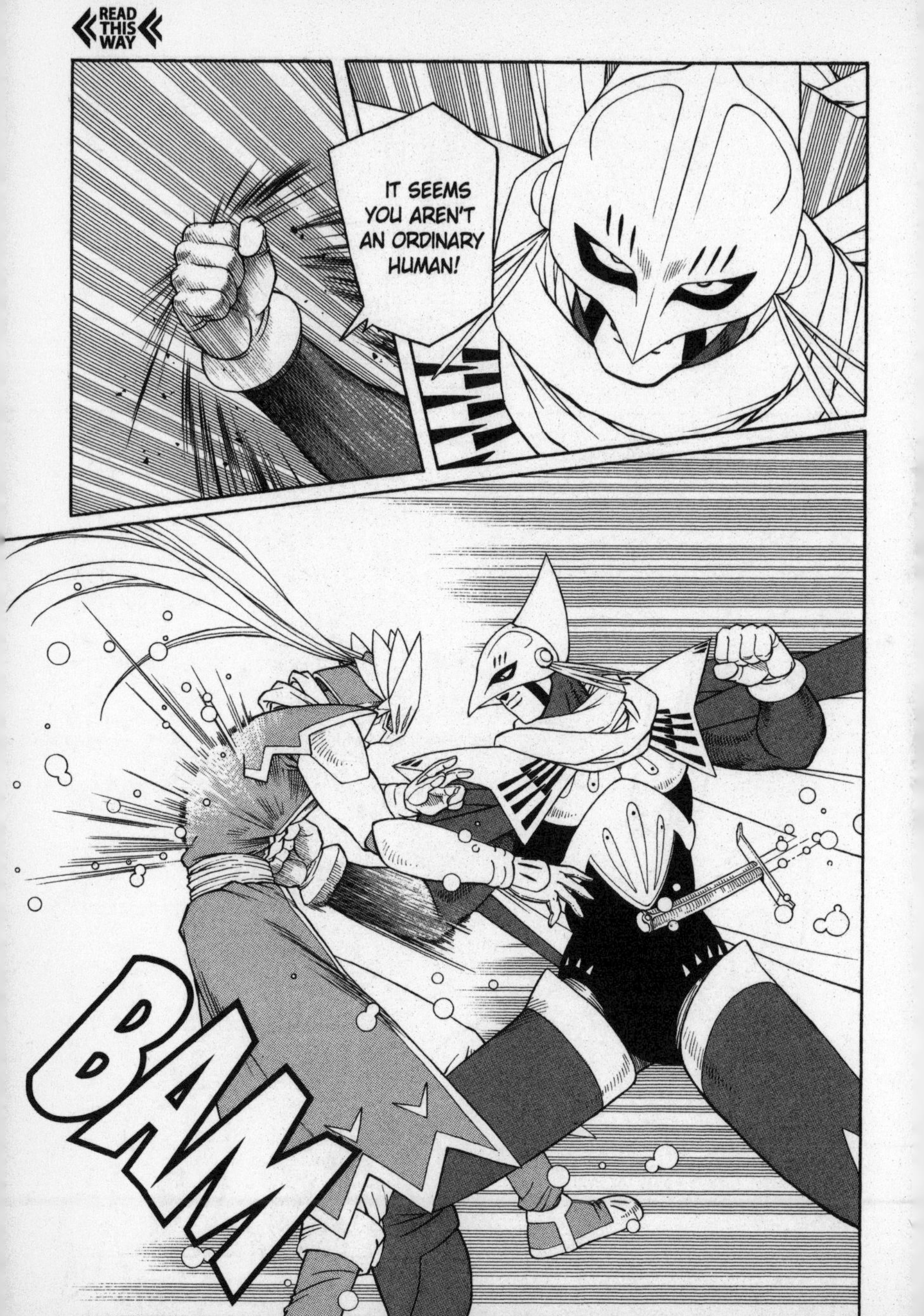
READ THIS WAY
IT SEEMS YOU AREN'T AN ORDINARY HUMAN!
BAM

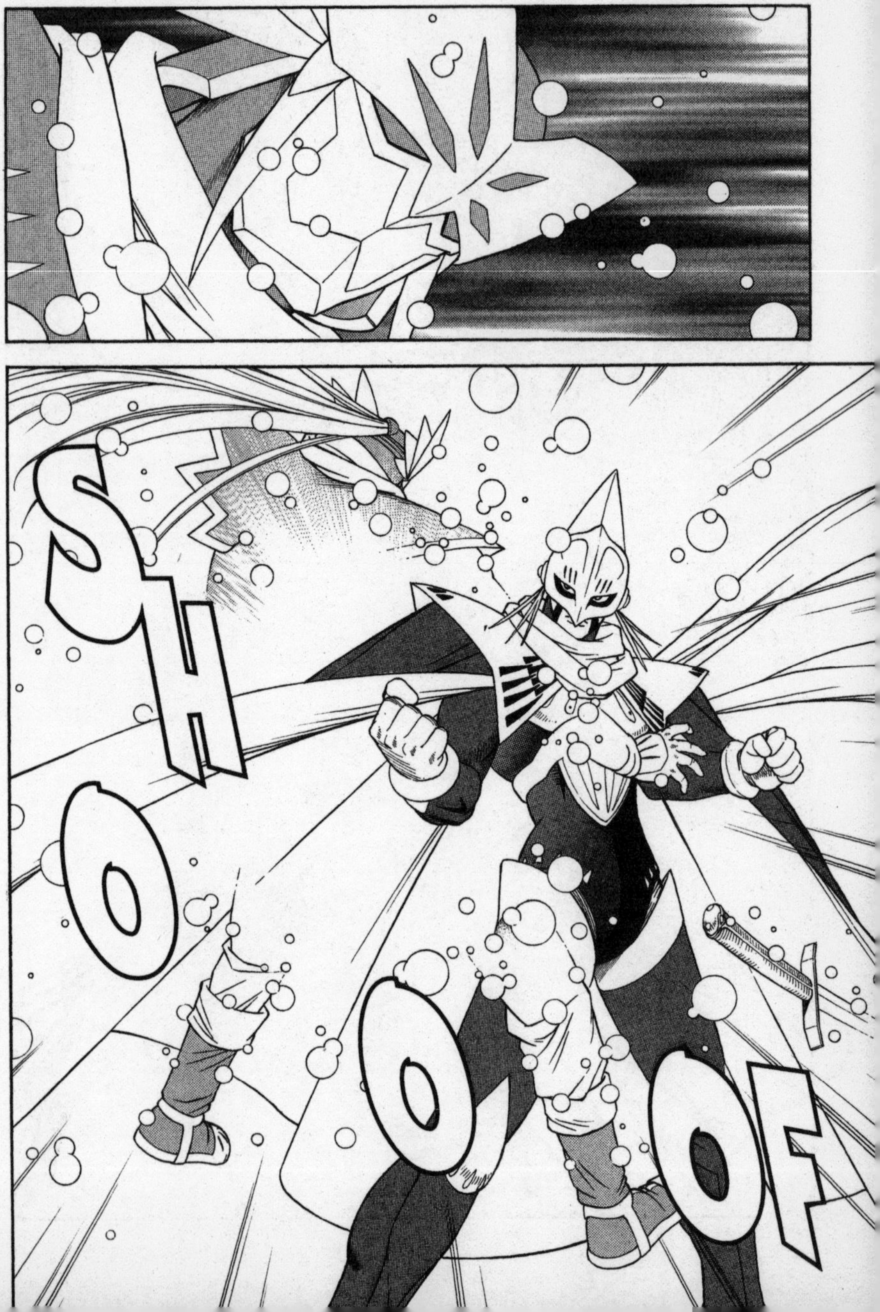
SHOOOF

READ THIS WAY

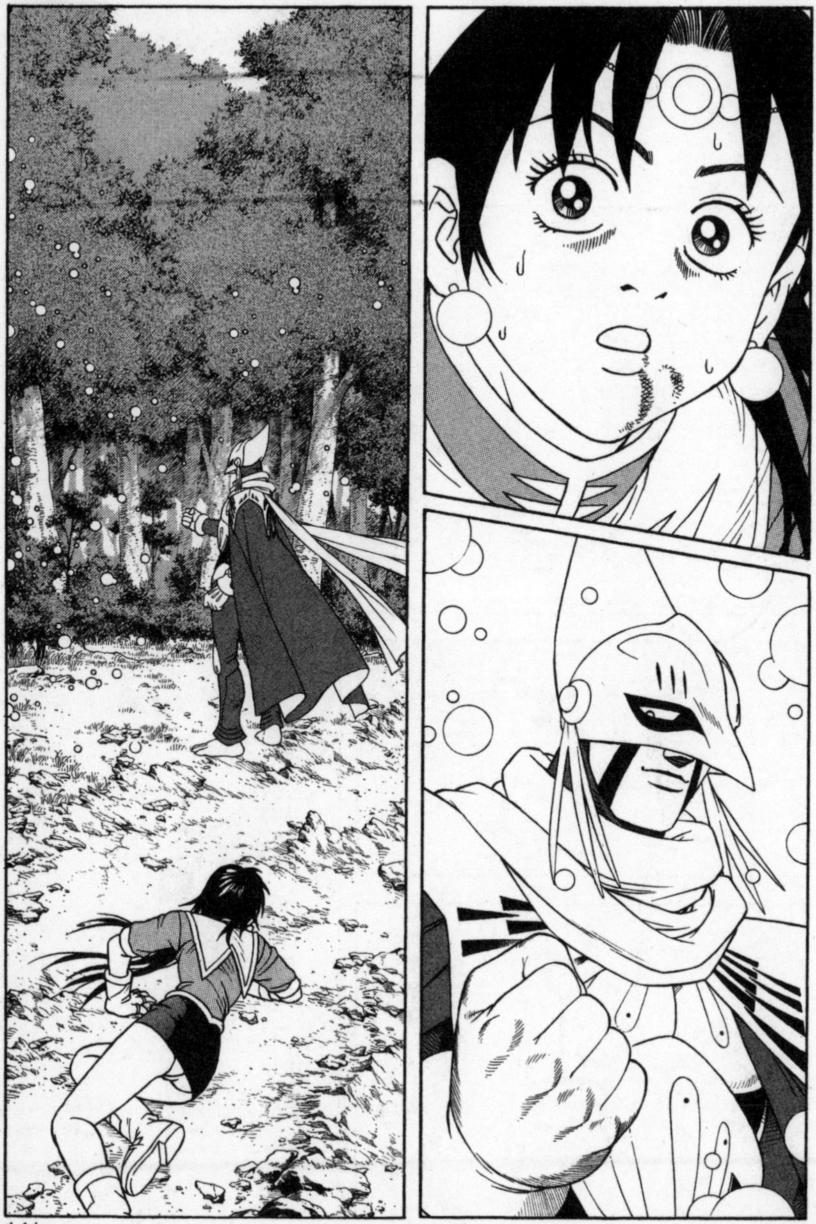

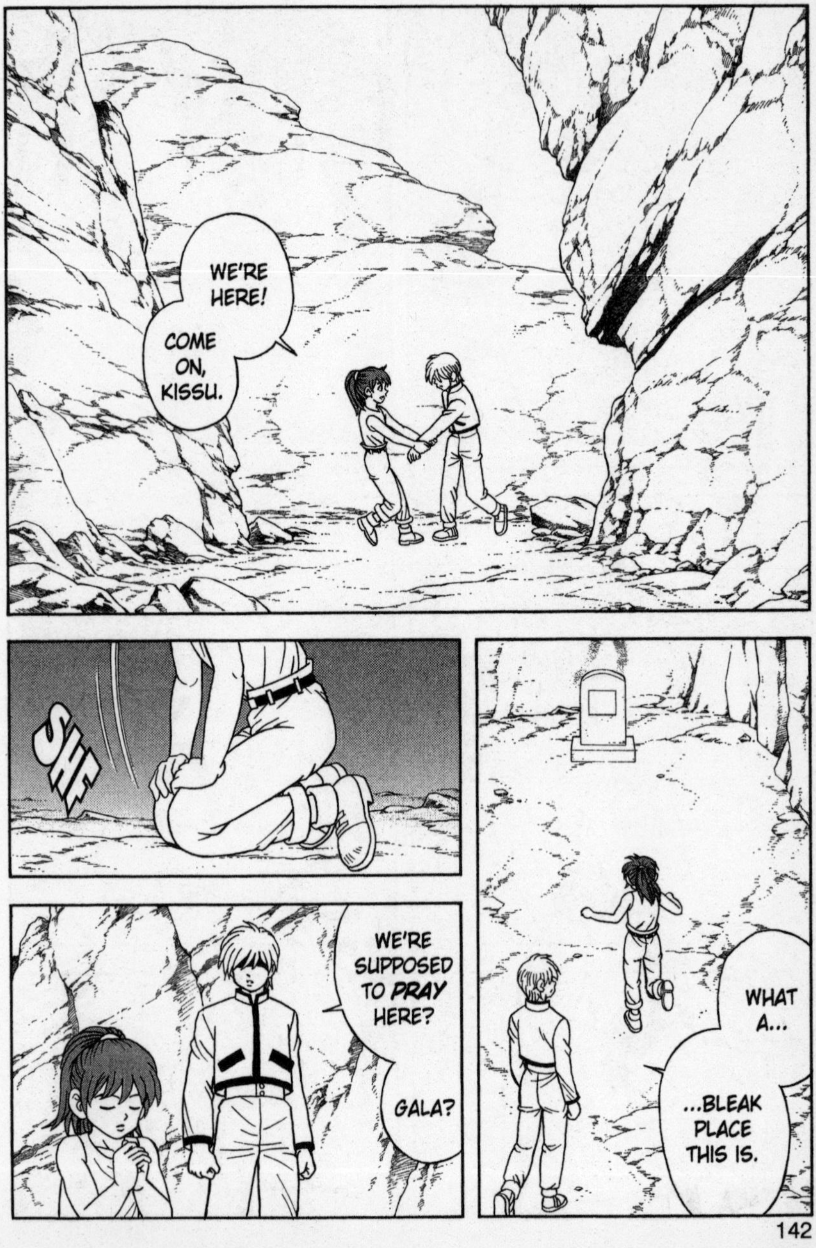
WE'RE HERE!
COME ON, KISSU.
WHAT A...
...BLEAK PLACE THIS IS.
SHF
WE'RE SUPPOSED TO *PRAY* HERE?
GALA?

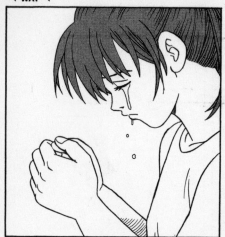

GALA?

I'M FINE...

...MOM!

YEAH.

I'M FINE.

...

MOM?

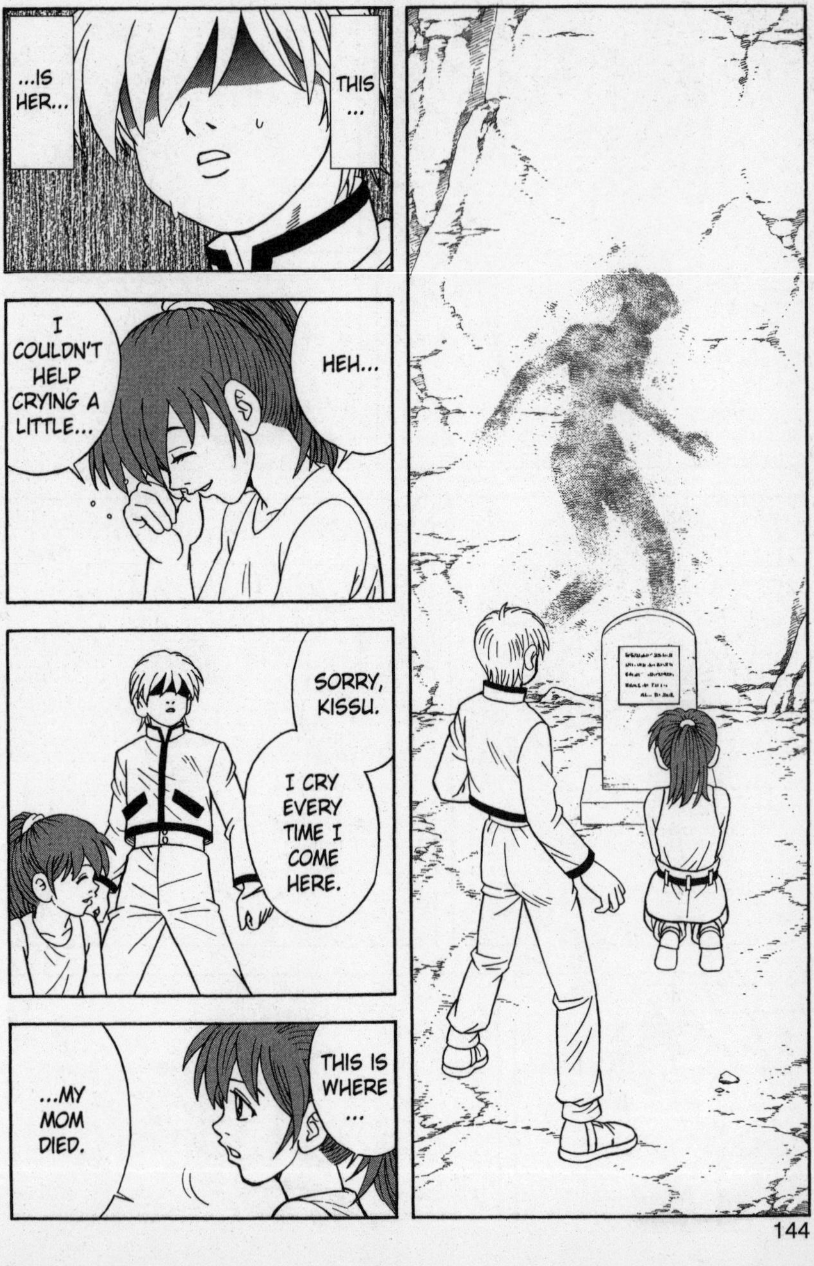
THIS ...
...IS HER...
HEH...
I COULDN'T HELP CRYING A LITTLE...
SORRY, KISSU.
I CRY EVERY TIME I COME HERE.
THIS IS WHERE ...
...MY MOM DIED.

READ THIS WAY

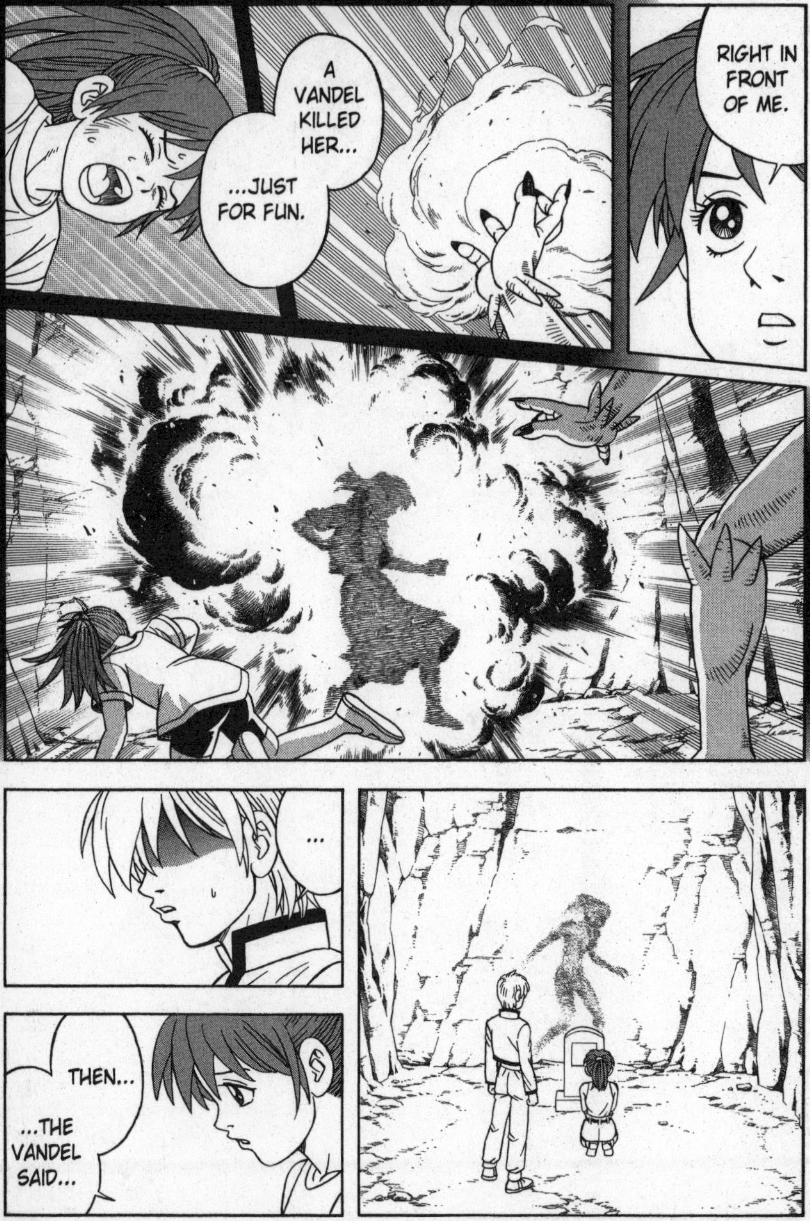
RIGHT IN FRONT OF ME.
A VANDEL KILLED HER...
...JUST FOR FUN.
...
THEN...
...THE VANDEL SAID...

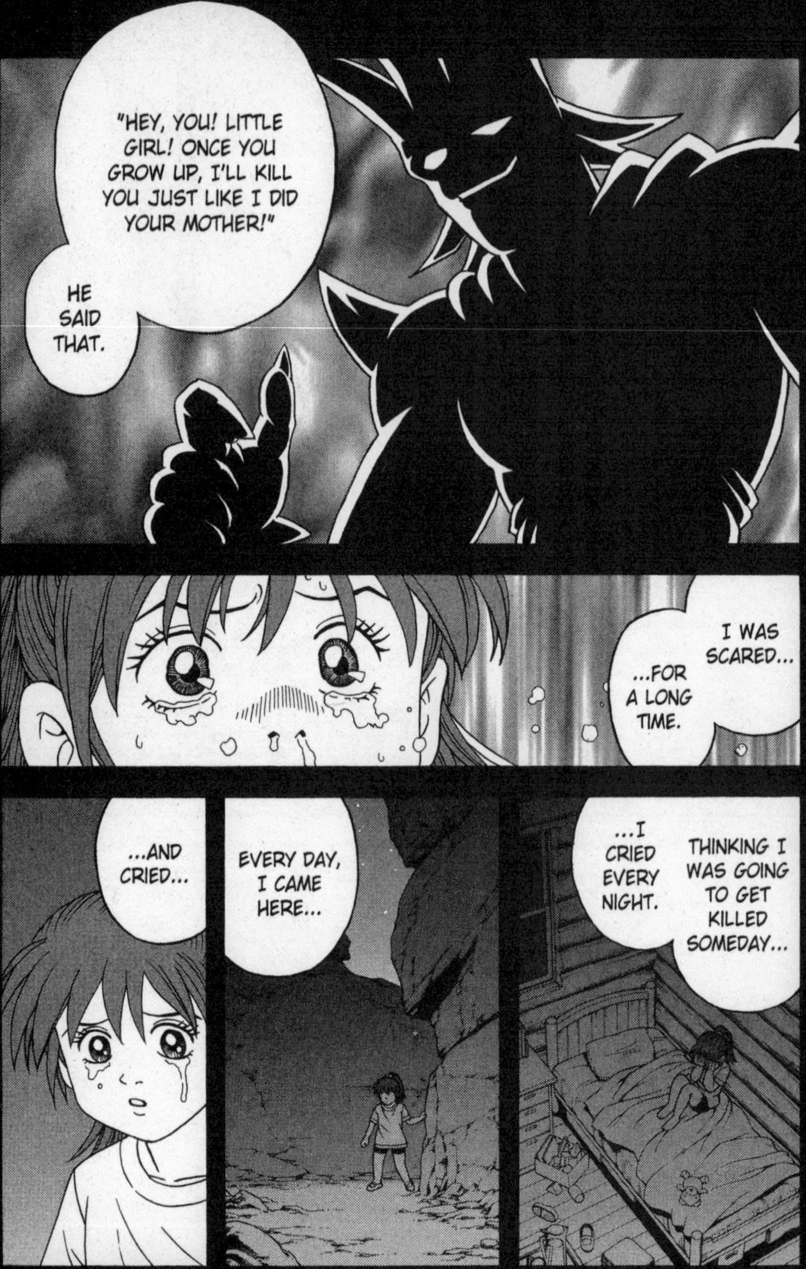
"HEY, YOU! LITTLE GIRL! ONCE YOU GROW UP, I'LL KILL YOU JUST LIKE I DID YOUR MOTHER!"
HE SAID THAT.
I WAS SCARED...
...FOR A LONG TIME.
THINKING I WAS GOING TO GET KILLED SOMEDAY...
...I CRIED EVERY NIGHT.
EVERY DAY, I CAME HERE...
...AND CRIED...

READ THIS WAY

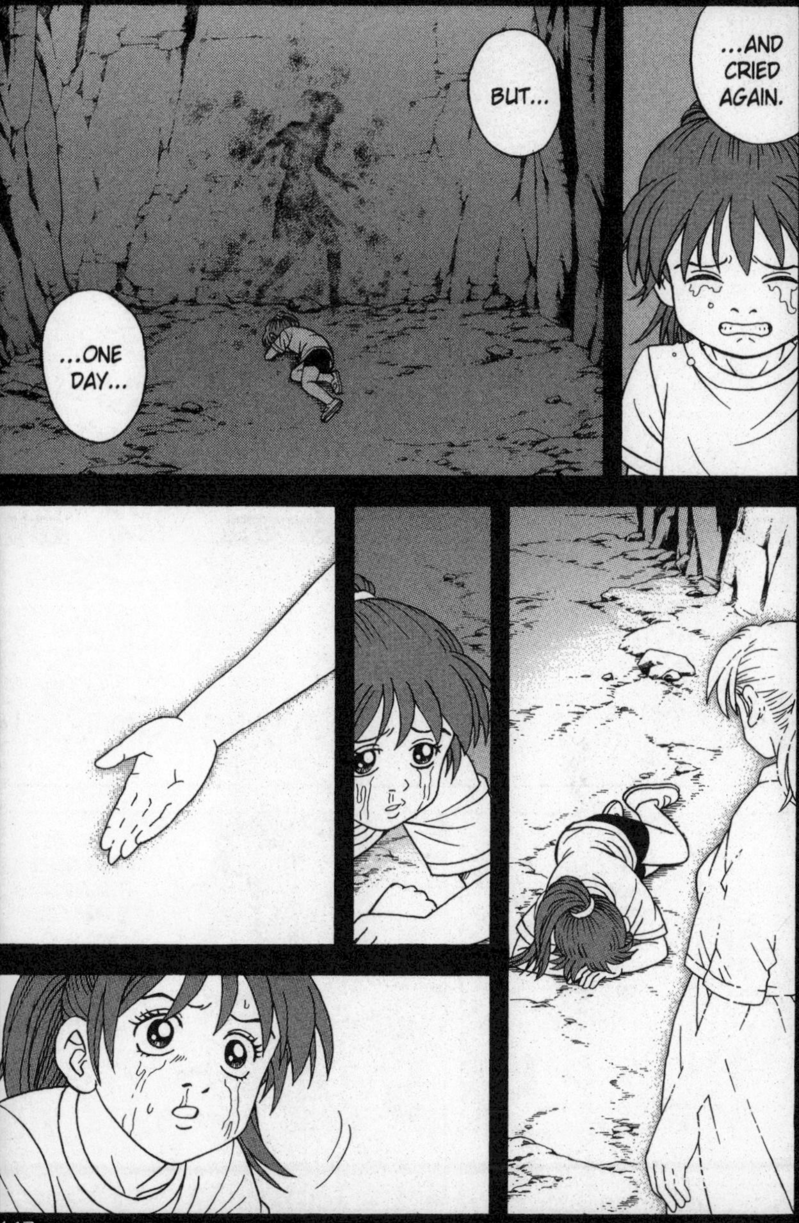
...AND CRIED AGAIN.
BUT...
...ONE DAY...

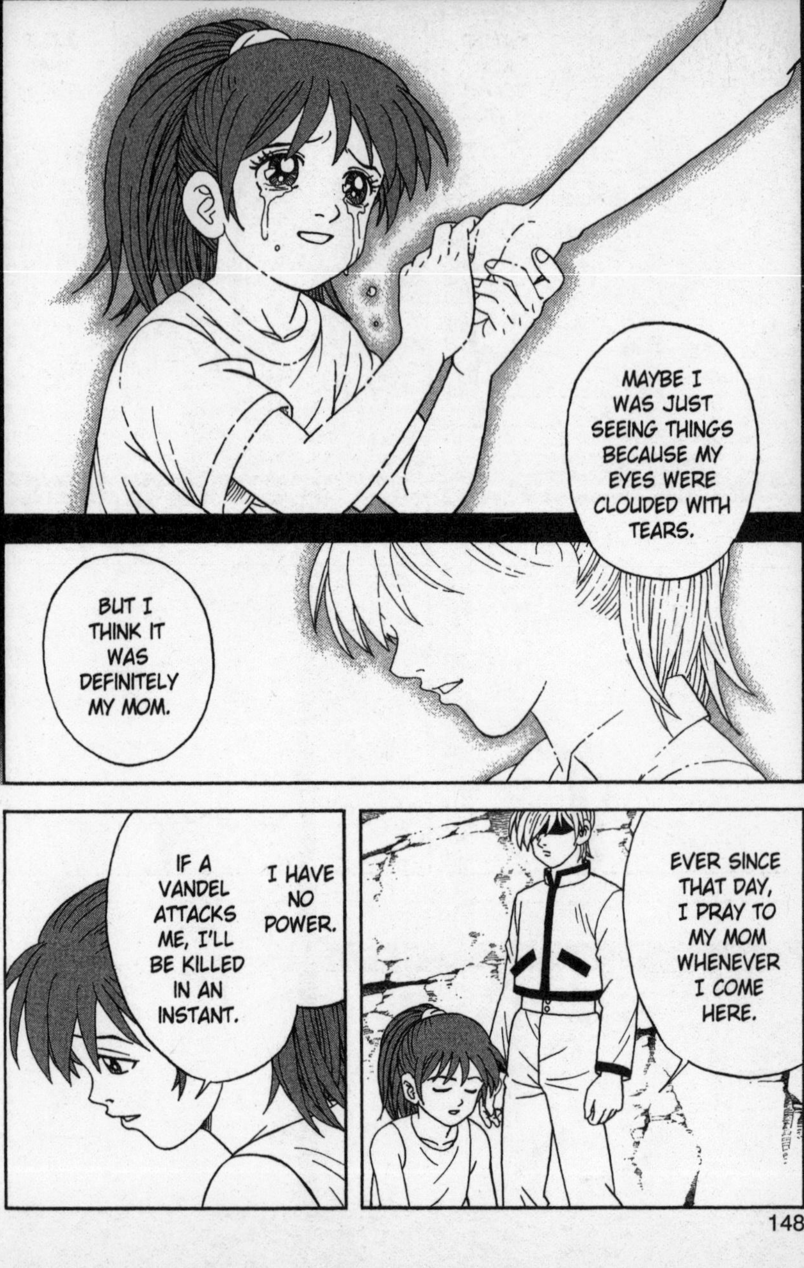
MAYBE I WAS JUST SEEING THINGS BECAUSE MY EYES WERE CLOUDED WITH TEARS.
BUT I THINK IT WAS DEFINITELY MY MOM.
EVER SINCE THAT DAY, I PRAY TO MY MOM WHENEVER I COME HERE.
I HAVE NO POWER.
IF A VANDEL ATTACKS ME, I'LL BE KILLED IN AN INSTANT.

READ THIS WAY

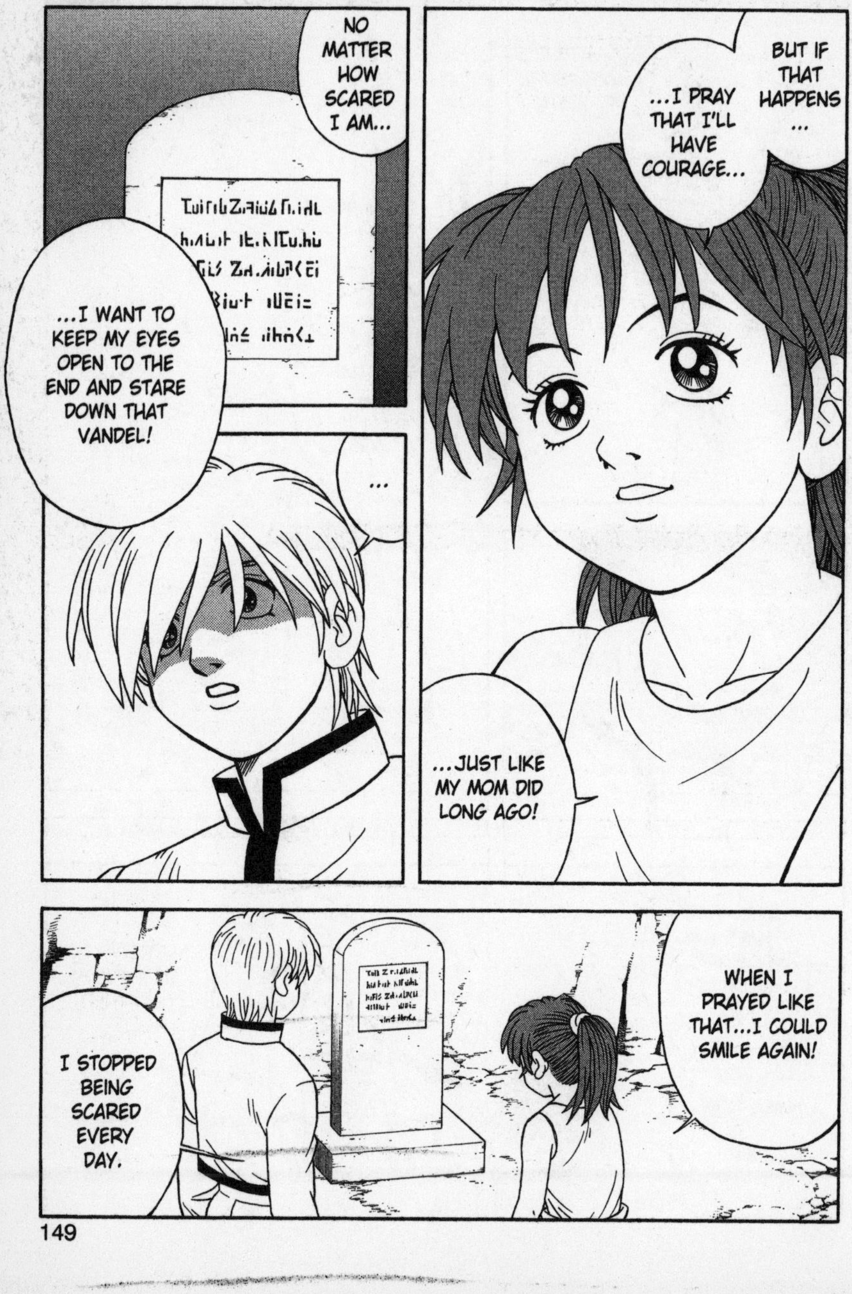
BUT IF THAT HAPPENS...
...I PRAY THAT I'LL HAVE COURAGE...
...JUST LIKE MY MOM DID LONG AGO!
NO MATTER HOW SCARED I AM...
...I WANT TO KEEP MY EYES OPEN TO THE END AND STARE DOWN THAT VANDEL!
...
WHEN I PRAYED LIKE THAT...I COULD SMILE AGAIN!
I STOPPED BEING SCARED EVERY DAY.

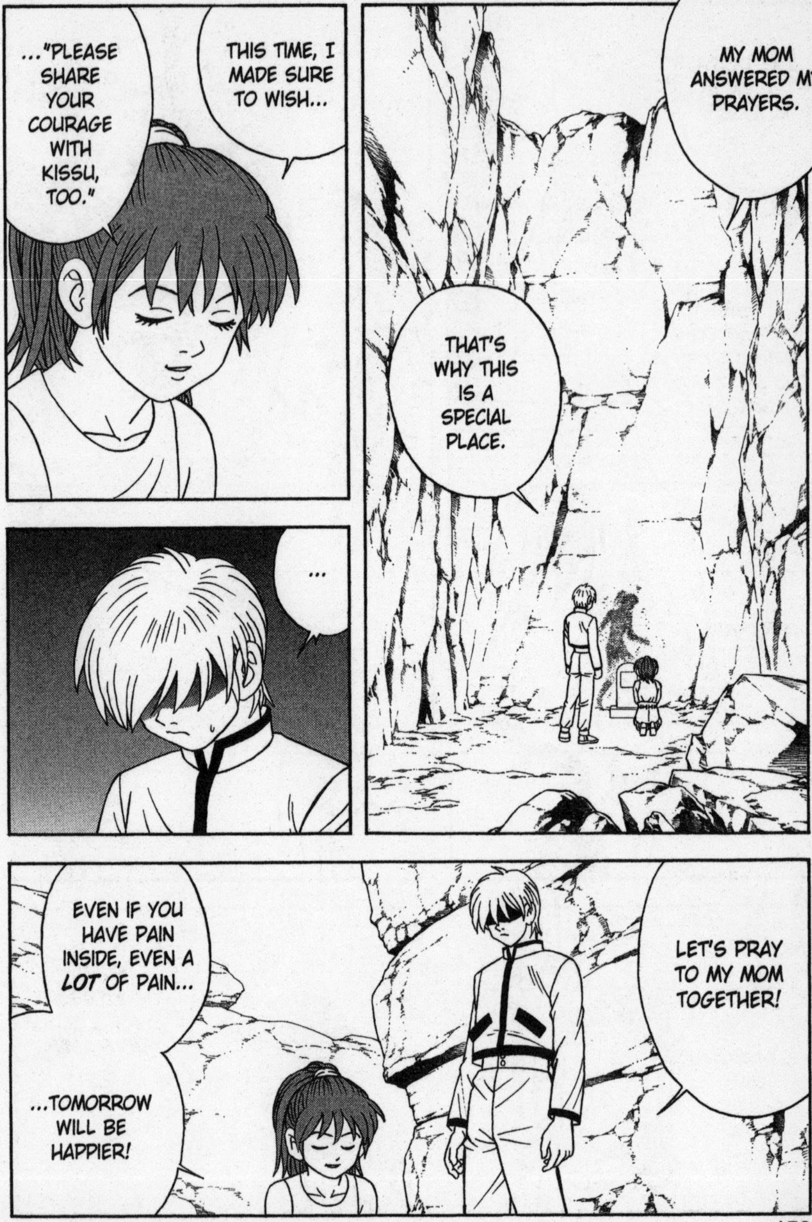
MY MOM ANSWERED MY PRAYERS.
THAT'S WHY THIS IS A SPECIAL PLACE.
THIS TIME, I MADE SURE TO WISH...
..."PLEASE SHARE YOUR COURAGE WITH KISSU, TOO."
...
LET'S PRAY TO MY MOM TOGETHER!
EVEN IF YOU HAVE PAIN INSIDE, EVEN A *LOT* OF PAIN...
...TOMORROW WILL BE HAPPIER!

READ THIS WAY

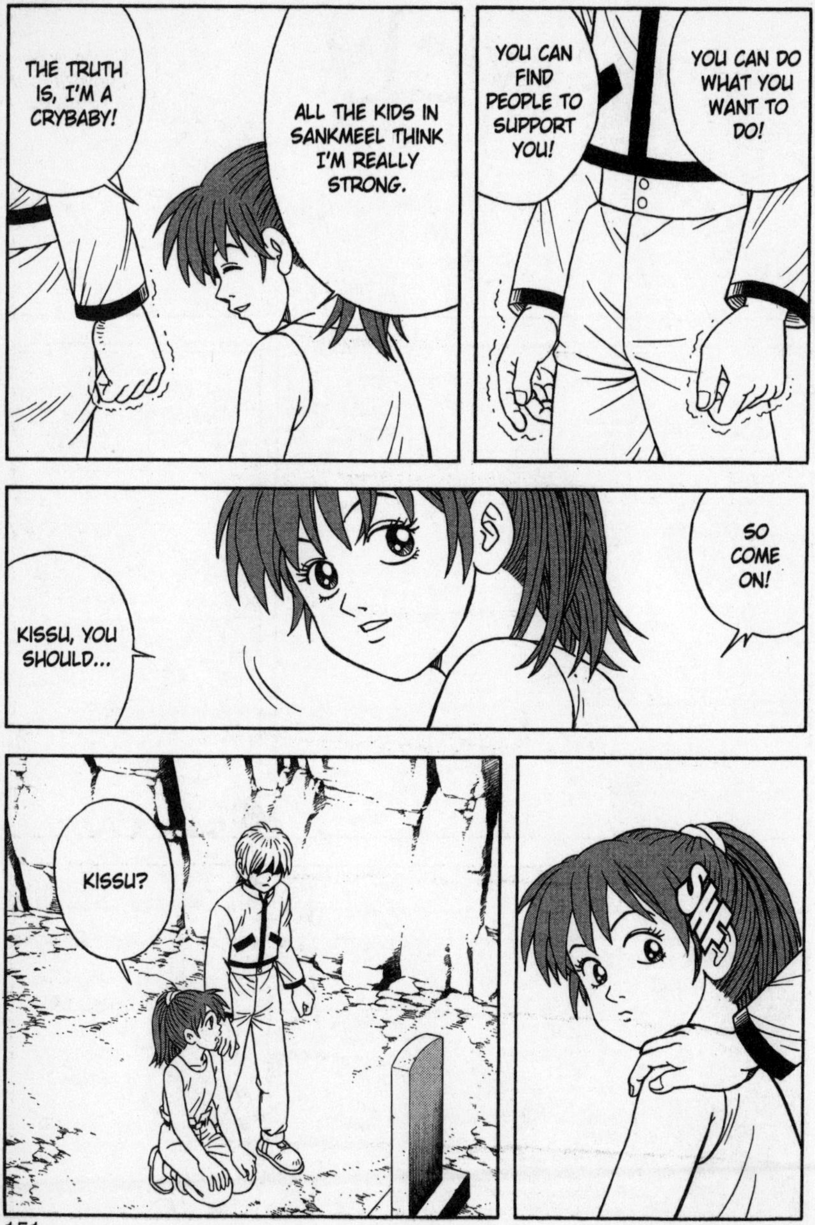
YOU CAN DO WHAT YOU WANT TO DO!
YOU CAN FIND PEOPLE TO SUPPORT YOU!
ALL THE KIDS IN SANKMEEL THINK I'M REALLY STRONG.
THE TRUTH IS, I'M A CRYBABY!
SO COME ON!
KISSU, YOU SHOULD...
KISSU?

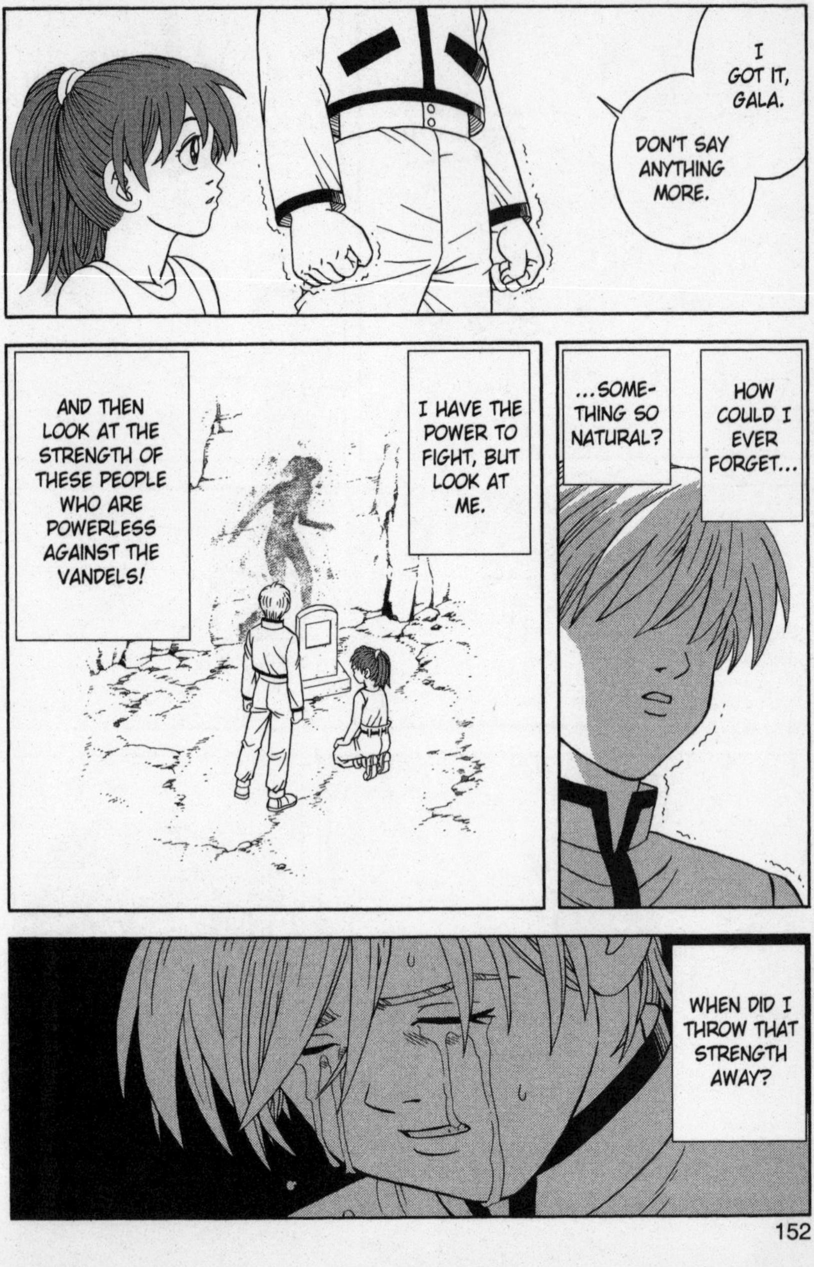
I GOT IT, GALA.
DON'T SAY ANYTHING MORE.
HOW COULD I EVER FORGET...
...SOME-THING SO NATURAL?
I HAVE THE POWER TO FIGHT, BUT LOOK AT ME.
AND THEN LOOK AT THE STRENGTH OF THESE PEOPLE WHO ARE POWERLESS AGAINST THE VANDELS!
WHEN DID I THROW THAT STRENGTH AWAY?

READ THIS WAY

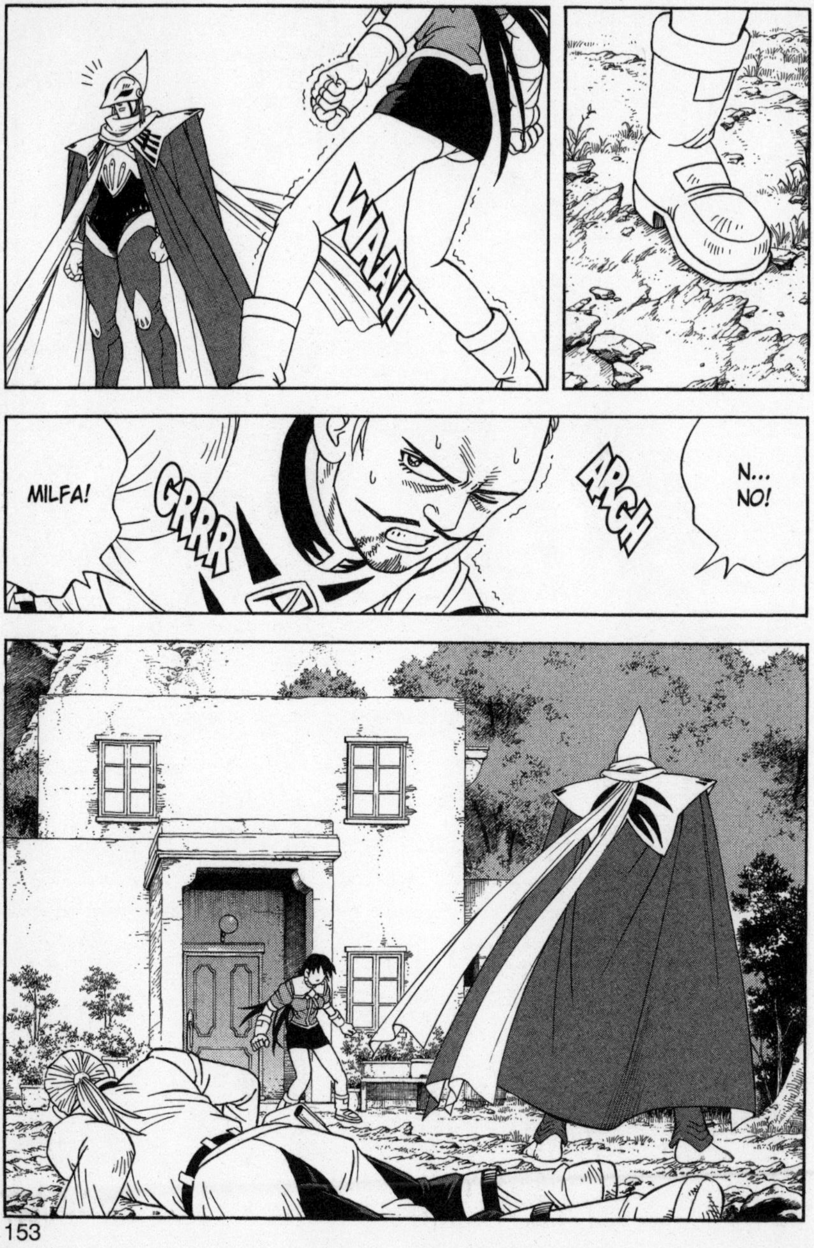

WAAH
N... NO!
ARGH
GRRR
MILFA!

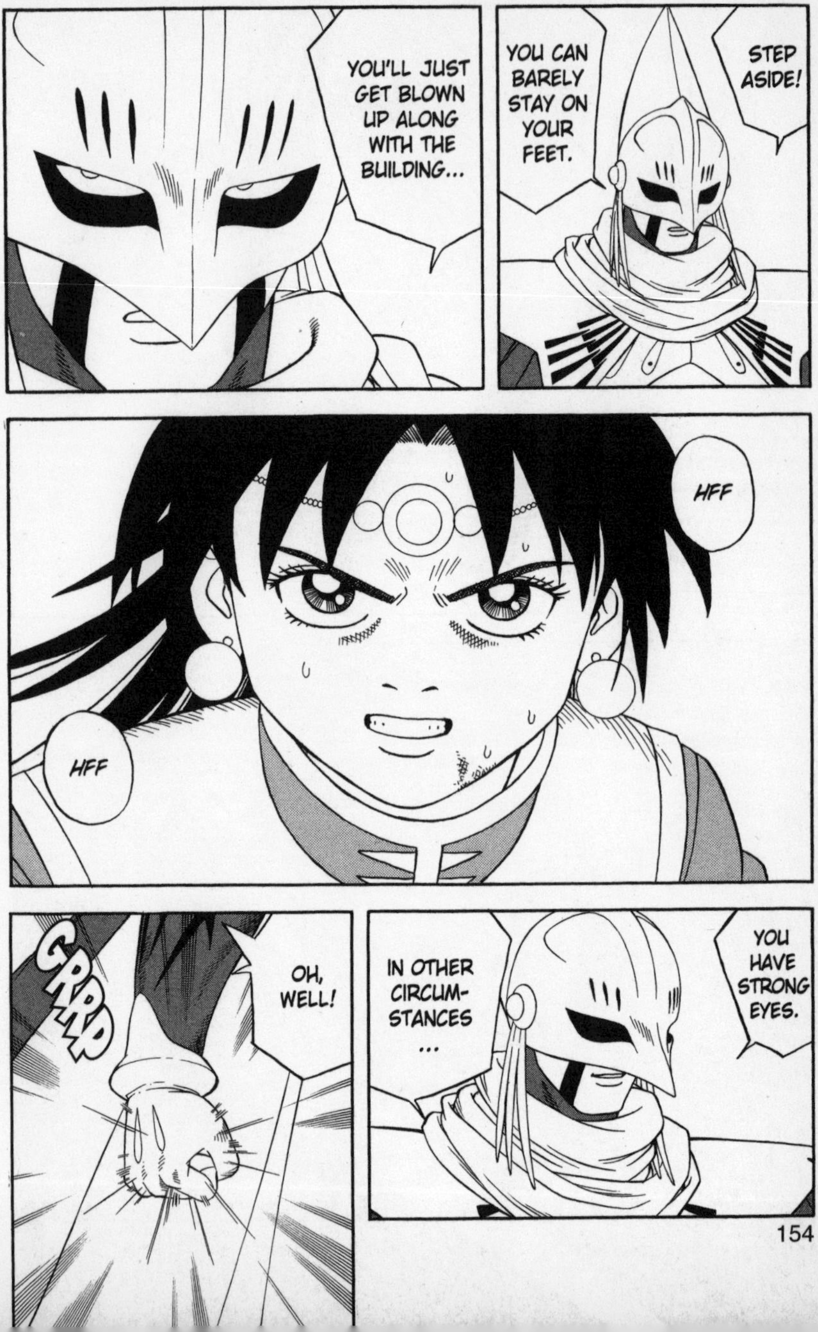
STEP ASIDE!
YOU CAN BARELY STAY ON YOUR FEET.
YOU'LL JUST GET BLOWN UP ALONG WITH THE BUILDING...
HFF
HFF
YOU HAVE STRONG EYES.
IN OTHER CIRCUM-STANCES ...
OH, WELL!
GRRP

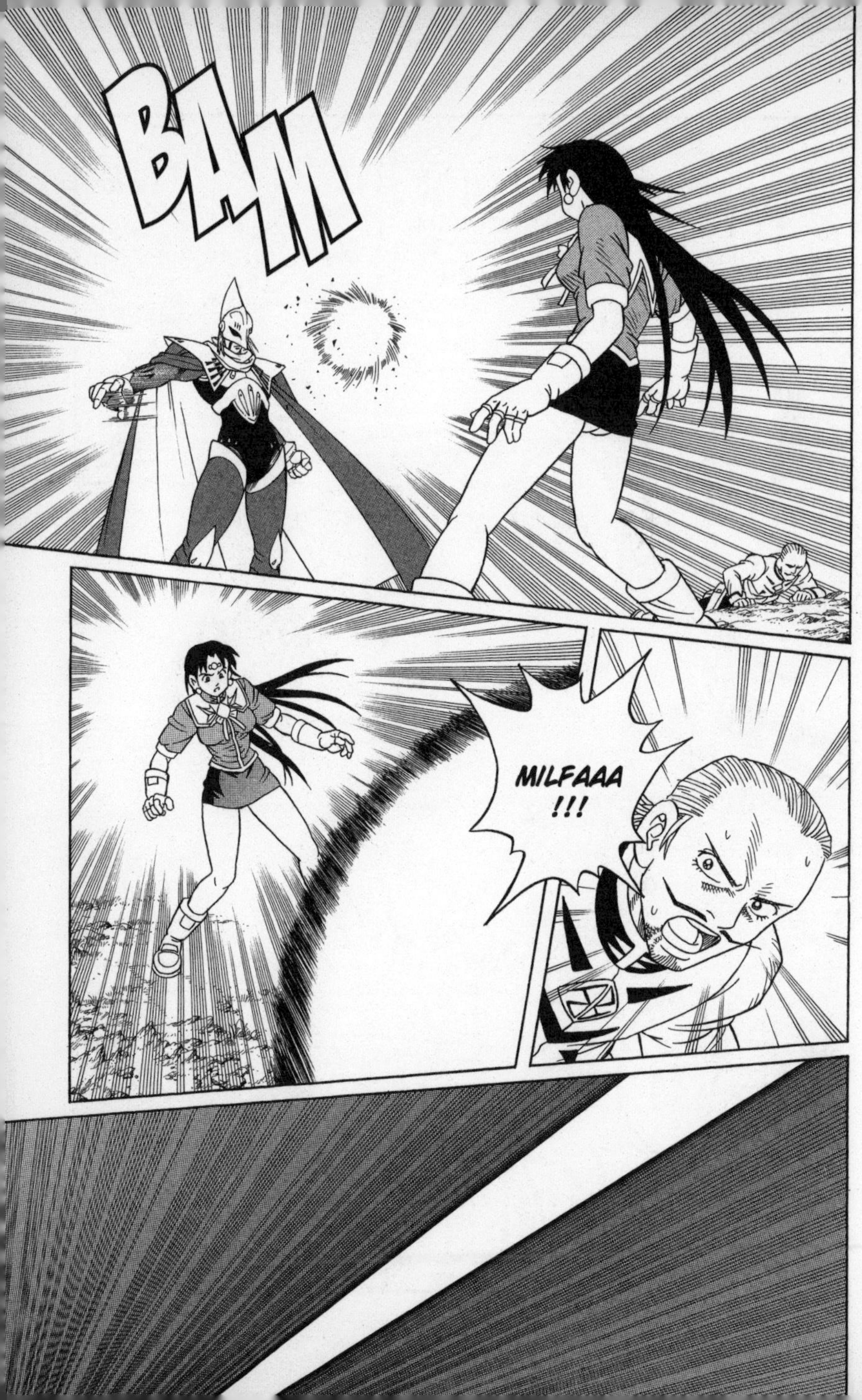
BAM
MILFAAA !!!

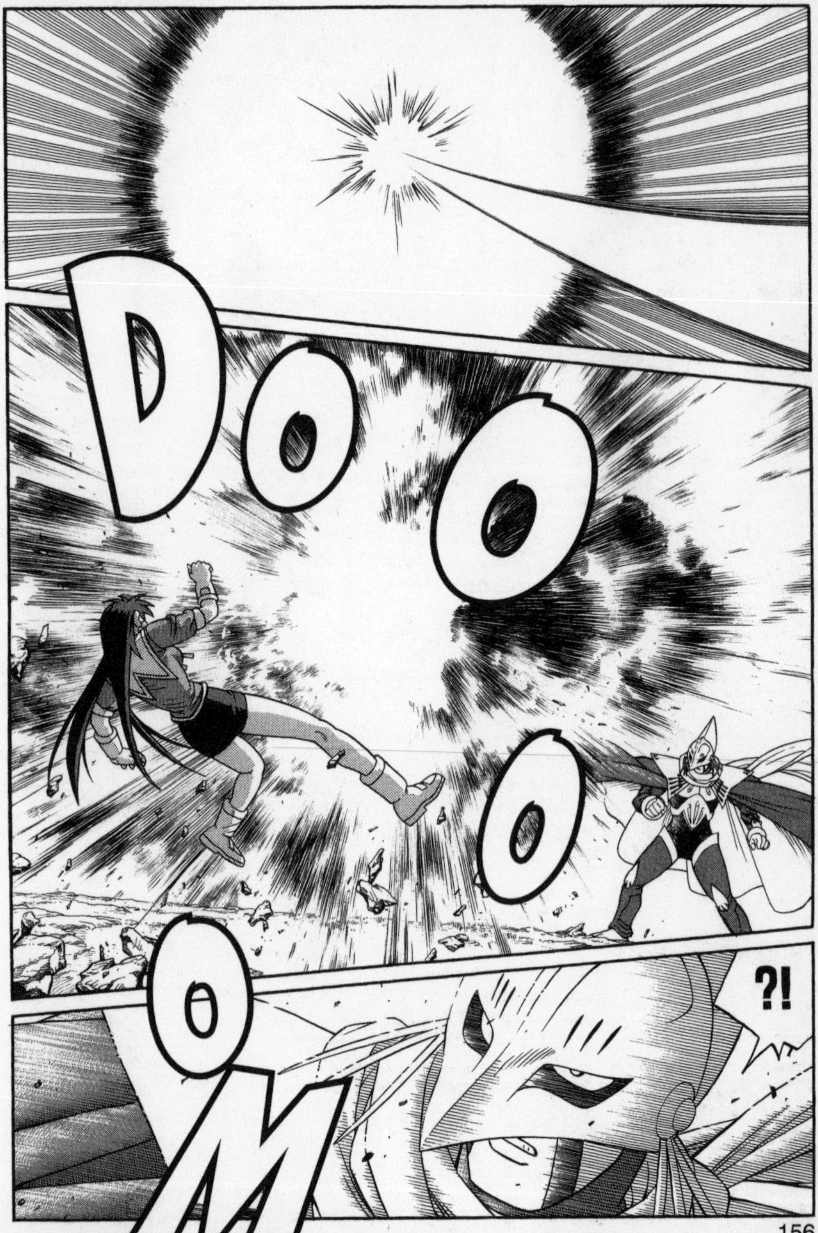
DOOOOOM
?!

READ THIS WAY

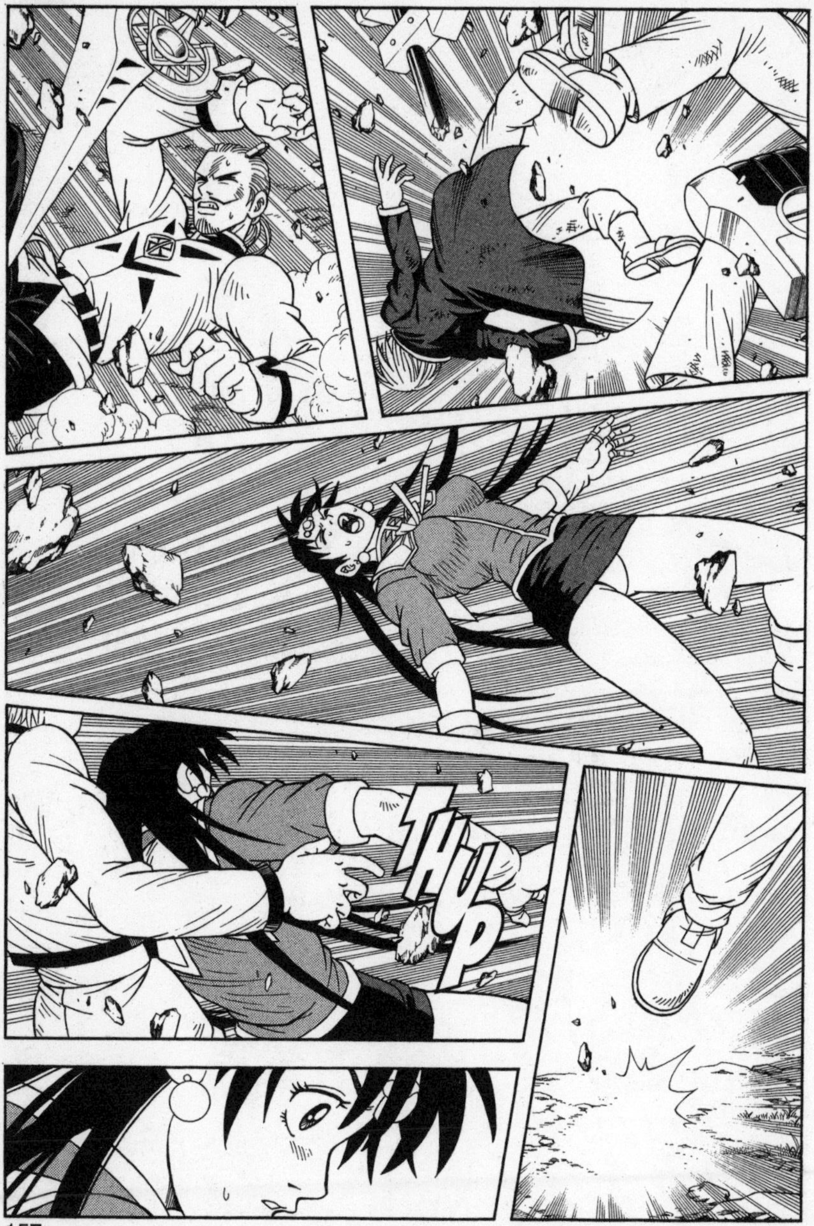
THUP

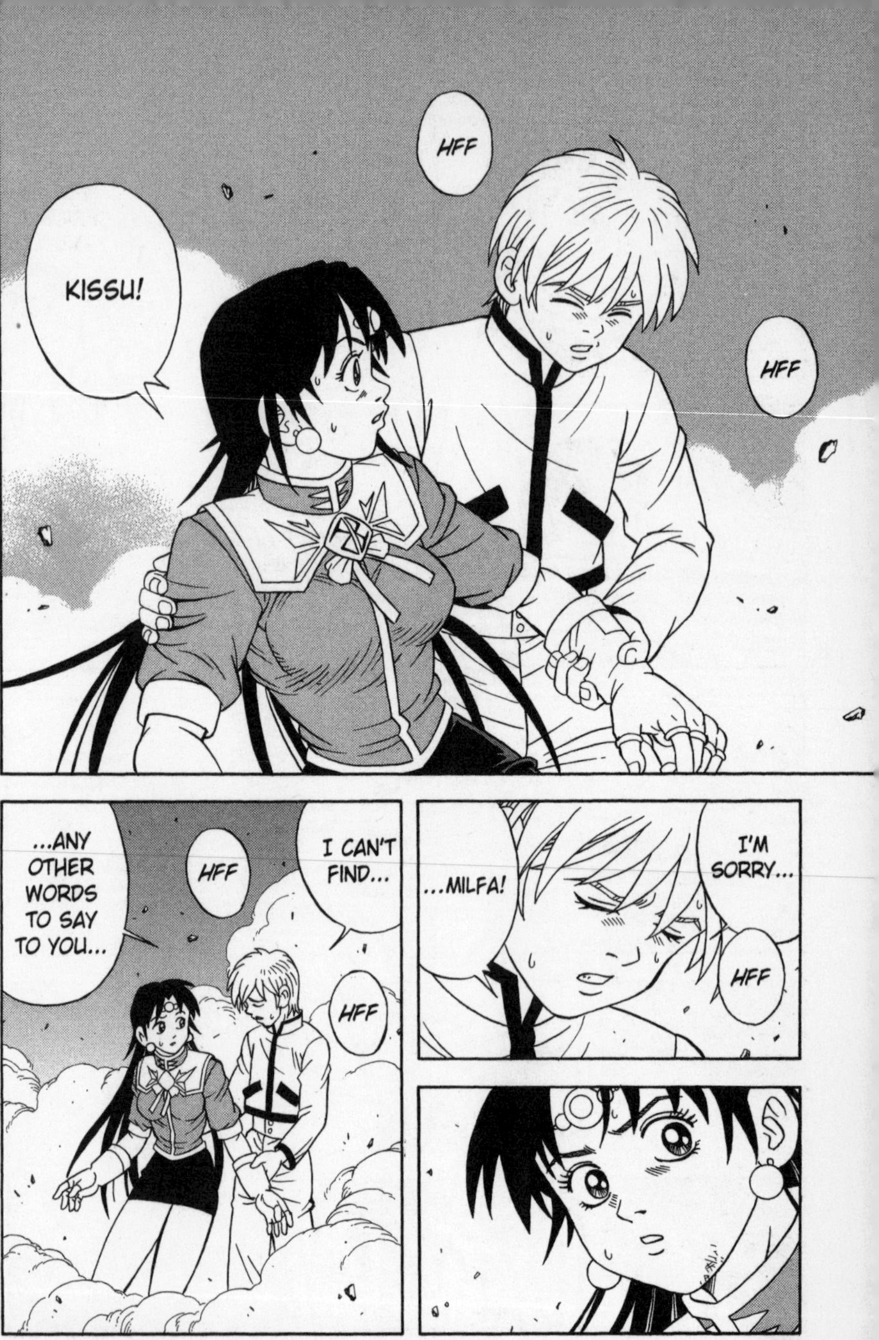
HFF
HFF
KISSU!
I'M SORRY...
HFF
...MILFA!
I CAN'T FIND...
HFF
...ANY OTHER WORDS TO SAY TO YOU...
HFF

READ THIS WAY

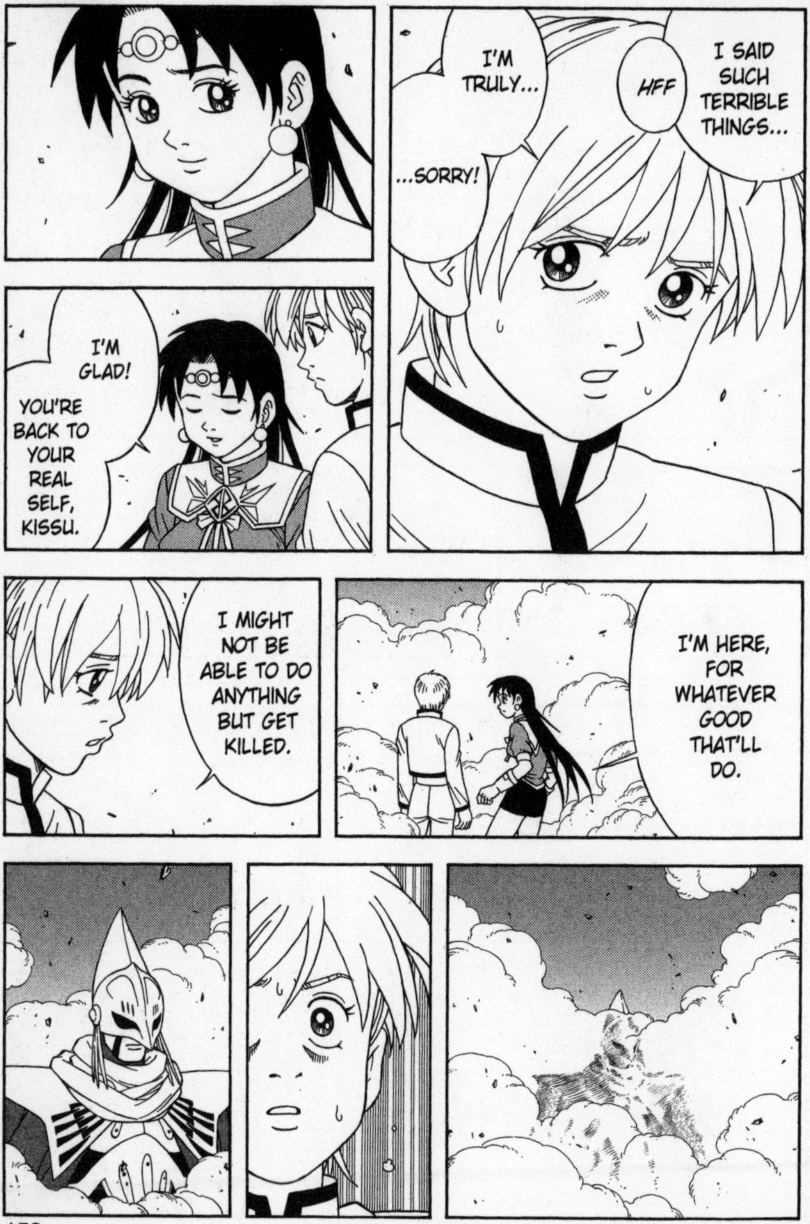

I SAID SUCH TERRIBLE THINGS...
HFF
I'M TRULY...
...SORRY!
I'M GLAD!
YOU'RE BACK TO YOUR REAL SELF, KISSU.
I'M HERE, FOR WHATEVER GOOD THAT'LL DO.
I MIGHT NOT BE ABLE TO DO ANYTHING BUT GET KILLED.

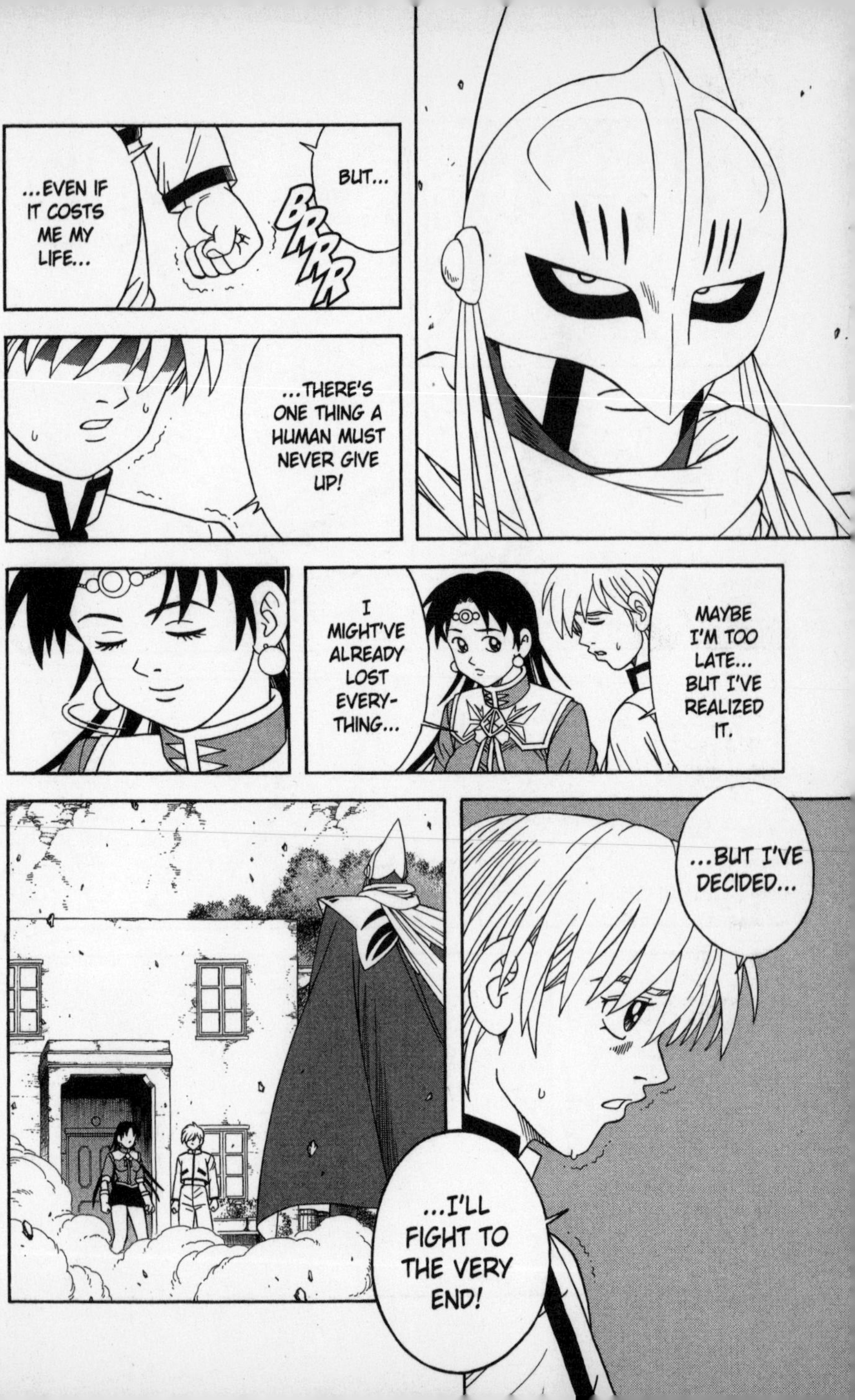
BUT...
BRRR
...EVEN IF IT COSTS ME MY LIFE...
...THERE'S ONE THING A HUMAN MUST NEVER GIVE UP!
MAYBE I'M TOO LATE... BUT I'VE REALIZED IT.
I MIGHT'VE ALREADY LOST EVERY-THING...
...BUT I'VE DECIDED...
...I'LL FIGHT TO THE VERY END!

READ THIS WAY

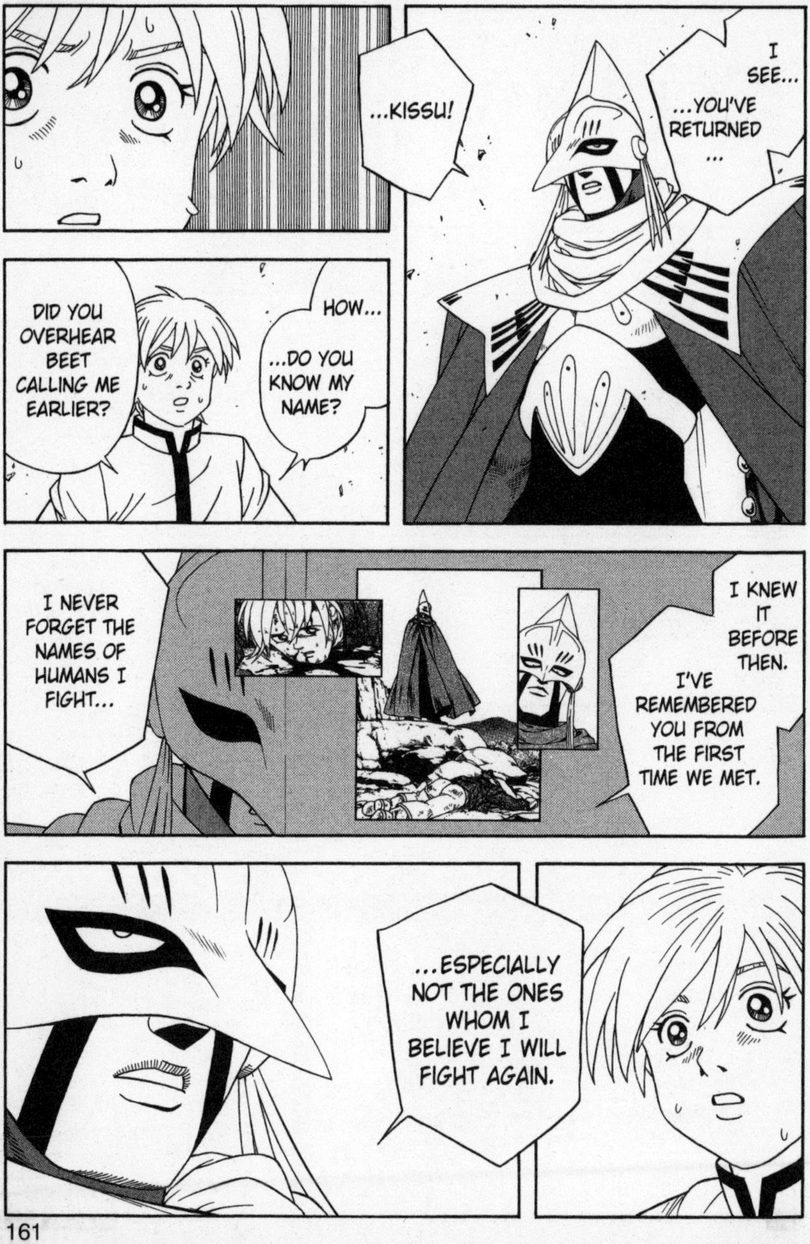
I SEE...
...YOU'VE RETURNED ...
...KISSU!
HOW...
...DO YOU KNOW MY NAME?
DID YOU OVERHEAR BEET CALLING ME EARLIER?
I KNEW IT BEFORE THEN.
I'VE REMEMBERED YOU FROM THE FIRST TIME WE MET.
I NEVER FORGET THE NAMES OF HUMANS I FIGHT...
...ESPECIALLY NOT THE ONES WHOM I BELIEVE I WILL FIGHT AGAIN.

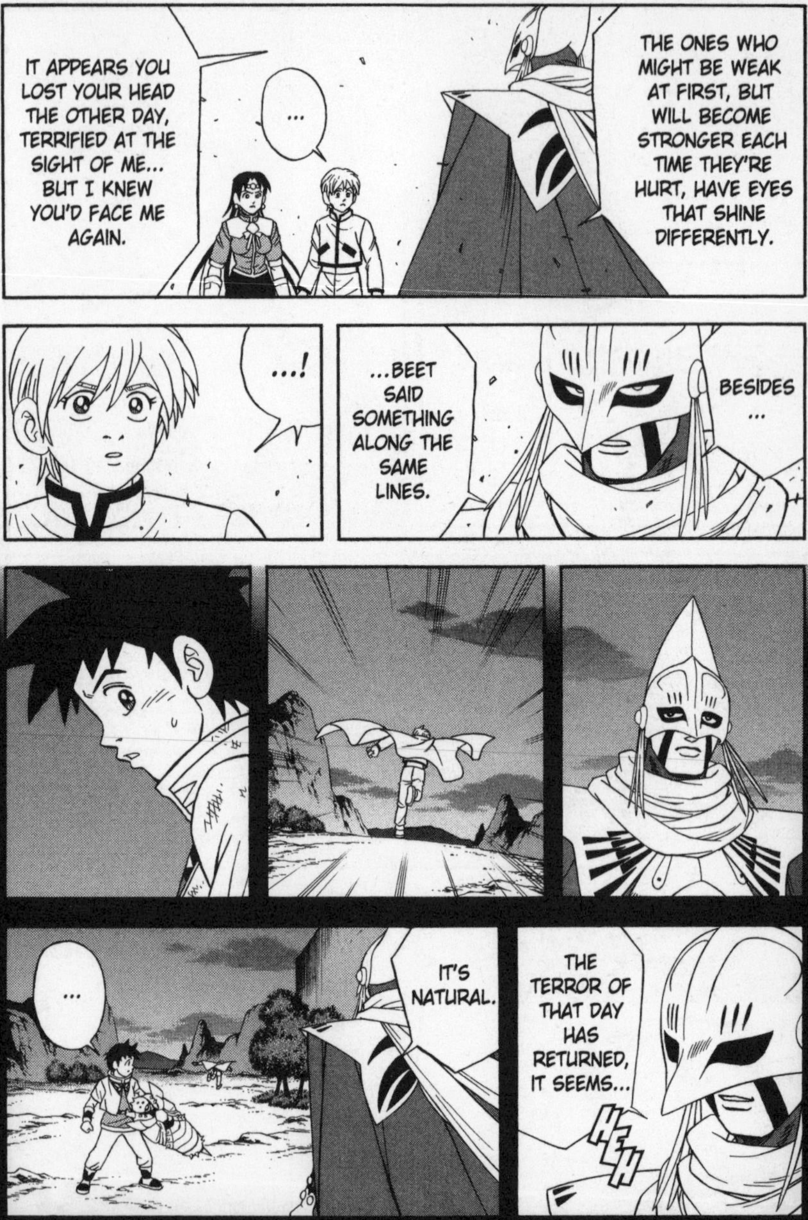
THE ONES WHO MIGHT BE WEAK AT FIRST, BUT WILL BECOME STRONGER EACH TIME THEY'RE HURT, HAVE EYES THAT SHINE DIFFERENTLY.
IT APPEARS YOU LOST YOUR HEAD THE OTHER DAY, TERRIFIED AT THE SIGHT OF ME... BUT I KNEW YOU'D FACE ME AGAIN.
...
BESIDES ...
...BEET SAID SOMETHING ALONG THE SAME LINES.
...!
THE TERROR OF THAT DAY HAS RETURNED, IT SEEMS...
HEH
IT'S NATURAL.
...

READ THIS WAY

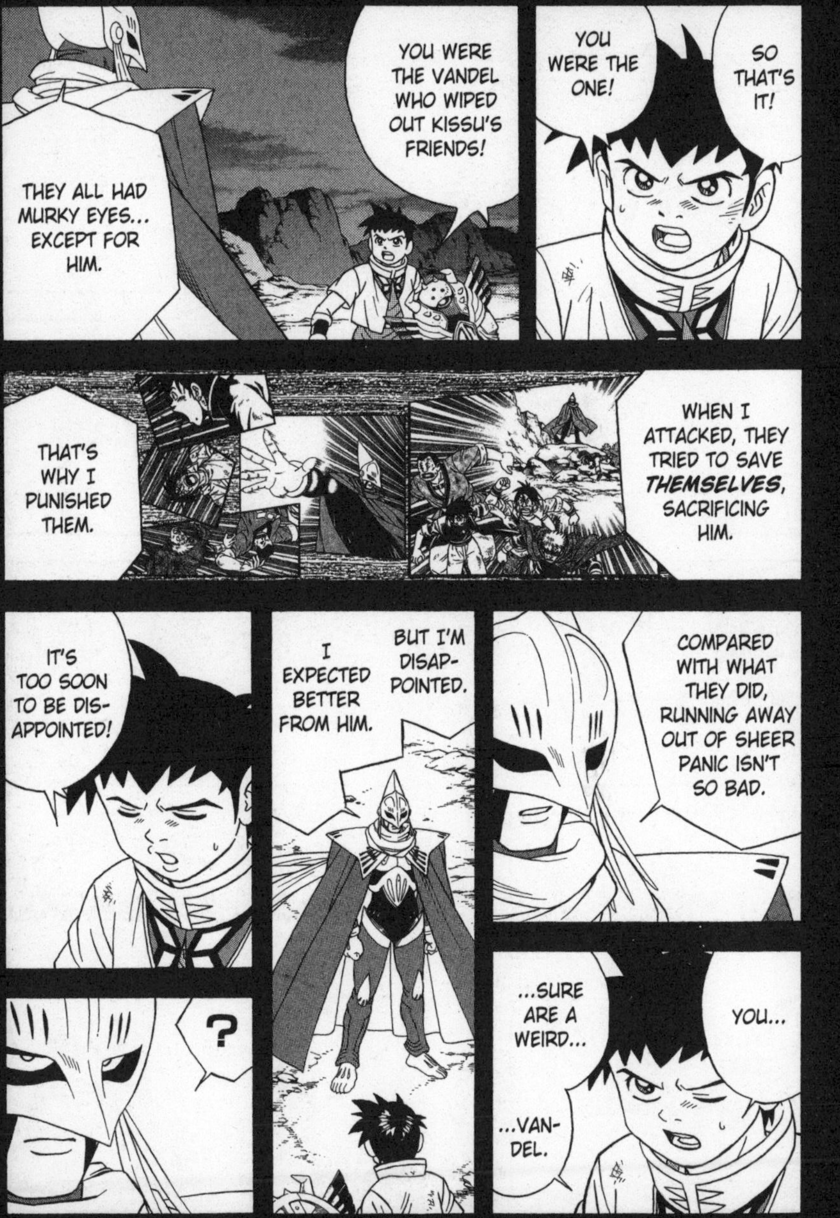
SO THAT'S IT!
YOU WERE THE ONE!
YOU WERE THE VANDEL WHO WIPED OUT KISSU'S FRIENDS!
THEY ALL HAD MURKY EYES... EXCEPT FOR HIM.
WHEN I ATTACKED, THEY TRIED TO SAVE *THEMSELVES*, SACRIFICING HIM.
THAT'S WHY I PUNISHED THEM.
COMPARED WITH WHAT THEY DID, RUNNING AWAY OUT OF SHEER PANIC ISN'T SO BAD.
YOU...
...SURE ARE A WEIRD...
...VAN-DEL.
BUT I'M DISAP-POINTED.
I EXPECTED BETTER FROM HIM.
IT'S TOO SOON TO BE DIS-APPOINTED!
?

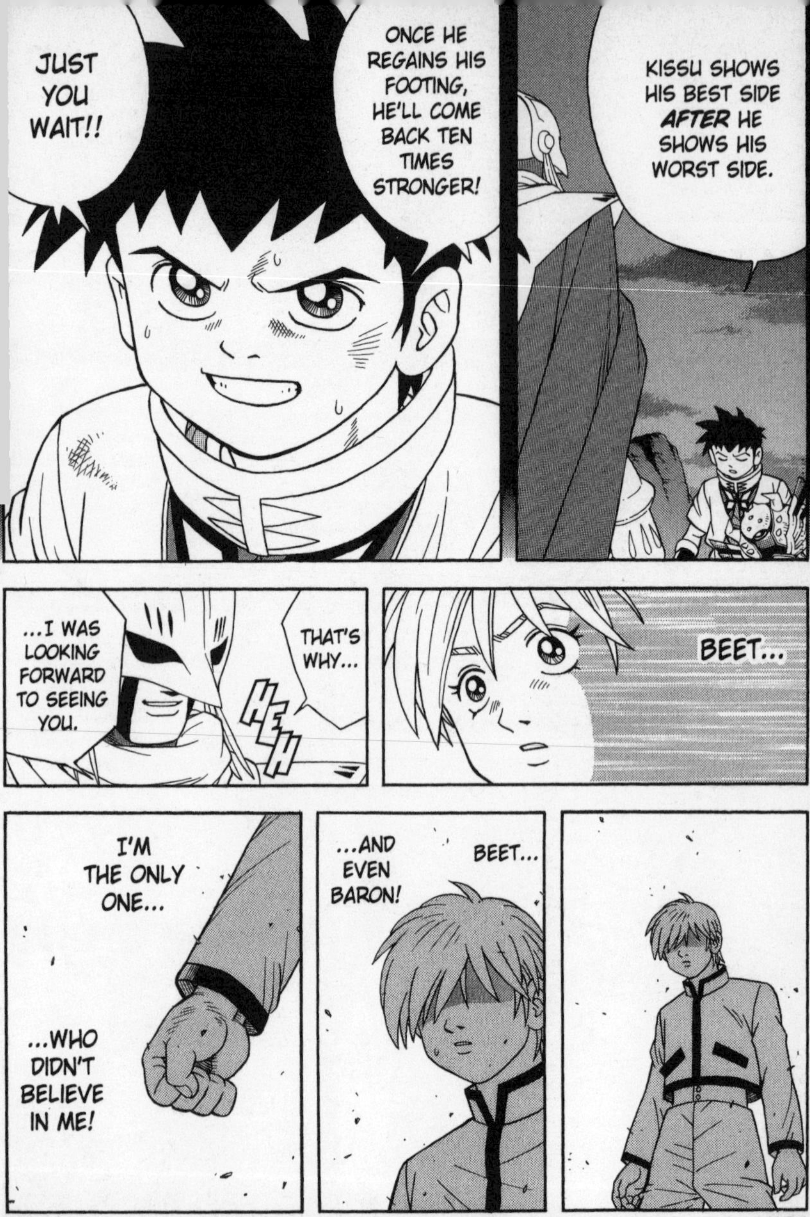
KISSU SHOWS HIS BEST SIDE *AFTER* HE SHOWS HIS WORST SIDE.
ONCE HE REGAINS HIS FOOTING, HE'LL COME BACK TEN TIMES STRONGER!
JUST YOU WAIT!!
BEET...
THAT'S WHY...
HEH
...I WAS LOOKING FORWARD TO SEEING YOU.
BEET...
...AND EVEN BARON!
I'M THE ONLY ONE...
...WHO DIDN'T BELIEVE IN ME!

READ THIS WAY

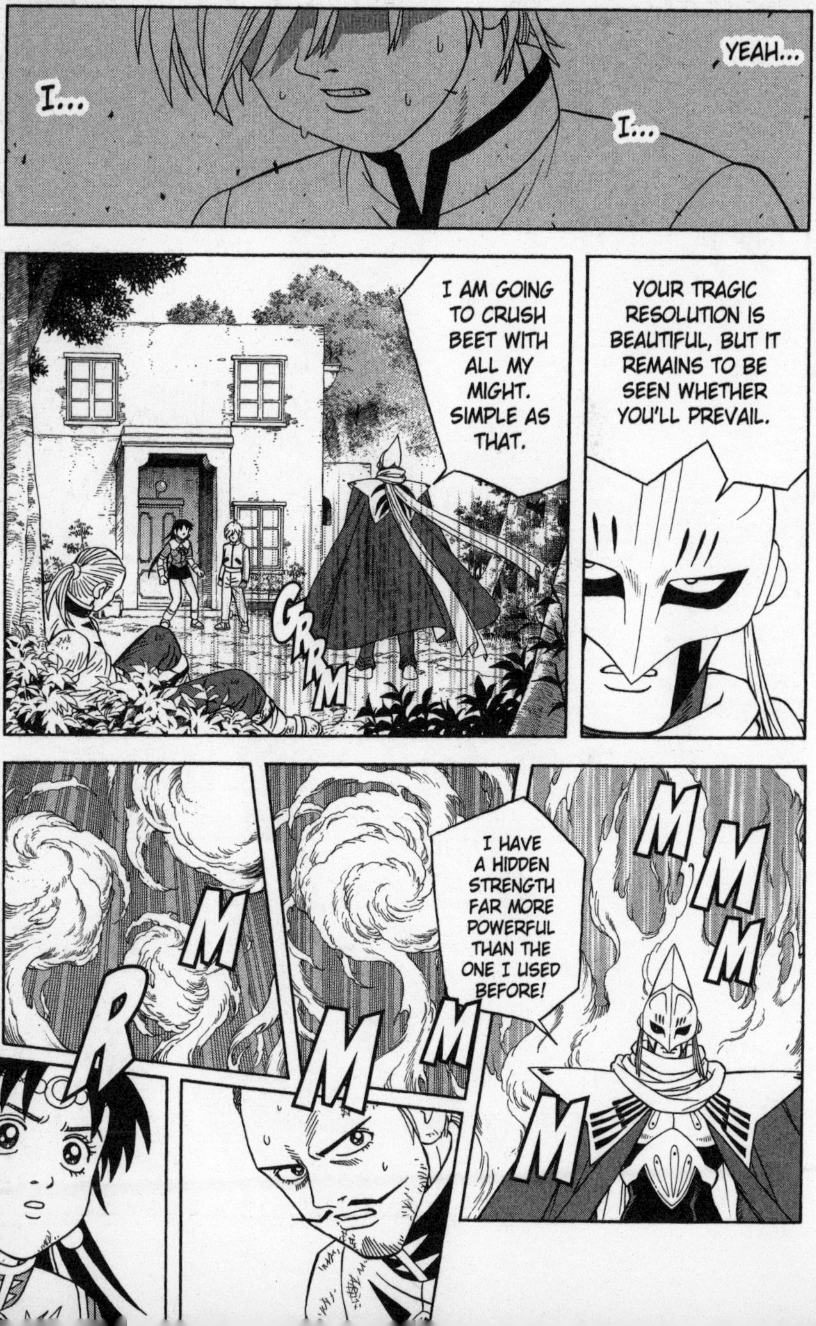
YEAH...
I...
I...
YOUR TRAGIC RESOLUTION IS BEAUTIFUL, BUT IT REMAINS TO BE SEEN WHETHER YOU'LL PREVAIL.
I AM GOING TO CRUSH BEET WITH ALL MY MIGHT. SIMPLE AS THAT.
GRRRM
MMMMM
I HAVE A HIDDEN STRENGTH FAR MORE POWERFUL THAN THE ONE I USED BEFORE!
MMM
RM

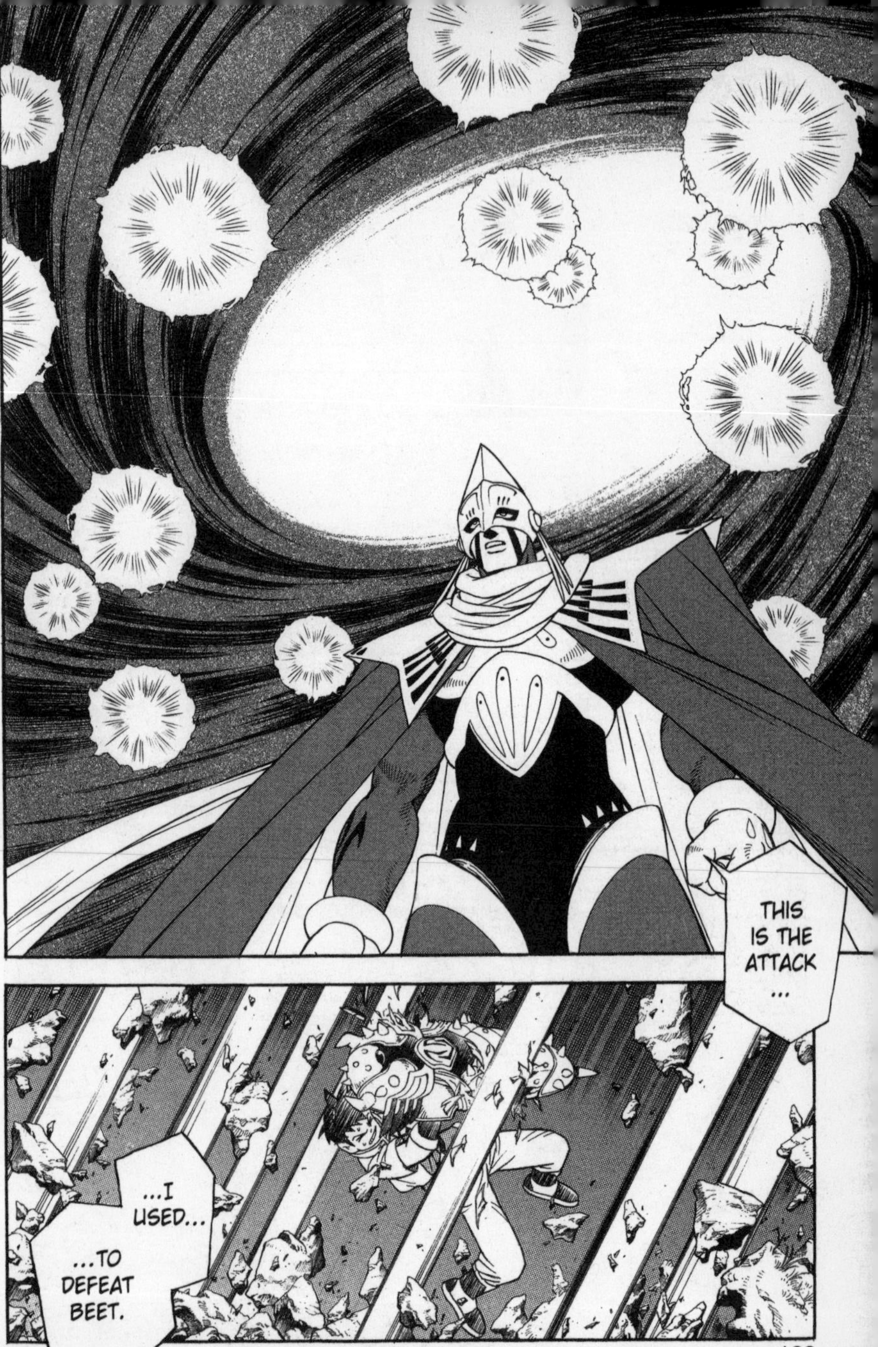
THIS IS THE ATTACK ...
...I USED...
...TO DEFEAT BEET.

《READ THIS WAY《

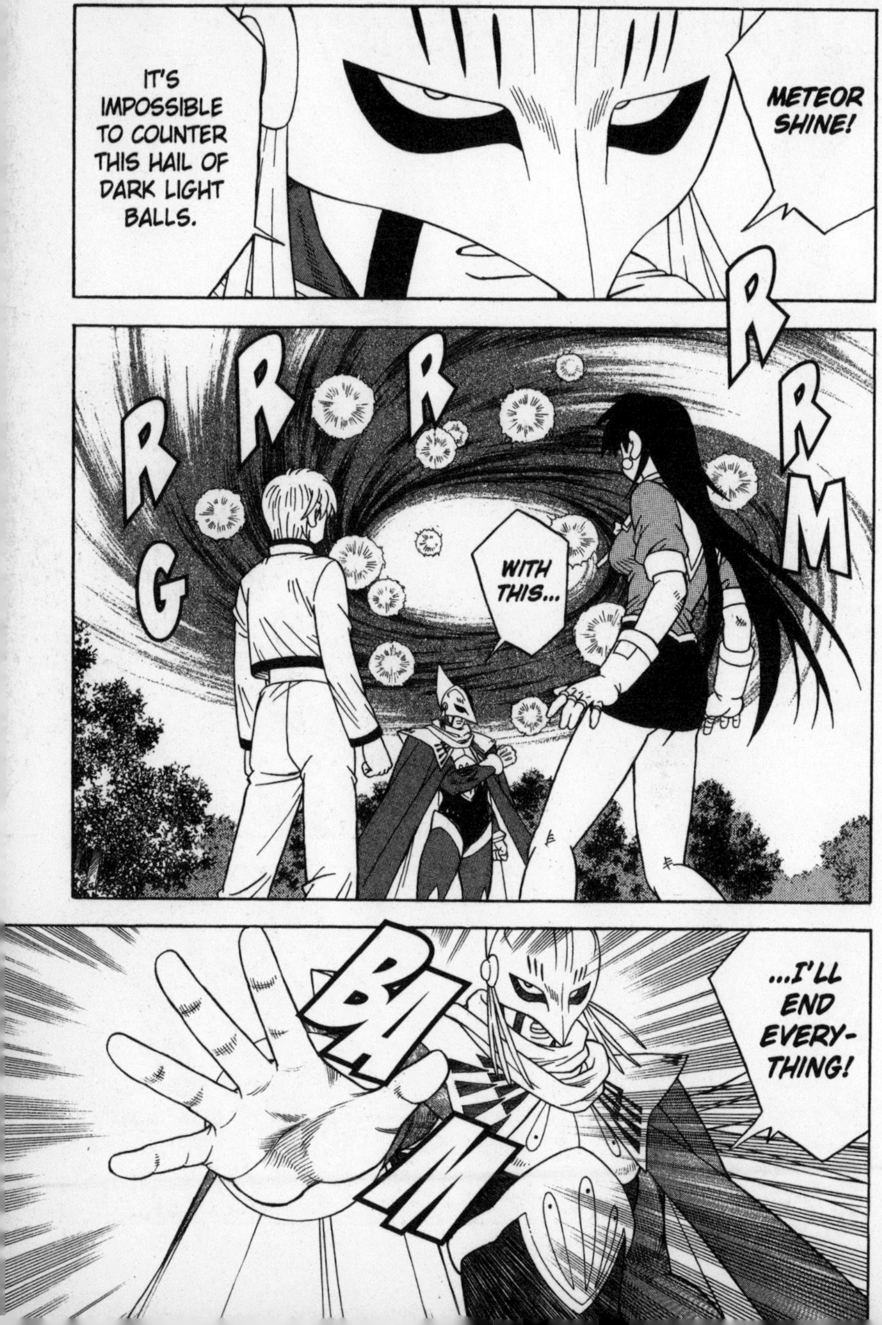
METEOR SHINE!
IT'S IMPOSSIBLE TO COUNTER THIS HAIL OF DARK LIGHT BALLS.
RRM
WITH THIS...
RRRG
...I'LL END EVERY-THING!
BAM

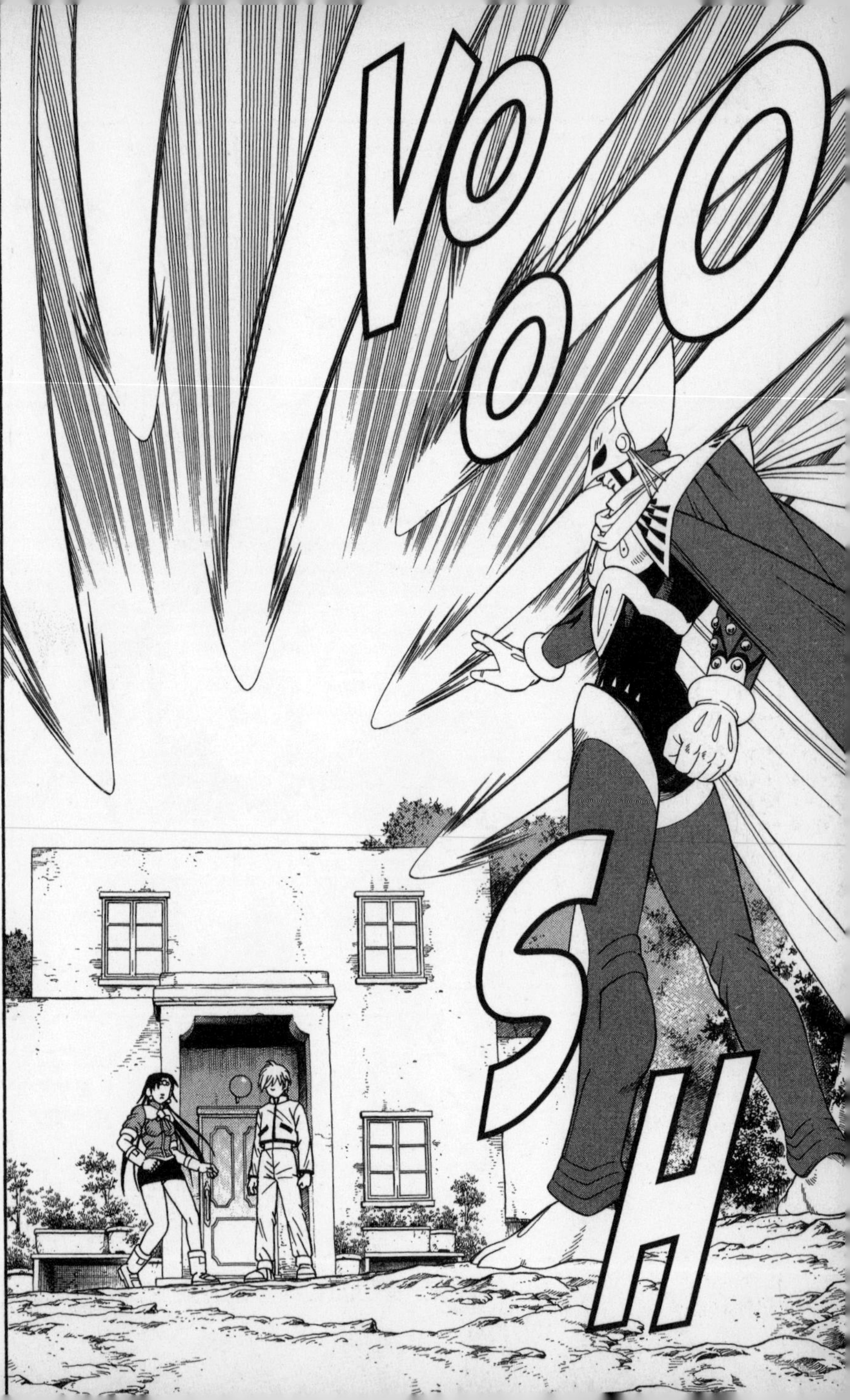
VOOOO
SH

READ THIS WAY

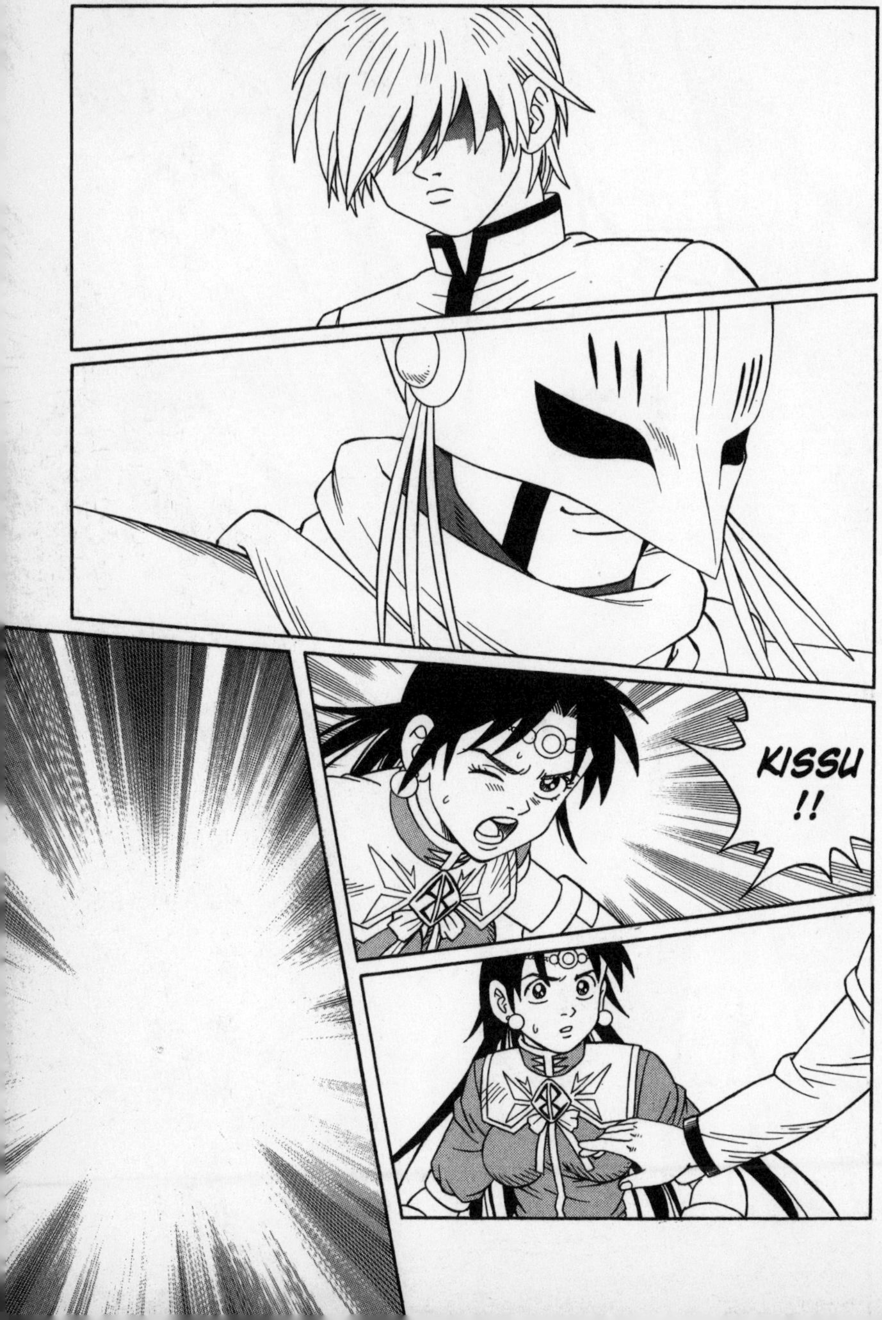
KISSU
!!

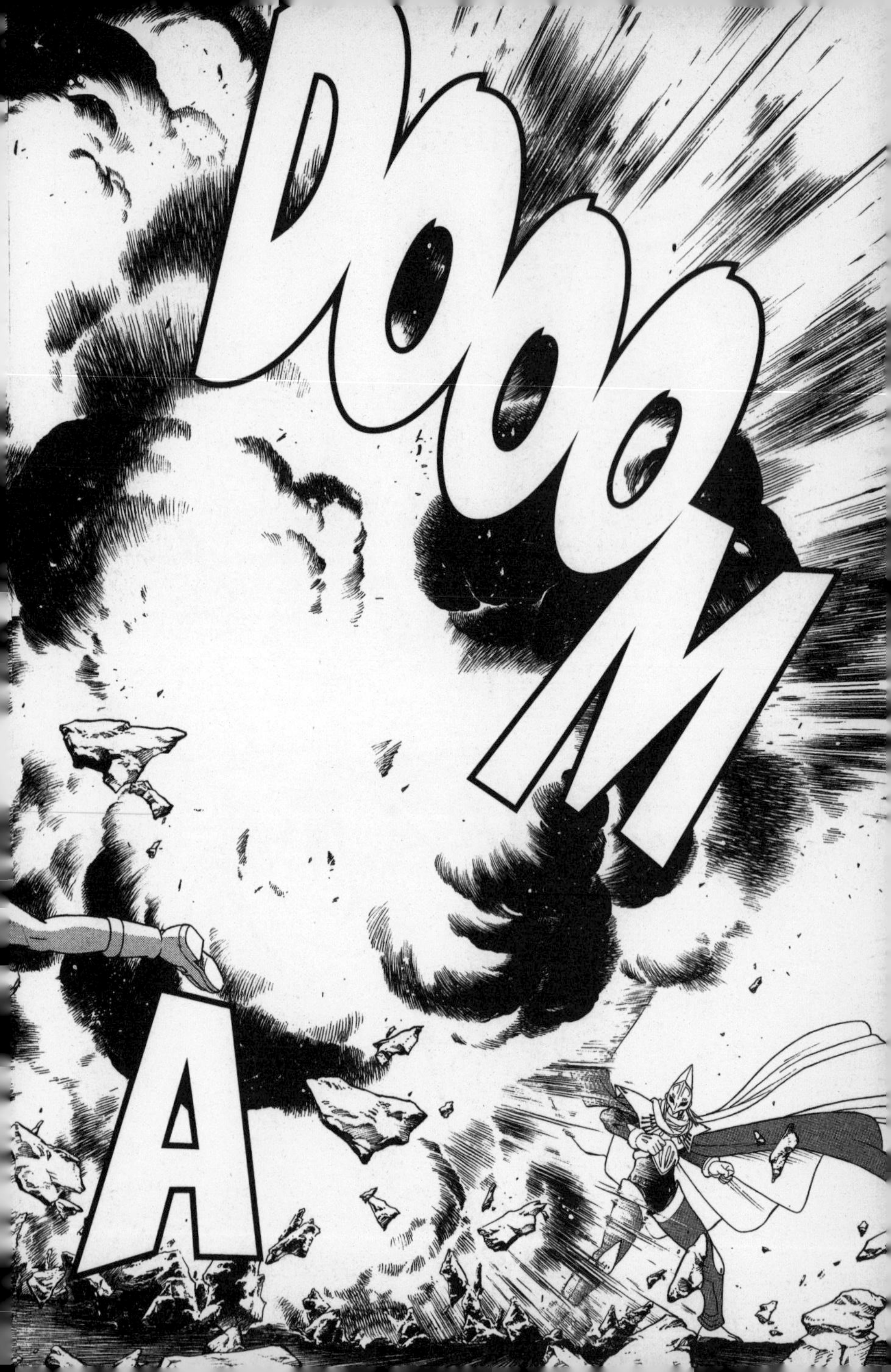
DOOOM
A

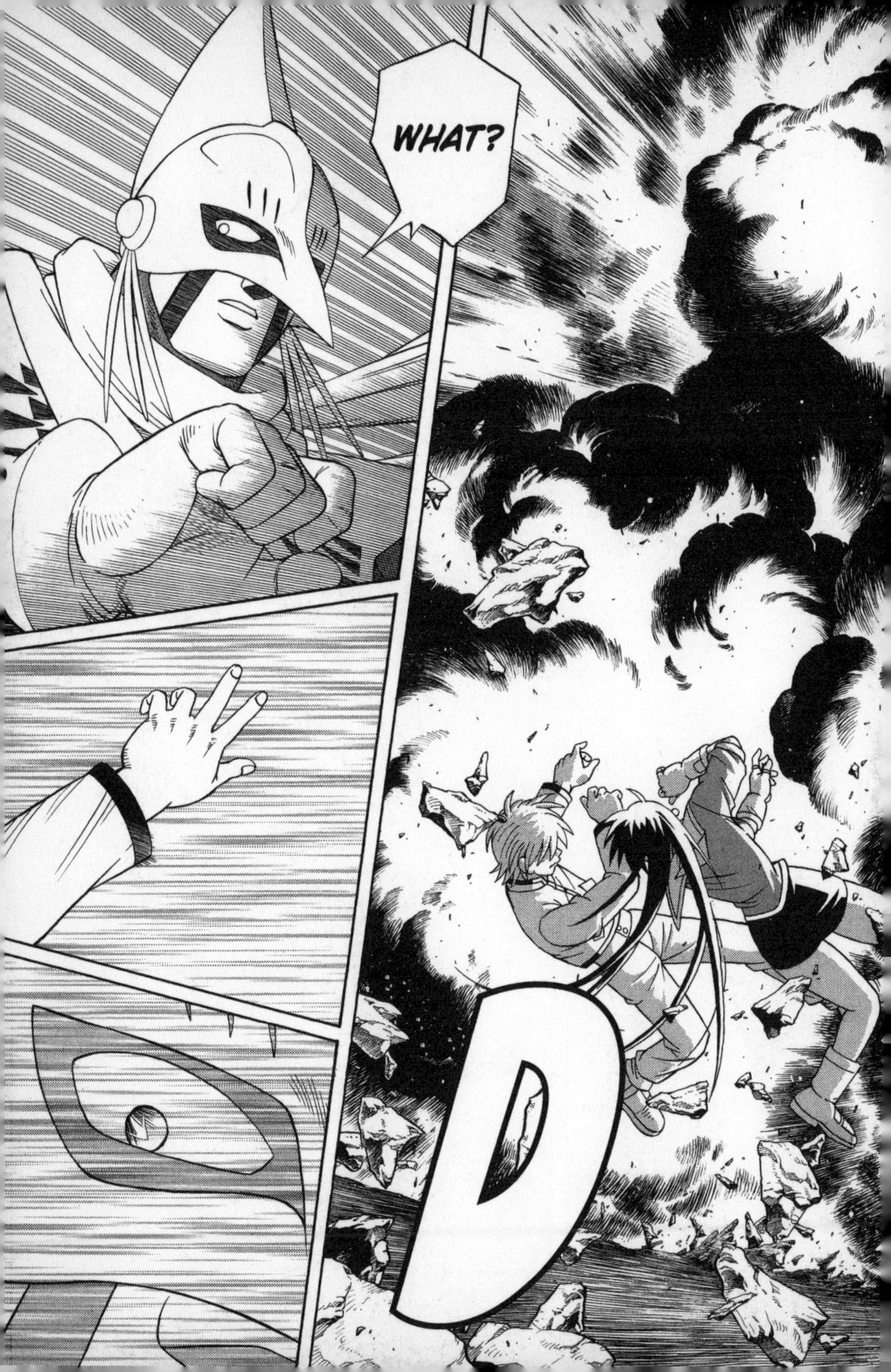
WHAT?
D

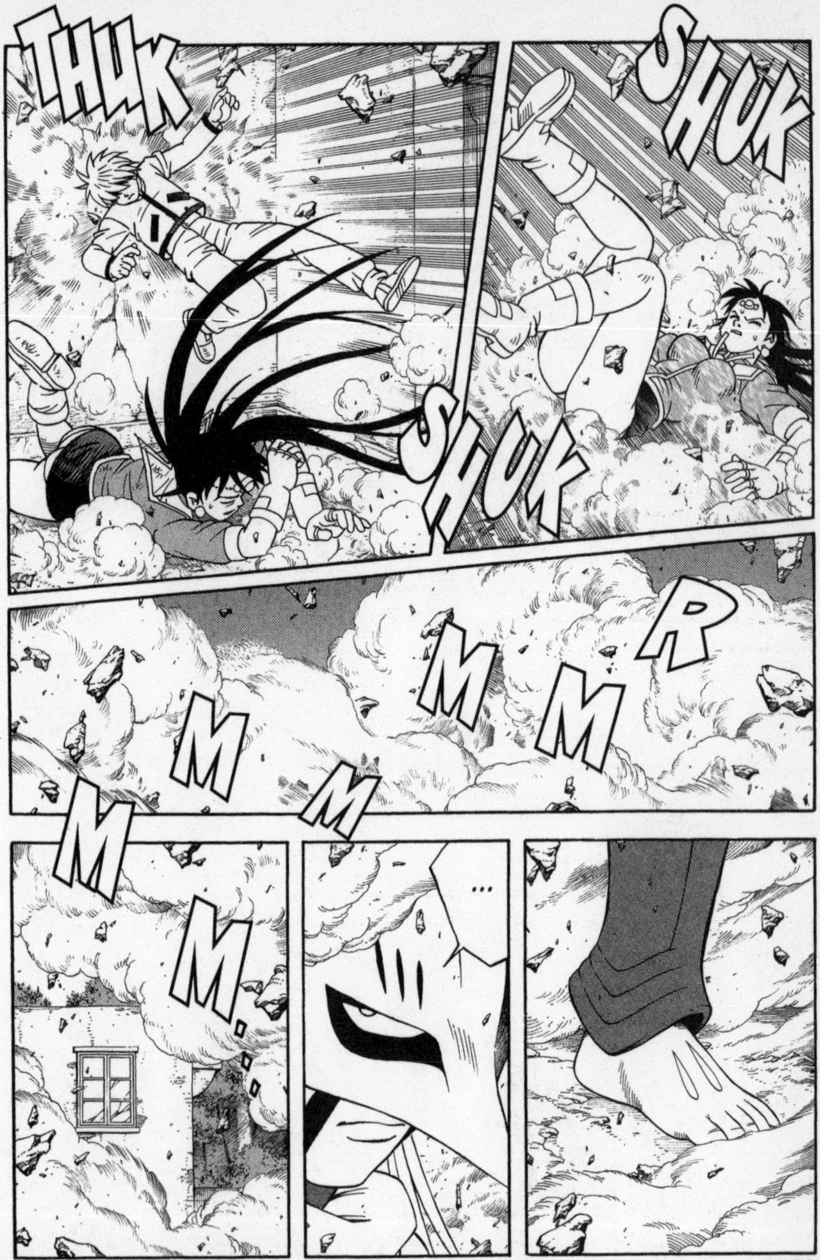
SHUK
SHUK
THUK
RMMMMMM...
...

READ THIS WAY

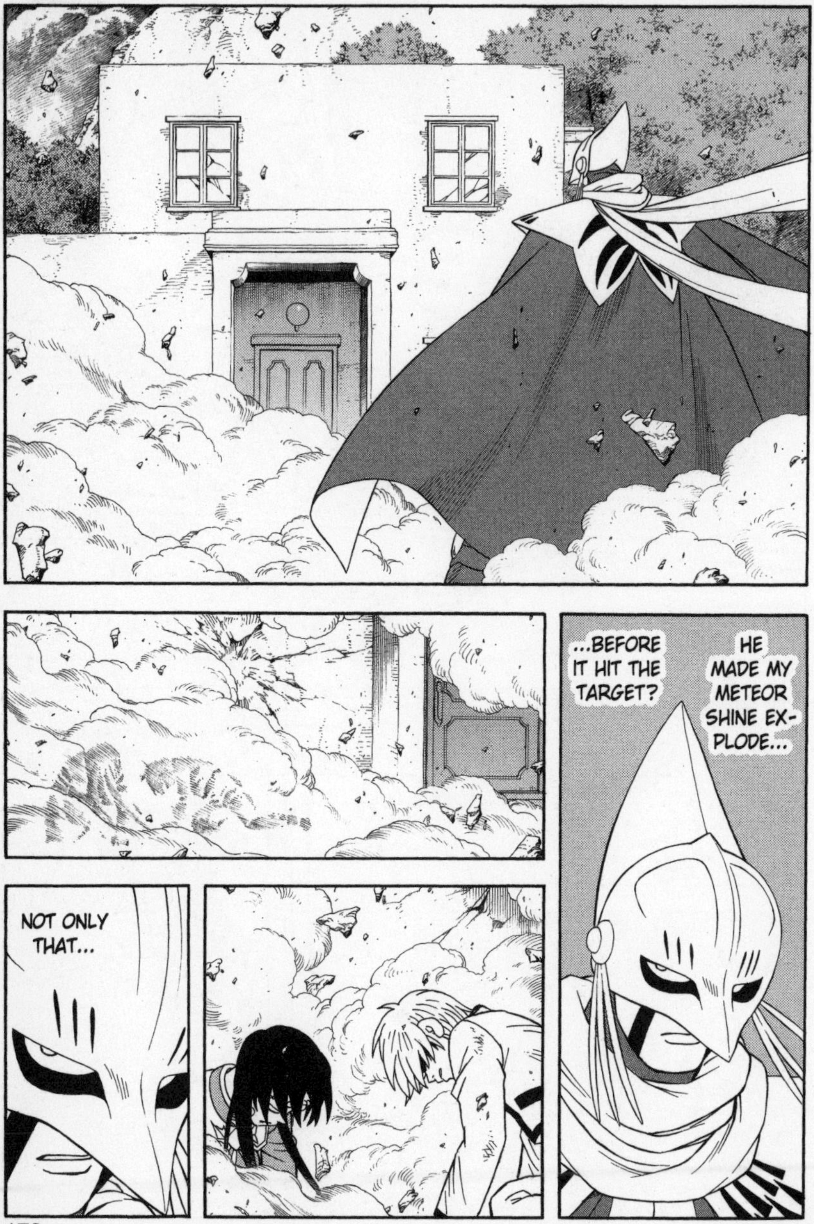
HE MADE MY METEOR SHINE EX-PLODE...
...BEFORE IT HIT THE TARGET?
NOT ONLY THAT...

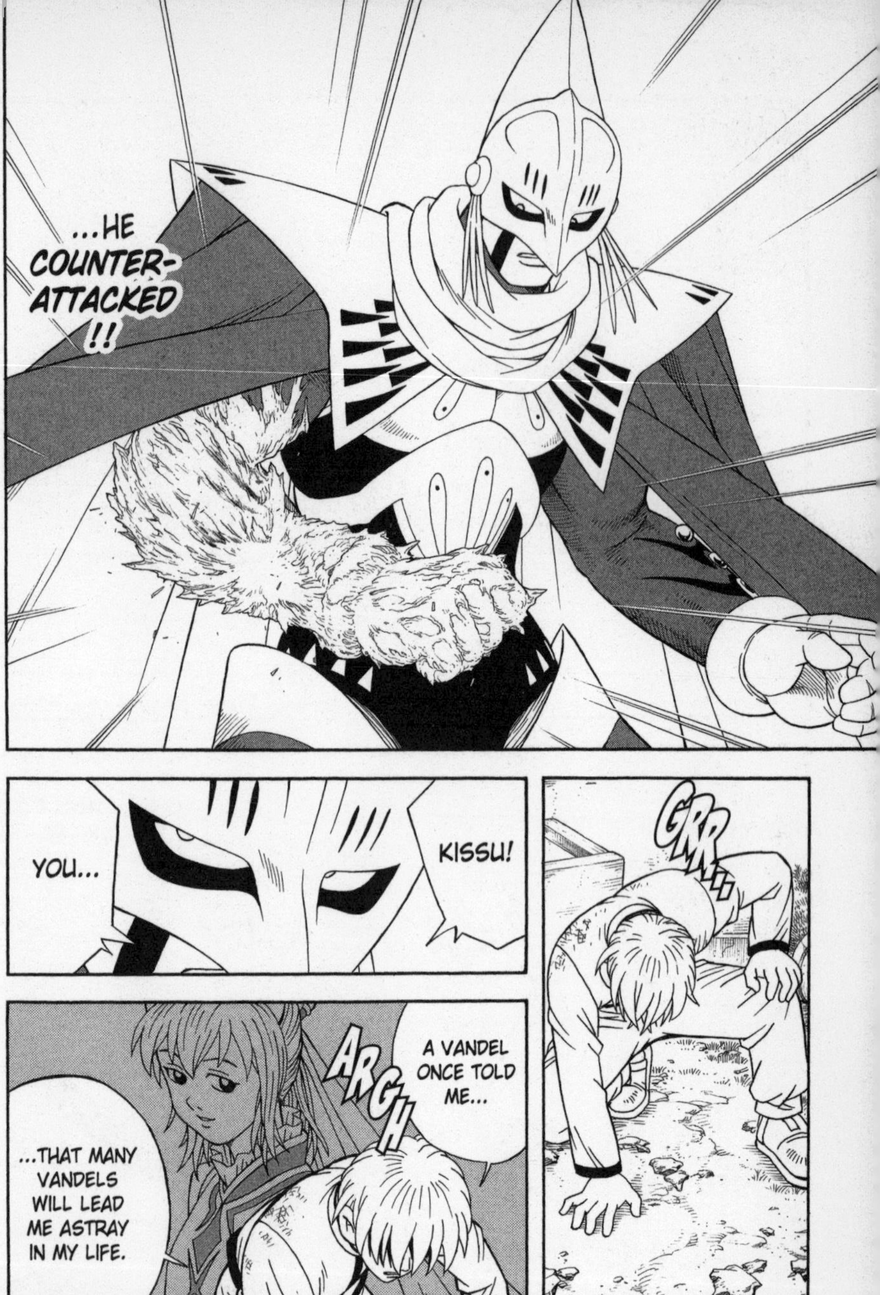
...HE COUNTER-ATTACKED!!
GRR
KISSU!
YOU...
A VANDEL ONCE TOLD ME...
ARGH
...THAT MANY VANDELS WILL LEAD ME ASTRAY IN MY LIFE.

READ THIS WAY

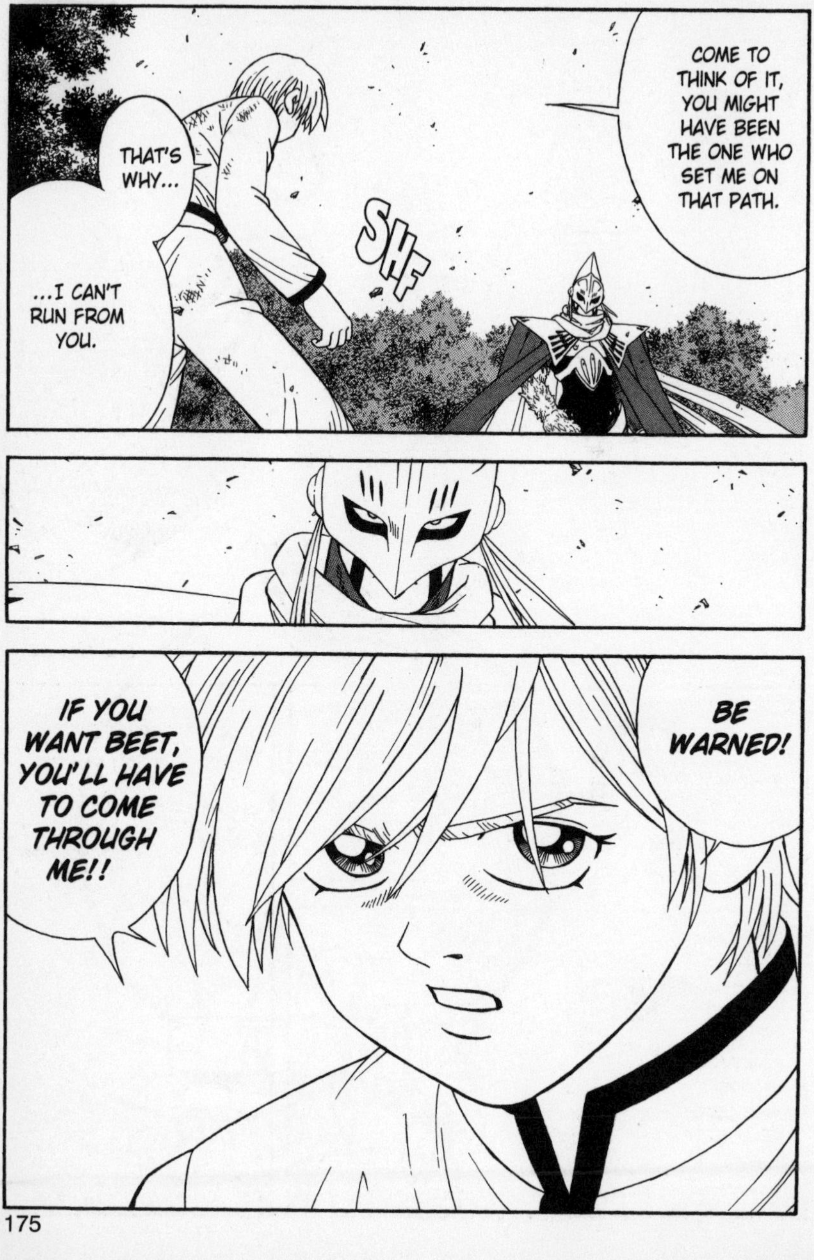
COME TO THINK OF IT, YOU MIGHT HAVE BEEN THE ONE WHO SET ME ON THAT PATH.
SHF
THAT'S WHY...
...I CAN'T RUN FROM YOU.
BE WARNED!
IF YOU WANT BEET, YOU'LL HAVE TO COME THROUGH ME!!

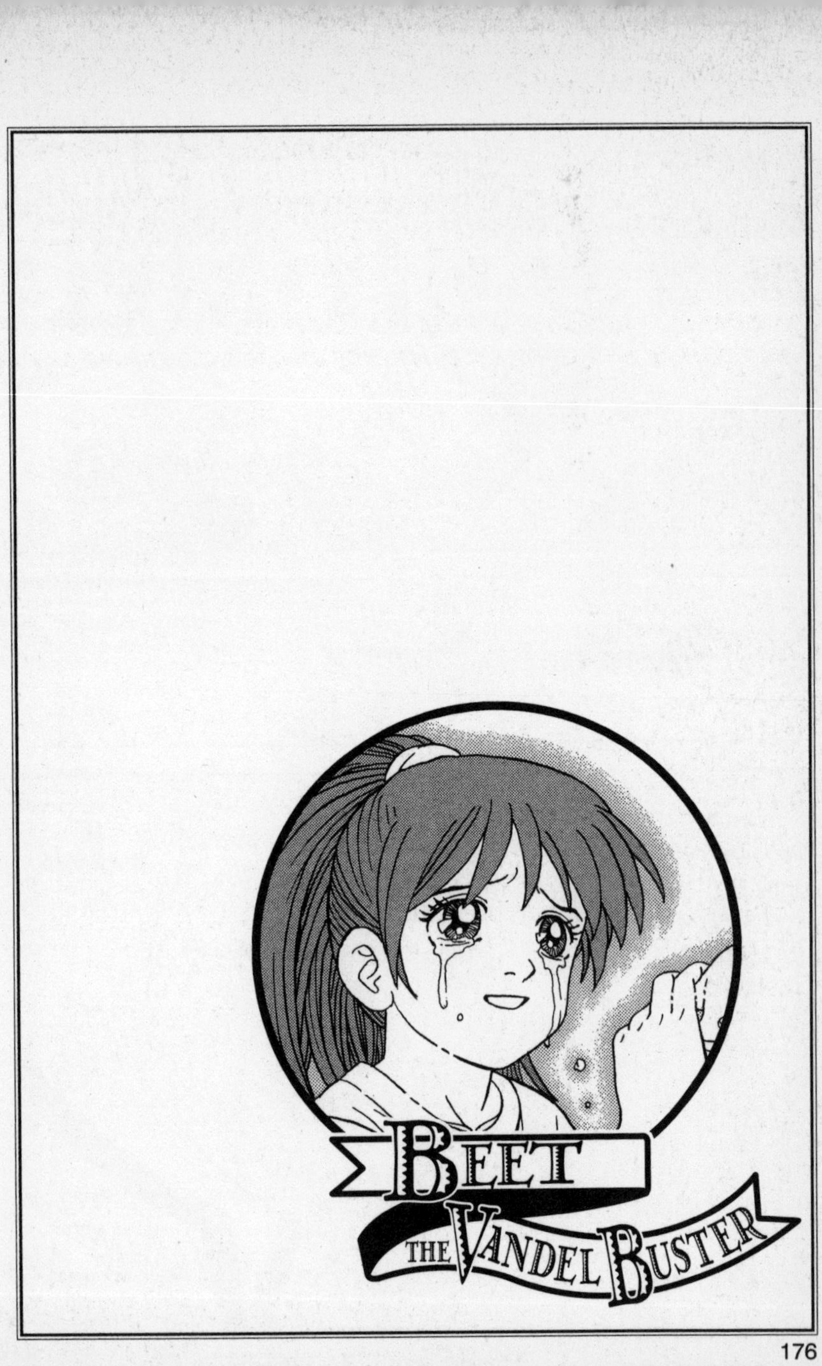
BEET
THE VANDEL BUSTER

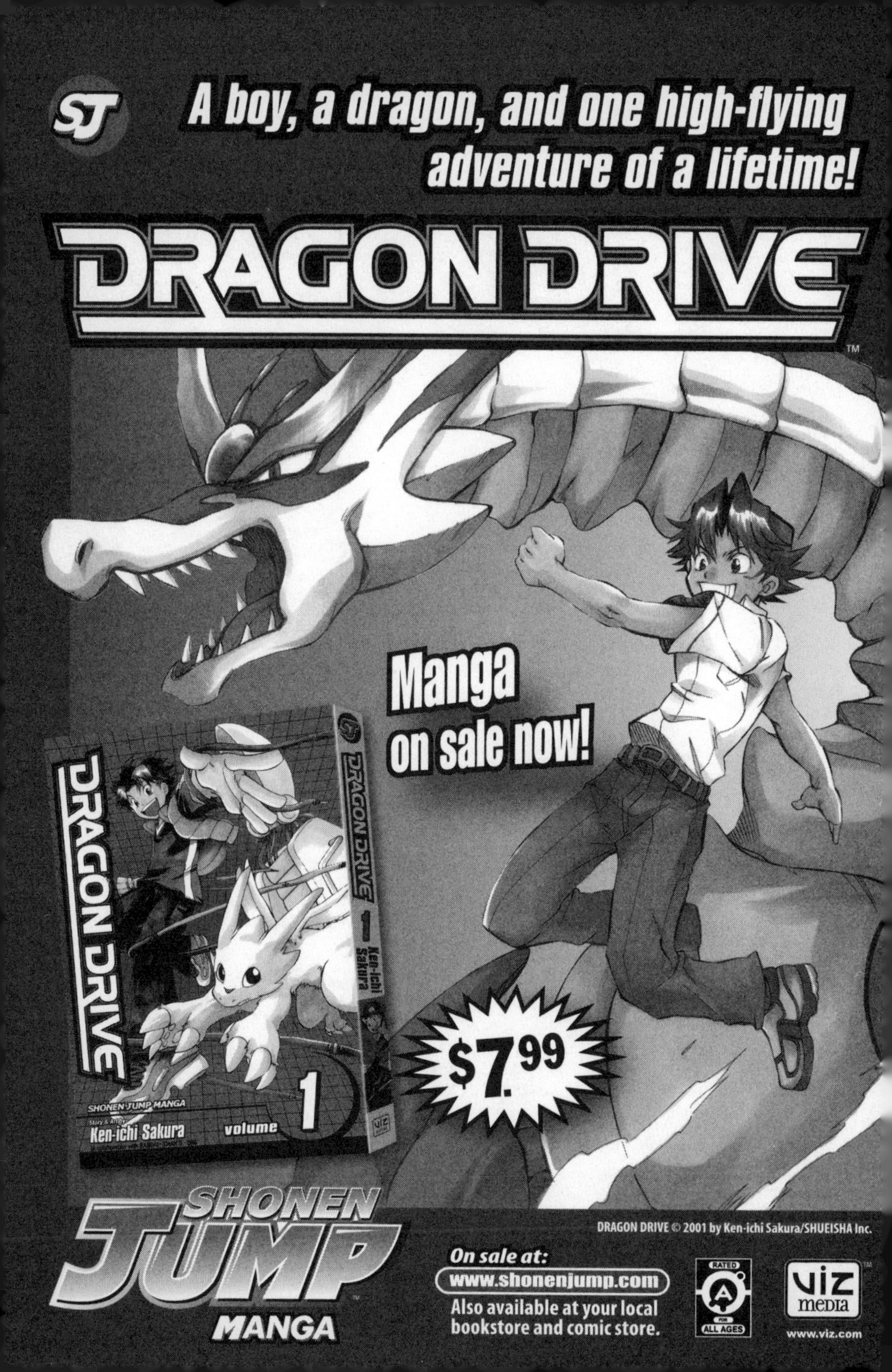

SJ
A boy, a dragon, and one high-flying adventure of a lifetime!
DRAGON DRIVE™
Manga on sale now!
DRAGON DRIVE
1
SHONEN JUMP MANGA
Story & Art by
Ken-ichi Sakura
volume 1
$7.99
SHONEN JUMP MANGA
DRAGON DRIVE © 2001 by Ken-ichi Sakura/SHUEISHA Inc.
On sale at:
www.shonenjump.com
Also available at your local bookstore and comic store.
RATED A FOR ALL AGES
VIZ media
www.viz.com

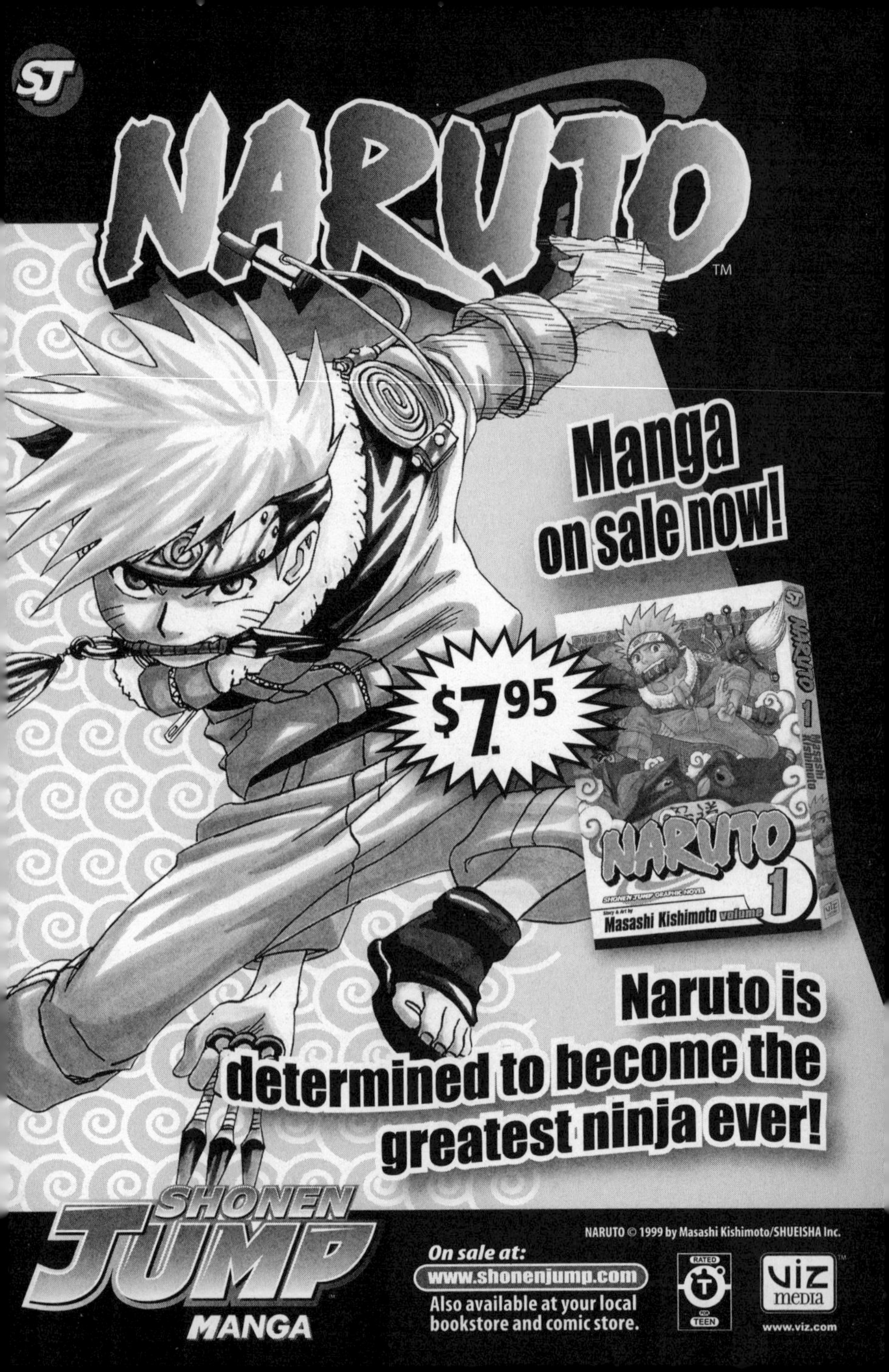
SJ
NARUTO™
Manga on sale now!
$7.95
NARUTO 1 Masashi Kishimoto
NARUTO 1
SHONEN JUMP GRAPHIC NOVEL
Story & Art by Masashi Kishimoto volume 1
Naruto is determined to become the greatest ninja ever!
SHONEN JUMP MANGA
NARUTO © 1999 by Masashi Kishimoto/SHUEISHA Inc.
On sale at:
www.shonenjump.com
Also available at your local bookstore and comic store.
RATED T FOR TEEN
VIZ media
www.viz.com

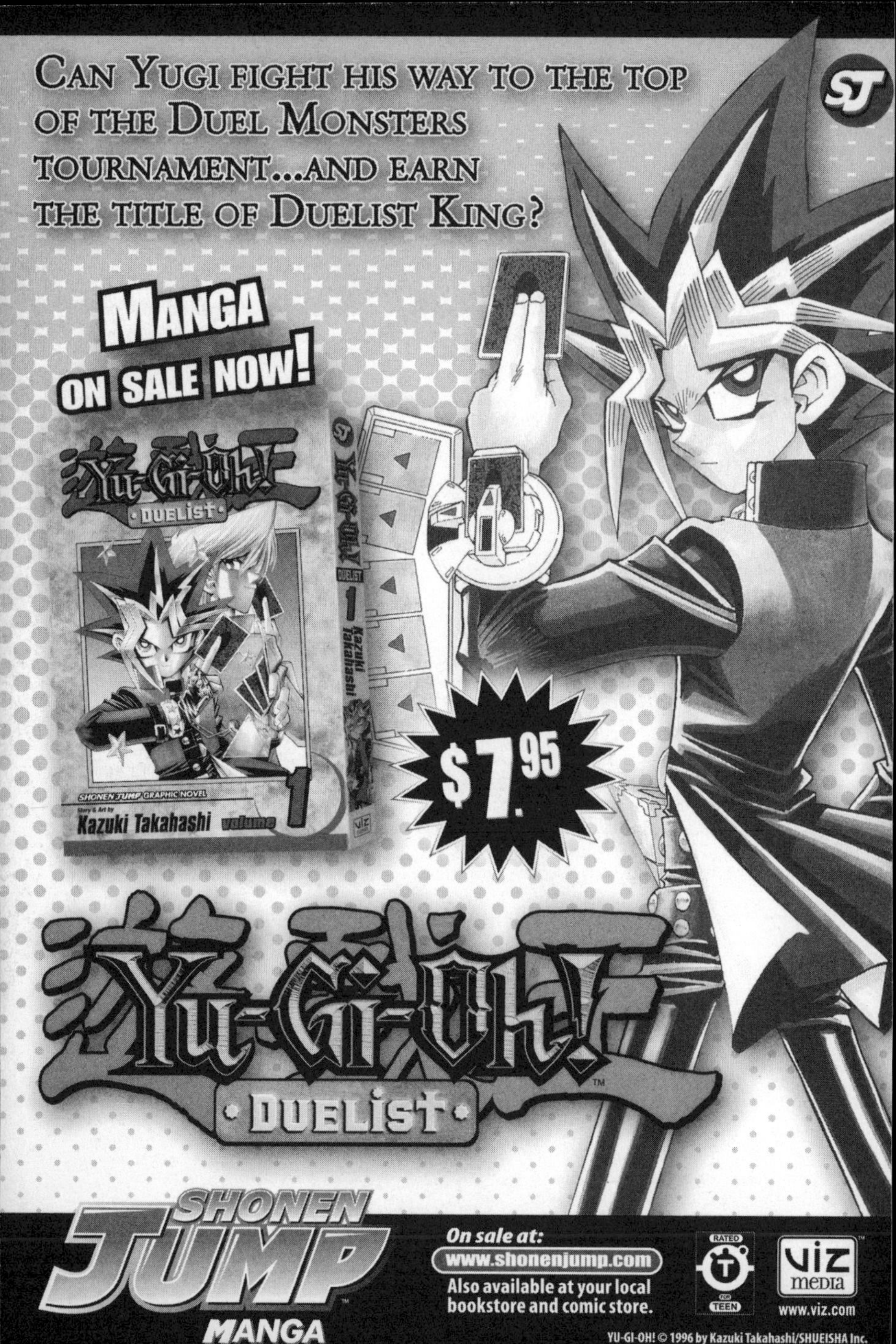

CAN YUGI FIGHT HIS WAY TO THE TOP OF THE DUEL MONSTERS TOURNAMENT...AND EARN THE TITLE OF DUELIST KING?
MANGA ON SALE NOW!
YU-GI-OH! DUELIST
SHONEN JUMP GRAPHIC NOVEL
Story & Art by Kazuki Takahashi
volume 1
$7.95
YU-GI-OH! DUELIST™
SHONEN JUMP MANGA
On sale at:
www.shonenjump.com
Also available at your local bookstore and comic store.
RATED T FOR TEEN
VIZ media
www.viz.com
YU-GI-OH! © 1996 by Kazuki Takahashi/SHUEISHA Inc.

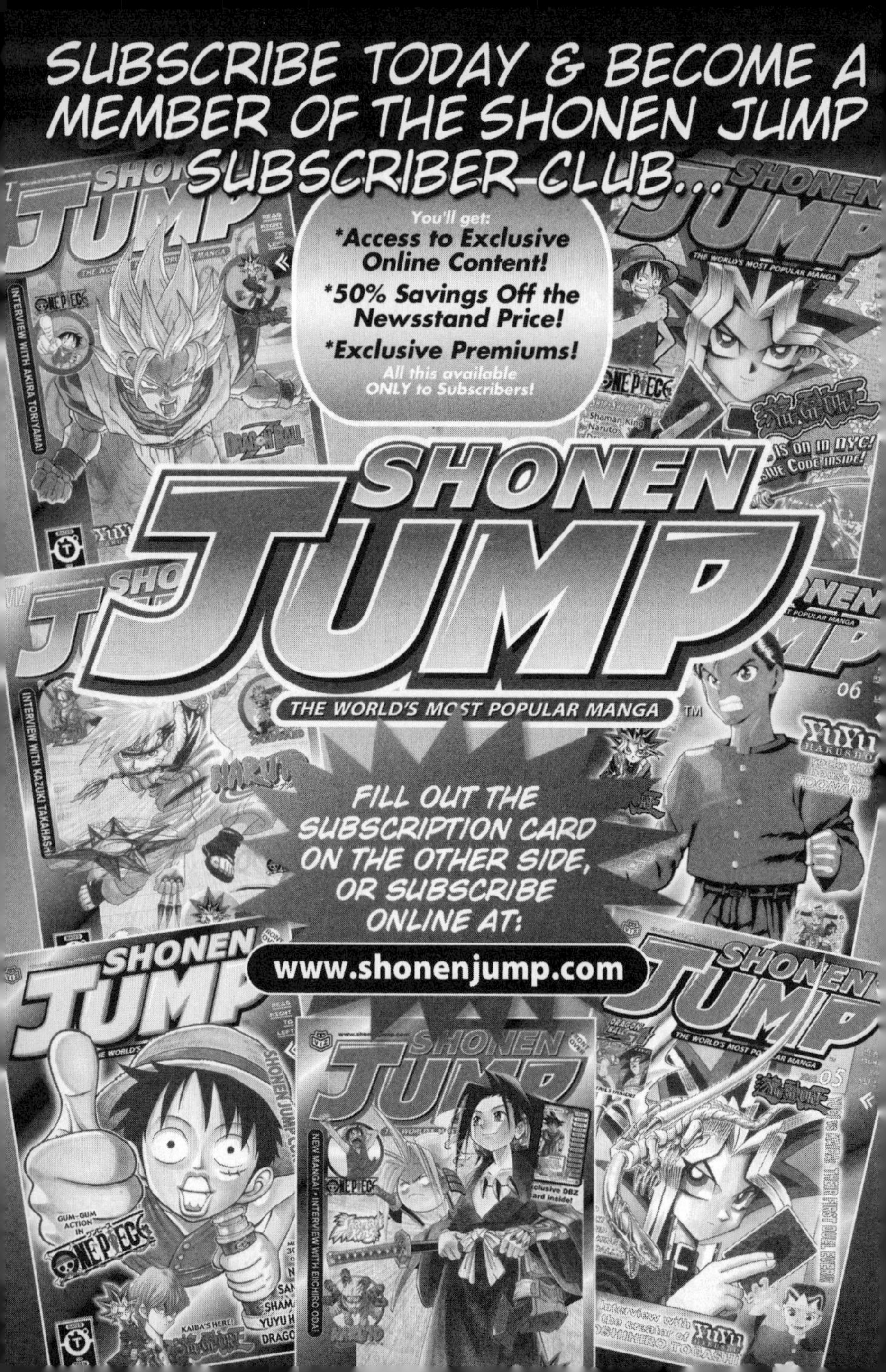
SUBSCRIBE TODAY & BECOME A MEMBER OF THE SHONEN JUMP SUBSCRIBER CLUB...
You'll get:
*Access to Exclusive Online Content!
*50% Savings Off the Newsstand Price!
*Exclusive Premiums!
All this available ONLY to Subscribers!
SHONEN JUMP
THE WORLD'S MOST POPULAR MANGA ™
FILL OUT THE SUBSCRIPTION CARD ON THE OTHER SIDE, OR SUBSCRIBE ONLINE AT:
www.shonenjump.com